Agrarian Policies in Central America

Also by Wim Pelupessy

THE LIMITS OF ECONOMIC REFORM IN EL SALVADOR

ECONOMIC MALADJUSTMENT IN CENTRAL AMERICA (*editor with John Weeks*)

PERSPECTIVES ON THE AGRO-EXPORT ECONOMY IN CENTRAL AMERICA (*editor*)

Also by Ruerd Ruben

SUSTAINABLE AGRICULTURE IN CENTRAL AMERICA (*editor with Jan P. de Groot*)

Agrarian Policies in Central America

Edited by

Wim Pelupessy
Senior Lecturer in Development Economics
Tilburg University, The Netherlands

and

Ruerd Ruben
Senior Lecturer in Development Economics
Wageningen Agricultural University, The Netherlands

First published in Great Britain 2000 by
MACMILLAN PRESS LTD
Houndmills, Basingstoke, Hampshire RG21 6XS and London
Companies and representatives throughout the world

A catalogue record for this book is available from the British Library.

ISBN 0–333–75386–0

First published in the United States of America 2000 by
ST. MARTIN'S PRESS, INC.,
Scholarly and Reference Division,
175 Fifth Avenue, New York, N.Y. 10010

ISBN 0–312–22426–5

Library of Congress Cataloging-in-Publication Data
Agrarian policies in Central America / edited by Wim Pelupessy and
Ruerd Ruben.
  p. cm.
Includes bibliographical references and index.
ISBN 0–312–22426–5 (cloth)
1. Agriculture and state—Central America. 2. Agriculture–
–Economic aspects—Central America. I. Pelupessy, Wim. II. Ruben,
Ruerd.
HD1798.A36 1999
338.1'8728—dc21   99–33838
                                                                                       CIP

This book is printed on paper suitable for recycling and made from fully managed and sustained
forest sources.

10   9   8   7   6   5   4   3   2   1
09 08 07 06 05 04 03 02 01 00

Printed and bound in Great Britain by
Antony Rowe Ltd, Chippenham, Wiltshire

Contents

List of Tables

List of Figures

Notes on the Contributors

Gerardo Barrantes is a researcher at the International Center in Economic Policy for Sustainable Development (CINPE) of the Universidad Nacional Autónoma, Costa Rica.

Edmundo Castro is a researcher at the International Center in Economic Policy for Sustainable Development (CINPE) of the Universidad Nacional Autónoma, Costa Rica.

Harry Clemens is a researcher at the Centro de Estudios para el Desarrollo Rural (CDR) of the Free University of Amsterdam in San José, Costa Rica.

Richard Eberlin is a researcher at the Department of Agricultural Economics of the Swiss Federal Institute of Technology, Zurich, Switzerland.

Jan P. de Groot is Senior Research Fellow in the Department of Development Economics of the Free University of Amsterdam, The Netherlands.

Wim Pelupessy is Senior Lecturer in Development Economics in the Faculty of Economic Sciences of Tilburg University, The Netherlands.

Peter C. Roebeling is a researcher at the Wageningen Agricultural University, The Netherlands.

Ruerd Ruben is Senior Lecturer in Development Economics in the Department of Economics and Management of Wageningen Agricultural University, The Netherlands.

Fernando Saenz is a researcher at the International Center in Economic Policy for Sustainable Development (CINPE) of the Universidad Nacional Autónoma, Costa Rica.

Arie Sanders is a researcher at the Centro de Estudios para el Desarrollo Rural (CDR) of the Free University of Amsterdam in San José, Costa Rica.

Jos Vaessen is a researcher at the Center of Development Studies of the University of Antwerp, Belgium.

Cor J. Wattel is a researcher at the Centro de Estudios para el Desarrollo Rural (CDR) of the Free University of Amsterdam in San José, Costa Rica.

Preface

In the last two decades of the twentieth century both interventionist and market-oriented agrarian policies have been implemented in the Central American economies. The results appear to be rather contradictory and little progress has been made in achieving an increase in agricultural productivity and a reduction in poverty in a sustainable way. In all six countries in the region government and market failures were and are widely present. This is also evident from the different chapters of this book, where policies on agrarian factor and output markets are evaluated by their effects at macro, sector, local and farm household levels respectively.

Analysts agree that social structures and underdeveloped institutions should be considered to 'get the policies right'. However, there exist a broad range of possible methodologies to apply, and there is much debate about the different ways to measure and judge the results of agrarian policy-making. The diversity of analytical procedures of the essays, which run from historical comparative analysis to farm household modeling, is one of the assets of this book. The careful treatment of each method and the identification of underlying economic and social causal relationships will give the reader a clear idea of the respective reaches and restrictions. The selection of the most appropriate approaches may depend on the type of questions to be addressed and instruments to be applied.

Four of the essays were selected from a seminar at the First Congress of European Latin Americanists in Salamanca, Spain, in June 1996 and were later updated and rewritten. The others were prepared for this book. They all originated from extensive research and fieldwork in the region done by European and Central American researchers. This collection will be useful for policy-makers, consultants and academics as well as agrarian organizations of the region.

Finally, we would like to acknowledge the support of Elisabeth van Tilburg for typing and editing the manuscript.

Tilburg   WIM PELUPESSY
Wageningen   RUERD RUBEN

1

A Critical Appraisal of Agrarian Policies in Central America

Wim Pelupessy and Ruerd Ruben

Introduction

The agrarian sector in Central America is accurately characterized by a high concentration of land ownership, fragmentation of rural factor and commodity markets and a limited degree of institutional development (Baumeister, 1987; Brockett, 1988). The traditionally polarized agrarian structure forced a large sector of the peasantry into production of basic grains for the domestic market, while agro-export production (coffee, banana, sugar cane, meat) and non-traditional crops are controlled by a small number of medium and large producers (Pelupessy, 1991: 160; 1997: 89). Agrarian reforms and other adjustment strategies only marginally changed rural society, since the economic conditions of production (relative prices, access to credit and services, availability of infrastructure) retained their agro-export bias. Relations of production of most of the rural working force and the main agro-export producers have remained unaffected by any kind of reform.

Consequently, technological progress in agriculture was relatively slow, local added value generation was low and development depended more on making agriculture more extensive by area expansion and only for export crops on improvements in yields. The great majority of small staple food producers had limited access to rural financial markets and had operational constraints for the adoption of improved production methods. These factors, as well as unfavorable internal terms of trade, proved to be major bottlenecks for agricultural investment and intensification. Therefore, rural employment and income levels lagged behind and degradation of natural resources is progressing.

A recent Japanese report identified the little progress in rural poverty reduction in the past 25 years as the principal problem for Latin American agriculture, despite its potentials (Takase and Watanabe, 1997: 4). The situation seems to be worse for Central America, since daily caloric and protein intakes are here 15 per cent below regional averages (ibid., 1997: 11). Under these conditions, rural development cannot be expected without the explicit recognition that policy interventions are required at macroeconomic, sectoral and regional level.

Agrarian policies are usually defined in terms of the incentives offered to producers (Ellis, 1992). A difference can be made between (1) the *level* of policy-making (macroeconomic, sectoral and regional policies) and (2) the *domain* of policy-making (market policies, structural policies, institutional development). For each type of policy, specific instruments are used and different effects are perceived with respect to welfare and income distribution. For our purpose agrarian policies are government actions specifically designed for the development of the agricultural and livestock sector. These policies are likely to induce adjustments in land use, technology choice and the creation of rural employment.

The cases included in this book offer a comprehensive overview of the current debate on the implementation of agrarian policies in Central America. Major attention is given to the interrelation with policy objectives at the macroeconomic level, the available policy instruments for the development of rural markets for land, labor and finance, and the adjustment of farming systems in tropical lowlands and hillside regions. Moreover, different analytical procedures for policy evaluation and appraisal are presented, although the main theoretical approaches of the studies seem to be rooted in (neo-)structuralist and institutionalist strands. The effectiveness of various policy instruments to induce a more dynamic and sustainable process of rural development will be discussed against the background of the ongoing structural adjustment programs in the region.

The use of case studies for policy analysis may be questioned, but is important because they may help 'to understand in more detail the nature of causal relationships' (Mitchell and Bernauer, 1998: 27). The particular cases are used for analytical-descriptive research to establish basic facts that may provide solid sources for research (Kannappan, 1995: 876–80). In this volume quantitative (partial equilibrium analysis mostly), qualitative and combinations of both methods are used and all have their respective advantages and disadvantages. When rigorously applied, qualitative case studies may have the potential to overcome the problems of 'being hostage to an a priori and mono disciplinary analytical framework' (Kannappan, op. cit.: 879–80; for guidelines to guarantee qualitative rigor see Mitchell *et al.*, op. cit.: 4–31).

In this introductory chapter we will summarize the main conclusions of the chapters 2 to 8 and address the implications for rural development strategies. Some general issues will be discussed here regarding the socio-political framework for priority-setting, the development of markets and institutional networks as major transmission mechanisms and the response reactions of rural farm households and estates to different types of policy instruments. The results of the case studies may be compared and then generalized in the light of recent research findings in the field. Therefore, attention is given to the structural position of agriculture within outward-oriented economic development strategies, rural tenancy and exchange relations, and the impact of market liberalization and privatization on the process of rural development. After a discussion on the effectiveness and constraints of different policy instruments, and the methodological difficulties of measuring effects adequately, major limitations of the current policy framework are acknowledged. Finally, it will be argued that an important part of agrarian policies in Central America failed to reach the perceived objectives, owing mainly to (1) the ruling conception of agriculture as an adjusting sector, (2) the incomplete character of market and institutional reforms, (3) the insufficient capacity and capability for policy making of the state, and (4) the limited understanding of the driving forces of farm household and estate behavior.

Policy framework

Central American governments demonstrate a strong and lasting bias in favor of commercial export agriculture. Overvalued exchange rates, liberal external trade regimes, as well as moderate fiscal levies and expansive monetary policies, represented the core ingredients for this outward-oriented pattern of economic development (Bulmer-Thomas, 1987). Exports were the main source of fiscal income and were also implicitly taxed by the overvalued exchange rates. Private investments and modernization were concentrated in export crop estates and their processing factories and were complemented by limited public investments. Public investment for rural development was strongly neglected; farm gate prices for food remained at a low level (to control wage labor costs in agriculture and other sectors) and access to land and credit was severely restricted.

The structural and political limitations of this agro-export model already became apparent in the 1960s, in spite of the introduction of inward-oriented policies and weak industrialization tendencies. Popular upheavals occurred in most countries, and growing social unrest and political pressure made attention to land reform and similar programs unavoidable. However, these programs had only a limited coverage in terms of both affected land and beneficiaries. Additional agrarian policies enabling the peasantry better access to rural markets and institutions were largely neglected (Dorner, 1992; Lipton, 1993; Thiesenhusen, 1995b). Therefore, patterns of land use did not substantially change, and input intensity (and yields) of agrarian production systems of food staples and small export growers remained extremely low. Survival of the peasantry in the Central American countryside thus mainly depends on further intensification of family labor within their own plots, along with temporary or permanent migration (export estates and off-farm employment) and – wherever possible – colonization into agrarian frontier areas.

During the 1980s, a number of additional economic limitations to the agro-export model became particularly important. Growing deficits on the current accounts of balance of payments and shortages in capital inflow and public budgets led to high inflation rates and external debt problems that could be corrected only with financial support from international agencies (IMF and World Bank) and foreign governments such as the United States. Loans were available only under conditions of structural adjustment of domestic economic policies and modernization of the state. Most programs include provisions for devaluation of the exchange rate and other export-promoting policies, liberalization of domestic food markets, budgetary limits for government spending and restrictive financial and monetary policies. Moreover, former state institutions for marketing, rural credit provision and agricultural extension are subject to privatization, while the supply of public services is being partially decentralized towards municipal authorities. Regional trade of food staples among Central American countries has been reactivated with the establishment of a system of price bands that permits unrestricted imports and exports of cereals.

While structural adjustment programs are intended – in principle – to reactivate agricultural production through improved traditional and non-traditional export possibilities and incentives for the production for the domestic market, small producers are not always able to reap the benefits. Major bottlenecks appear when market or institutional failures prevent the adequate transmission of price signals to primary producers, and thus traders and middlemen increase their margins. It is interesting to note also that international trading companies use such mechanisms to increase their margins. Preliminary estimates show export revenue losses for coffee from 7.5 per cent to 25.9 per cent of the total exports in 1993–4 for Costa Rica and Guatemala (Morisset, 1997: 18–24). The primary commodity export model of Central America did not generate positive equity effects and neither did its structural adjustment variant. Liberalized product markets in combination with extra-economic coercion in labor markets gave extraordinary rents to a minority (Pelupessy and Weeks, 1993: 2–3). Consequently, at the end of the 1980s about 60 per cent of the rural population was still living in conditions of extreme poverty, while the rural poor represent more than 70 per cent of the total population in this sector (Menjívar and Trejos, 1990).

Within Latin America the economies of Central America belong to the group with the higher Gini coefficients (0.46 to 0.59) and, with the exception of Costa Rica, with the lowest human development index (HDI < 0.600). Moreover, in some countries (e.g. Nicaragua) purchasing power constraints have resulted in a general economic stagnation. Structural adjustment programs without adequate policy instruments to improve farmers' access to markets, measures to enhance real competition and procedures to establish genuine local institutions (farmers' unions, credit and savings cooperatives, etc.) are likely to meet their limitations sooner or later.

Policy analysis

Economic theory provides a wide variety of approaches for the analysis of agrarian policies. Decision-support systems (i.e. cost–benefit and multi-criteria analysis) are commonly used for the assessment of rural investment programs, but these instruments have their restrictions for policy analysis, owing to their static and partial nature. Therefore, a number of other analytical procedures have been developed to account for growth and equity effects and occasionally also some others (like sustainability) that are likely to occur.

At the national and sectoral levels, major questions refer to the role of agriculture within the process of economic development and the changes in the agrarian production and social structures. Comparative approaches offer insight into the economic, political and historical factors that influence success or failure of similar policy interventions under apparently dissimilar conditions (see Chapter 2 by Pelupessy). A highly interventionist reform of the land market executed by a sufficiently autonomous state will be needed when tenancy structures have become dysfunctional and distributional outcomes broadly unacceptable (see also Binswanger *et al.*, 1995: 2718). Both economic and political effects on rural class relations should be considered and will affect the effectiveness and the tactics of implementation if there is political sensitivity (Killick, 1990). The reform and its complementary (macro) policies should establish mechanisms for resource transfers to develop agriculture. To make this happen measures should be taken to reduce rural insecurity and to guarantee policy continuity. A structural adjustment program could be introduced as a complementary macro strategy. The impact of this program on private and social (shadow prices) profitability has been estimated using a policy analysis matrix PAM on agricultural incomes and (inter)national trade for two food crops (see Chapter 3 by Eberlin). In the two cases both types of benefits were found positive after the implementation of structural adjustment. An improvement of the real terms of trade of both tradables generated a favorable supply response. However, the period of analysis of three years is relatively short and it seems as if results were also affected by a decrease of external input use, which may decrease yields in the long run. Also, the study warns for market imperfections and other institutional constraints. Some of the latter are even consequences of the applied macro policies and may hamper the sustainability of the results. Farm household modeling is a useful procedure for the *ex ante* evaluation of the expected supply response of different types of small farmers to sectoral agrarian policy instruments of the structural adjustment type, taking into account both production and consumption objectives at the micro level (see Chapter 4 by Roebeling and Saenz). Assuming that price signals of policies are transmitted to the agricultural producers, it appears that supply responses enhance the cash crop orientation and profitability, at the expense of soil nutrient fertility losses and rising input use. Constraints include limited capital and especially labor availability. A combination of policy measures seems to be more effective than the effects of the individual policies.

In the field of technological development, farming systems approaches and cost–benefit analysis are still useful tools for the assessment of the attractiveness of alternative crops or technologies for settlers at the agrarian frontier (see Chapter 5 by De Groot). Increasing (export) demand provokes supply responses towards more productive and sustainable land use systems of settlers at the maturing frontier, which is an area already integrated into the market economy, with adequate infrastructure and high market values of land and wealth. New market and credit opportunities could reduce migration from older to new frontier zones. But smaller settlers often lack the capacity to translate intensification into more sustainable land use. Low external input technologies and credit programs may be useful to enhance this capacity. The adoption of new technologies mostly requires additional incentives as access to credit, extension and tenancy security, that can be evaluated with econometric and multi-variate methods (see Chapter 6 by Ruben and Vaessen). Instead of looking exclusively at supply aspects, demand by small farmers for conservation practices is central in this study. For each practice a different set of factors is relevant. But for most knowledge and information of the new technique are important. Also, institutional and wealth variables and access to credit may be of influence, depending on the type of conservation activity and farmer.

The functioning of surrounding rural financial or labor markets proves to be an important factor in the process of agricultural change. A detailed analysis of the supply and demand conditions on rural financial markets offers insight into the level of market segmentation (see Chapter 7 by Sanders and Wattel). Financial reforms applied within the framework of structural adjustment generally did not enhance the access to rural credit in Central America. Imperfect domestic financial markets, lack of control of monetary authorities and the openness of the economies meant that only the position on the international financial markets improved. Banking spreads and segmentation of rural financial markets remain high, while increasing real interest rates may have shifted resources from the informal into the formal market. The shift could reduce the access of small farms to credit. Appropriate credit policies should look for solutions to the institutional barriers and market imperfections. A multi-market framework can be used to analyze the importance of rural markets for off-farm employment and the derived expenditure and investment effects at farm household level (see Chapter 8 by Ruben and Clemens). Similar procedures have been used for the analysis of rural land markets (Carter and Mesbah, 1993). Rural off-farm employment could play a major role in obtaining food security and it also provides a means to overcome the credit and product diversification constraints. Except for rural households unable to escape abject poverty, off-farm employment creation could be highly relevant as an additional source of income.

The selection of the most appropriate approaches for policy analysis finally depends on the type of questions to be addressed and the instruments that can therefore be applied (Sadoulet and De Janvry, 1995). At macroeconomic level, domestic prices and internal terms of trade can be considered as endogenous variables that can be used for enhancing rural development. Exchange rate policies and public investment are major instruments for modifying the competitiveness of agro-export producers. At sectoral level, linkages between agricultural producers, input delivery networks, traders and processing industry become most important, and policy interventions are likely to address transaction costs and rural infrastructure development. Finally, at microeconomic level, producers have to be considered as price-takers and thus aspects of risk in, access to, and information on, factor and commodity markets become of major importance. Also, differentiation between farm households and sustainability of natural resource management regimes have to be taken into account.

Major drawbacks that are common to most frameworks for policy analysis refer to difficulties in assessing *microeconomic responses* by rural households and their aggregates to different types of policy incentives (see Schiff and Montenegro, 1997), *interactions* between market policies and institutional development, and the *dynamic development dimension*. The first question refers to the fact that different types of farm households may show broadly opposite response reactions, for example to price policies, depending on their net supply or net demand situation on the market. Net producers are likely to benefit from rising food prices, while net consumers face a welfare decrease (De Janvry *et al.*, 1991). Similarly, higher rural wages or better-off farm employment opportunities may lead to improved welfare for households that hire labor out, but they will tend to increase production costs for farmers relying on wage laborers. Guaranteeing an adequate degree of targeting efficiency in agrarian policies therefore requires a detailed understanding of farm household relationships with factor and commodity markets.

The second question refers to the political economy framework for agrarian policy-making, where 'markets are social institutions whose distributional effects occur within given political and institutional hierarchies' (Weeks, 1995: 6). While certain interventions in the landholding structure or the access conditions to rural markets would be desirable from a welfare or sustainability viewpoint, political conditions often do not permit their full implementation. Most modeling approaches are not able to recognize the interaction between the political structure and the 'choice' of policy instruments. Therefore, agrarian policies frequently suffer from implicit biases in favor of dominant rural classes (Lipton, 1993; De Janvry and Sadoulet, 1992; also Chapter 2 by Pelupessy) and thus are facing a great deal of inconsistency at the level of their implementation. The third question refers to problems of including the following factors in the analysis: dynamic comparative advantages, complementary policies whose effects are conditional one on another, strategic measures and the long-term impact of non-economic factors (Schiff and Montenegro, 1997: 407; Thorpe, 1995: 223–4).

Policy instruments

In the evaluation of the effectiveness of policies it is necessary to distinguish clearly between the instruments to be manipulated by the government and its targets or objectives. The possibility of reaching a certain objective will depend on the existence of restrictions that are not likely to be affected by policies and institutions that could only be changed by structural policies in the long run (Pelupessy, 1997: 178–82). World market commodity prices are restrictive for the Central American policy maker, who can influence the current income of export growers by manipulating the tax rate. A redistributive land reform may be introduced to enhance the structural earning capacity of these growers.

Programs for agricultural growth and rural development can rely on a broad number of possible agrarian policy instruments. Selection of suitable incentives requires a detailed understanding of their implications at macroeconomic, sectoral and local level. But macro policies may also affect agriculture and sometimes they neutralize or contradict the effect of sectoral agrarian policy. Central America offers a wide range of experiences – both successes and failures – with different types of policy instruments and it is often almost impossible to isolate the effects of each separate measure or to distinguish between these and the influence of (external) restrictions. The most important policy instruments that have affected agriculture in the region will be briefly reviewed to draw conclusions regarding their effectiveness.

At macroeconomic level, the exchange rate and foreign trade regulations represent major trade policy instruments. Despite the traditional outward-oriented development strategy, exchange rates have usually been overvalued, but export producers receive special facilities, like US dollar certificates for coffee producers, tax deductions for banana companies and producers of non-traditional crops. The foreign exchange regime offered, however, limited incentives for the intensification of farming systems to improve the efficiency of agricultural production. After structural adjustment, import prices for agricultural inputs tended to rise, and a tendency towards reduced input applications for non-tradable basic grains can even be expected (Wattel and Ruben, 1992). For agricultural tradables the situation may be the opposite and will depend on the combined effect on the external output and input markets (see Chapters 3 to 6 in this volume).

Budgetary policies at the government level are related to taxation regimes, public spending and investment priorities. Since most government revenues are derived from indirect taxes, a clearly regressive effect has been noticed. Administrative weaknesses and widespread evasion reduce income from direct taxation as property taxes on houses, livestock and land. Guatemala especially is well known for its extremely low tax rate of less than six per cent of GDP. Consequently, government spending is severely limited and budgets for most public agencies only cover salaries but almost no operational costs. Public expenditures for social services such as health and education, stagnated during the last decade (exceptions are Costa Rica and Sandinista Nicaragua), while infrastructure development had to be financed primarily from national and international lending. Chapters 2 to 6 of this book emphasize the key role of public and/or private investments for the development of agriculture at the micro, meso and macro levels in Central America. An increase of public expenditure in agriculture of developing countries has also had positive effects on the aggregate supply response (Schiff and Montenegro, 1997: 407). Recent international cross-country research has confirmed the importance of fixed capital as a determinant of agricultural growth (Mundlak *et al.*, 1997). Another interesting conclusion of this study is that prices had little direct impact on agricultural growth, beyond the effects through inputs and the choice of technology. Access to public extension and financial services remained restricted to better-off farmers. Local community organizations, non-governmental agencies and externally funded rural development projects try to fill this gap. A systematic analysis of the role of a variety of these organizations at different levels of rural development has been carried out by Uphoff (1993). The role of the state as a development agent can be considered fairly restricted. Privatization of some former state activities like banking, extension and internal commerce therefore meets limited opposition, while decentralization can be a suitable device for bringing these services closer to the intended beneficiaries. The efficiency of domestic markets could be achieved in principle through more or less intervention (Singh, 1995). However, high concentrations, rent-seeking mechanisms and food security problems may not be automatically solved by privatization.

Commercial policies have been widely applied in Central America, particularly those controlling internal food prices for the urban population. In the 1970s most countries established state agencies in charge of purchasing basic grains (rice, maize, beans) from peasant producers at more or less stable prices. The state also influenced processing, transport and wholesale and retail activities to reduce the market power of the intermediaries. Local producers could only marginally benefit from the price guarantees, since high transaction costs and all kinds of quality standards reinforced a strong market segmentation, leaving ample room for informal intermediaries to dominate the market. Moreover, a major share of price subsidies finally accrued to consumers, while the government budget for internal trade showed a marked increase. To reduce the state deficit, internal trade was liberalized again and most former state agencies were abolished, while facilities for free intra-regional trade in cereals within certain price bands guarantee supply at the lowest prices.

Structural policies were important during the 1980s, when several countries launched interventionist programs of land reform and when some public investment was done in rural development. At the end of this period, even while a substantial part of the rural population still had no access to land, political conditions for further land reform were almost absent. Attention was now devoted to the formal registration of property rights. Land titling is considered an important condition for enhancing farm-level investments and guaranteeing access to financial institutions that usually require collateral for borrowing. Cost recovery for financial and technical assistance services proved to be viable only for medium and large size farmers.

Institutional development received more attention when budgetary limitations of the central government forced privatization and decentralization of activities. Most former rural development banks have been privatized and rural assistance programs are subject to decentralization towards NGOs or municipalities. However, real competition on rural markets is still restricted. Owing to low population densities and the limited size of the agrarian surplus, markets tend to remain relatively thin and delivery networks can be easily monopolized. Even in the sphere of financial intermediation, where sometimes local initiatives for village banking and credit cooperatives had some success, it remains difficult to guarantee adequate linkages with higher-level clearing institutes. For rural community services the establishment of social funds has been an important incentive. While relying essentially on self-selection mechanisms, local public works and start-up credits for rural non-agricultural enterprises proved to be effective instruments for targeting assistance towards poor households (Van der Walle and Nead, 1995).

Some general conclusions can be drawn with respect to the adjustment of the framework for agrarian policy-making in the Central American region. While exchange rate policies, foreign trade liberalization, privatization and market reforms reinforced the open character of the economy, institutional policies lagged behind. Economic reforms stimulated overall economic growth and reestablished equilibrium in government accounts (Irwin, 1991). However, the diminishing role of the state in Central America has brought about a sensible reduction in the provision of public goods, the management of positive and negative externalities, actions to enhance competitiveness of rural markets and institutions and support for rural investments. The chapters in this book show the urgent need for these policy instruments, because the dysfunctional internal structure of the agrarian sector has only been slightly modified, and only minor adjustments took place in terms of land use or production technologies. The 'crowding-in' effect of public investment on private investment is of fundamental importance in Central American agriculture (De Janvry *et al.*, 1993: 574). There is now a real possibility of creating complementarity and synergy between society and (central) government actions, especially in the small-farm rural sector (Evans, 1996; Tendler, 1993).

Effectiveness

The effectiveness of policy reforms has to be evaluated from the viewpoint of the objectives perceived and their impact on the behavior and performance of economic agents. We will focus here on the latter perspective and therefore address two major questions: first, what type of response reactions to different policy incentives can be registered at the level of individual farm households, and second, which factors or environments affect differences in response between farm households, and how are the positive and negative effects distributed over various agents?

Several studies indicate that supply response to economic policy incentives tends to be low in situations of frequent market or institutional failures. The availability of competitive inputs and outputs, including consumer goods markets and public goods as technology, is crucial for the efficiency of reforms (Binswanger *et al.*, 1995: 2732). Transaction costs for access to land, credit and inputs are generally high in Central America, and local markets are strongly segmented (see Chapters 2, 5 and 7 of this book). Under these circumstances, market liberalization alone cannot bring about sufficiently competitive conditions to improve welfare, but is most likely to result in increasing price differences and segmentation. Consequently, small peasants might reduce the market-orientedness of their agrarian production and economize on the purchase of market inputs, especially fertilizers. Subsistence agriculture may increase. These tendencies are reinforced by the registered institutional failures that limit access to information and constrain the coverage and outreach of technical assistance and extension programs, occasioning more risk-averse behavior by peasant households. Finally, the overall reduction in the availability of (formal) credit and the preference of most private financial agencies for non-agricultural investment point in the same direction. Supply response reactions may thus be rather low for smaller producers located in hillside areas who are more specialized in basic grains production, whereas a higher response can be expected from medium producers who devote a larger area to traditional and/or non-traditional agro-export crops.

Two reactions to policy incentives are usually distinguished: an income effect (the result of changes in relative input and output prices) and a substitution effect (Singh *et al.*, 1986). The latter effect refers mainly to adjustments in technology choice, in market orientation and in input use that occur with changing market opportunities. After structural adjustment, technologies applied for basic grains production – especially for small farmers in hillsides and remote regions – generally made less use of purchased inputs and relied on the substitution of labor for inputs (Chapters 5 and 6). As noted before, the rate of commercialization of basic grains production also decreased. Wherever opportunities for exports to neighboring countries arise, however, market production is strengthened (Chapters 3 and 4). In order to maintain household income, engagement in wage labor and off-farm employment becomes more important (Chapter 8 by Ruben and Clemens). Higher opportunity costs of labor – due to labor demands from the more dynamic agro-export sector – may compete with growing demands for on-farm labor use. This implies that the intra-household division of labor will also be affected.

Besides implications for welfare and efficiency, attention should be given to the distributional impact of agrarian policies. While market policies are characterized by their generic nature, structure policies permit – in principle – better targeting. Price incentives proved to be more effective in those countries and sectors where marketing and infrastructure are better developed (especially in Costa Rica and El Salvador). Financial reforms led to an overall decline in the availability of rural credit in all countries. Sanders and Wattel (Chapter 7) argue that the reduction in (formal) credit mostly affected two groups: the rent-seeking elite (i.e. cattle holders and traditional agro-export producers) and land reform beneficiaries who formerly had a preferential access to credit. Consequently, their land use patterns will become more extensive and constraints on the land market are likely to appear. Otherwise, small and landless farmers, as well as tenants, already facing severe limitations in obtaining access to land (as demonstrated by Pelupessy in Chapter 2) and now receiving less support for access to yield-enhancing inputs, will be more inclined to engagement in the rural or peri-urban labor markets. Once they become net purchasers of food, they are driven away from their traditional class interest. The 'struggle for land', which has been a major motive for social and political mobilization during the last decades, now becomes an issue of secondary importance. Local and national peasant organizations increasingly focus their attention on issues of rural finance, self-management of marketing networks and decentralization of services to guarantee direct benefits for their members (Tangermann and Valdés, 1994).

Finally, long-term implications of agrarian policy reform depend mainly on the prospects for the establishment and maintenance of viable family farms. The current structure of economic incentives favors a process of labor intensification within and outside the farm boundaries. Changes in cropping pattern are restricted to a small segment of medium-size farms that more or less successfully started production of non-traditional crops (Weller, 1993). Small farms may have lower costs in producing these crops, but have less or insecure access to external factors and services such as transport and marketing (Collins, 1995: 1105–10). Growth rates of cereal yields and changes in livestock stocking rates remained generally low, however. With declining levels of input applications these agricultural production systems will also become less sustainable (De Groot and Ruben, 1997). For non-marketable inputs it will be almost impossible for commonly applied agrarian policies to become efficient. Negative nutrient balances, declining organic matter stocks and degeneration of seed systems already demonstrate the fragility of peasant production systems (Pasos, 1994; Leonard, 1987). When soil erosion further threatens productive capacity, farmers will finally be left with no other alternative than to sell their land. Agrarian policies without a more explicit focus on sustainable land use will leave at least the Central American peasantry in disarray.

Agrarian policies and rural development

Macroeconomic adjustment policies and sectoral reforms should have created conditions for agricultural growth in Central America, although they could not bring about a fundamental change in the dynamics of the rural development process. The case studies have shown that exchange rate policies and market liberalization favored some reactivation of the agro-export economy based on the corresponding price and income incentives. But rural market failures and segmentation, the absence of delivery networks and appropriate local institutions strongly reduced the effectiveness and efficiency of policies. The causes of this inconsistency between strategies for agricultural growth and rural development can be found in underinvestment in public goods, constrained access to financial institutions and limited development of externalities and inter-sectoral linkages (Chenery, 1974). In the 'plundering of agriculture' argument, past economic policies were even held responsible for the underdevelopment of agriculture in developing countries (Schiff and Valdés, 1992).

Apparently this was related to the agrarian transformation process whereby the sector would generate a surplus for industrial development (Timmer, 1988). This implies that real producers' prices are maintained at low levels and that the importance of the creation of rural purchasing power is neglected. However, the real problems are the absence of previous resource transfers towards agriculture to foster rural development, and the lack of employment opportunities in other sectors in Central America. Direct and indirect taxation were not an impediment for the development of an export sector in agriculture. So the economic variables do not tell the whole story. In the region, agrarian policies cannot be seen as totally independent from the social structure (Pelupessy, 1997: 173–5).

For the selection of suitable agrarian policy instruments, detailed understanding of the rural social structure and of the motives of farm household behavior is required. Most farmers maintain multiple relationships with land, labor, capital and commodity markets and derive their income from various farm and non-farm sources (Devé, 1990). This plurality creates a variety of interests and class positions that may limit perspectives for collective private action.

Central America's agrarian reform can be characterized as an 'incomplete' process, because privatization and decentralization were not accompanied by a parallel development of competitive market frameworks and the establishment of effective institutions. In these circumstances, local authoritarian elites can easily take control of rural institutions and traditional contractual relations may be re-emerging. Market reform under conditions of low market development thus requires a far more active role from the state. Both public and private actions are necessary to create a sustainable market 'order' or 'system' in the rural economy (see the important contributions of Grabowski, 1995, and Platteau, 1994). It can also be argued that liberalization of the small-farmer sector should be introduced gradually. Market-oriented policies should be imposed on those who can afford them.

2
Institutional Constraints and Internal Dynamics of Land Reform in El Salvador and Taiwan

Wim Pelupessy

Introduction

The agrarian reform that took place throughout the 1980s in El Salvador and its continuation in the 1990s is generally considered unsuccessful and restricted in nature, and is plagued by inefficiencies and internal as well as external constraints (Diskin, 1989; Reinhardt, 1989; Montoya, 1991; Acevedo *et al.*, 1995). Nevertheless, a recent study has suggested a reconsideration and deepening of this reform, paying due attention to the elimination of institutional constraints. Complementary sectorial and macro policies could play an important role, while the effects of economic and political variables should be considered as well (Pelupessy, 1997: 268–9).

At the heart of agrarian reform lies land reform, which is broadly defined as an effort of the government to modify land ownership and tenure relationships in agriculture, which include interventions directed towards increasing land ownership and land use equity (Grindle, 1986: 212). According to Lipton (1993: 647), it is 'state action to induce substantial transfers of land rights to, and consequent rises in real income or power for, the rural poor.' Hayami (1991: 164) mentions reduction of rural poverty and inequality, the adjustment of unequal asset distribution and the increase in employment and labor income per unit of land area as important goals of redistributing land reform. An agrarian reform also includes complementary sectoral policies such as the pricing and marketing of crops, technical assistance, the allocation of credit and other inputs and other productivity-raising measures. This should accelerate the agrarian transformation process.

This chapter focuses on the institutional constraints to land reform and its far-reaching effects on the dynamics of the agrarian transformation in

El Salvador. These are analyzed in the light of Taiwan's successful land reform project of the 1950s. An examination of the motives, design and (long-term) results of the Taiwanese reform may provide useful insights into the problems of Salvadoran agrarian policies. Attention is given to the historical differences of agrarian and social structures, and the domestic and international political environments. It will be shown that the study of the economic and political mechanisms that accelerated the agrarian transformation in Taiwan will also be relevant for the Salvadoran case.

Before we proceed, it is useful to explain some basic concepts used in the present analysis. Agrarian transformation may be seen not only as the change from an agrarian to an industrial economy as, for instance, in Dorner (1992: 4), but should be considered a more fundamental process where agrarian production and distribution become progressively based on wage labor, restricted (private) ownership of the means of production and the operation of markets for commodities and factors of production (Pelupessy, 1997: 7).

This institutional change is affected by state policies, but the former may also influence the latter, depending on the presence and extent of relative state autonomy. This autonomy is the capacity of states to adopt policies that affect the interests of the dominant social classes negatively or that at least are not geared to these interests. This capacity may be related to the influences of more than one social class in the state, to the control of state institutions over economic resources such as foreign exchange and infrastructure and to the influence of external agents.

Some authors stress the importance of politics, using the concept of the developmental state, which is one 'whose politics have concentrated sufficient power, autonomy and capacity ... to shape, pursue and encourage the achievement of explicit developmental objectives.' (Leftwich, 1995: 500) The presence of this autonomous state is seen as the explanation for the successful transformation in countries like Taiwan in the postwar period (Leftwich, 1995: 501).

Land reform seems to be one of the fundamental development strategies, although there is still no unanimity on this issue, let alone how it should be constituted. Therefore the next section of this chapter will summarize the recent discussion on the theory and practice of land reform as the base of any agrarian development process. In the section that follows, the initial conditions in the pre-reform period of El Salvador and Taiwan will be compared. It will be demonstrated that structural restrictions hampered agricultural development in both countries. The direct and more cyclical or temporary motives for the reforms will be discussed next. After this we will compare the design and implementation of the land reforms of El Salvador and Taiwan. It will be argued that existing institutions essentially determine the design of reforms. The choice of instruments could serve economic as well as political objectives, both of which should be considered. On the other hand, the character of implementation and the different stages of the process will be mainly affected by specific and short-term economic and political considerations at the start. External political agents were important in both cases where the reforms had an anti-communist motivation and the United States was an important stakeholder. Social turmoil was a common feature when the reforms were introduced. The next section compares the impacts of both reforms. The affected land, labor and crops and their weight compared with those in the non-reformed agricultural sector provide useful indicators. A more or less comparable time-frame of a ten-to fifteen-year period of implementation is assessed.

The changes in the use of technology, current inputs, credits, technical assistance and their effects on the growth of production and productivity provide insights into the compliance with growth objectives of the reform. The impact on employment and income generation, rural organization and state involvement indicates the equity effects that influence the social structure of rural areas. The consistency between land reform and other policies may also reflect the degree of autonomy of the respective states.

In the following section, the long-term effects of the land reforms of both countries will be evaluated. In this case, we will try to use the results of Taiwan to make a kind of prediction of possible trends in El Salvador. Again, the development of rural classes, intersectoral linkages and resource transfer mechanisms from agriculture to other sectors may give indications of the long-term impact on agrarian transformation. The future integration of agriculture in the rest of the economy depends also on complementary actions of the (developmental) state. Finally, conclusions will be presented in the last section for future policies to extend and deepen the land reform process in El Salvador.

Land reform at the end of a millennium

According to a review article of Thiesenhusen: 'Land reform lives!' (1995a: 193–209). The question is, for what purpose and under what conditions? A correctly designed and applied reform may facilitate, for example, efficiency-increasing changes in agricultural factor and product markets, technologies and power structures (Lipton, 1993: 642).

However, some authors see the justification of land reform more on social and political than on economic grounds (El-Ghonemy 1990: 282; 299: Timmer, 1991: 16; Sobhan, 1993: 115). Hayami has constructed a model where political (marginal) revenues and costs of reform are downward and upward functions respectively of the degree of land redistribution. An optimal level of land distribution may follow, given its political revenues and costs. Undefined preference functions, highly unequal distribution of (political) market power of participants and institutional changes make the approach less applicable (Pelupessy, 1997: 131). On the other hand, equitable redistribution of ownership rights of land to individual families is often considered the only rational method of reform (Prosterman and Riedinger, 1989; Prosterman *et al.*, 1990). The possibilities of scale, organizational, distributional and technical advantages can make other methods relevant, as a potentially positive relationship between size and productivity cannot be ruled out a priori (Platteau, 1992: 45–50; Binswanger *et al.*, 1995). Furthermore, it should be noted that the income of the rural poor depends not only on access to land and efficiency in its use, but also on the distribution of the generated rents (Bell, 1988: 763). This means that other agricultural and sectoral policies, as well as macro policies, must be considered in the analysis. The direct impact of reforms should be measured in growth, efficiency and equity terms: production and productivity in agriculture, productive employment, marketable surpluses, income distribution and rural poverty. Political effects such as changes in stability in rural areas, social polarization and class structures may have a more indirect and long-lasting character than the economic factors mentioned earlier and may affect the sustainability of these. However, it goes too far to qualify land reform as a 'political exercise with surprisingly few solid economic underpinnings' (Timmer, 1991: 16). It will be argued in the following sections that institutions and adequate management of their change are of fundamental importance for the economic successes of reform.

The initial conditions[1]

With an area of about 20 000 square kilometres, El Salvador is the smallest republic in Central America. Taiwan has a territory 1.7 times this size. Both are tropical, northern-latitude countries (El Salvador 15°

and Taiwan 23.5°), have a mountainous character, and are densely populated. Despite the difference in total area, the size of the respective farmlands was 1 089 000 hectares of livestock and cropland at the end of the 1970s in El Salvador and 870 000 hectares cropland in Taiwan at the end of the 1940s. El Salvador still had a reserve of 200 000 hectares of potential farmland.

With 407 000 rural families, El Salvador had an average 2.7 hectares per family farm, while the average was 1.2 hectares for Taiwan, with 665 000 rural households. If pre-reform trends had continued in El Salvador, all land reserves would have been consumed in the 1990s, when average land intensity would have dropped to 1.7 hectares per family. This point had been already reached in the 1940s in Taiwan. Before reform, one-fifth of the Taiwanese farmland (181 000 hectares) was owned by the state as a consequence of the expulsion of Japanese landlords after the second World War, before which Taiwan had been a Japanese colony since 1896. The remaining 80 per cent or 682 000 hectares was private land, of which 260 000 hectares were in the hands of Taiwanese (absentee) landlords. All Salvadoran land was privately owned, of which 40 per cent (about 560 000 hectares) belonged to big landowners (70 hectares or more).

Access to land was highly unequal in both countries, as is shown in Table 2.1. Owing to discrepancies in information, slightly different size categories of landholding are used. Still, the similarity between the two countries in the relative distribution of access of rural families to land is striking. However, the magnitudes of the landholding were much larger in El Salvador than in Taiwan. The increasing trend of land concentration in El Salvador meant a strong increase in landless families, a decrease in the number of tenancies, and concentrated property ownership by landlords. In the fifteen years before reform, landlessness among rural families in this country increased from 12 per cent to 41 per cent of the total, while the number of tenants declined by 50 per cent. In 1971, 60 per cent of the landholdings were still occupied by tenants or lessees. After the Second World War, the agro-export crops were modernized by new technologies, higher input intensity and improved seeds. Coffee yield per hectare reached the highest levels in the world. Growth rates had also been enhanced by import-substituting industrialization and regional economic integration. The dynamics of these strategies lasted only one decade. The extremely skewed distribution of land and the accelerated expansion of rural poverty restricted the possibilities for further growth and made the economy vulnerable to temporal shocks.

Table 2.1 Pre-reform distribution of landholdings in El Salvador and Taiwan

El Salvador (1975)[a]		*Taiwan (1950)[b]*	
Size	%	Size	%
Landless	40.9	<0.5 ha	25.6
<1 ha	34.1	0.5 to < 1 ha	45.0
1 to 1.9 ha	15.3	} 1 to 4.9 ha	27.3
2 to 4.9 ha	6.0		
5 to 9.9 ha	1.9	} 5 to 20 ha	1.9
>10 ha	1.8		
		>20 ha	0.2
Total	100	Total	100
Absolute amount (1000 families)	407	Absolute amount (1000 households)	665

Sources: Pelupessy (1997); Wang Rong (1992); Ho (1966).
Notes:
[a] El Salvador – number of families (incl. landless).
[b] Taiwan – number of households (one plot per household presumed).

On the other hand, the increase in population in Taiwan led to a proliferation of subleasing systems and the informal transfer of rights from owners and tenants. This complicated the tenancy relationship and weakened the control of landowners. Tenancy rates increased to between 50 and 70 per cent of the harvest and landlords tried to undermine contracts, refusing written agreements and often asking for deposits or advanced payment. In this way the tenancy system became unsustainable and agricultural growth stagnated. In 1948, 30 per cent of the farm families in Taiwan were owners, 26 per cent partial owners and 38 per cent tenants.

Both countries were agro-export economies. In El Salvador, agriculture and livestock products counted for 25 per cent of real GDP before reform and export crops for ten per cent, of which coffee was the main product, contributing about seven per cent. The production and export of coffee have been the economic base of the dominant land-controlling class, the so-called oligarchy. The export crops coffee, cotton and sugar cane occupied 40 per cent of the cultivated land (coffee 23 per cent), showed higher output growth rates than the basic grains and earned 60 to 70 per cent of total export income. The export crops were normally grown on farms of ten hectares or more, while the most important estates had at least 50 hectares. The basic grains of El Salvador were cultivated on smaller plots and had far lower profitability per hectare. Because of this, rural income was more concentrated than land ownership and the development was of a bimodal nature.

Taiwan's main crop was rice, which occupied 60 per cent of the farmland and produced 15 per cent of real GDP. For agriculture, the proportion was 35 per cent. The main crop was even more dominant than in El Salvador. The cultivation of rice had been stimulated since colonial times, when Taiwan served as an important supplier of cheap food for the colonizer (Byres, 1989). The Japanese introduced new cultivation technologies, improved seeds and trading systems, and organized the small peasants so that high yields were obtained. In this way, Taiwan relieved the problems of stagnating agriculture and growing population in Japan. During the Japanese occupation, rice was not only a staple to feed the local population, but also an export crop with a relatively advanced technology. The situation changed drastically in the 1940s. The scarcity of land, the disorder in the tenancy system, the disappearance of the Japanese market and the damage caused by the Second World War restricted further modernization and growth of Taiwanese agriculture. Agricultural development in El Salvador and Taiwan reached its limits at the end of the 1970s and 1940s respectively.

Motives for reform

The unequal development of Salvadoran agriculture provided the structural motivation for reform. The agrarian reform that was introduced in 1980 was to be the backbone of a new strategy to reactivate and restructure the stagnating economy. An explanation for the occurrence of this turning point can be found in short-term economic and political factors. Examples of the former include the failure to reactivate the import substitution model, the downturn of regional integration, the two world oil crises, the cyclical crisis of the developed economies and its effects on the world commodity markets, and the problems in the international capital markets in the second half of the 1970s.

Structural imbalances in the economy also caused domestic political unrest, aggravated by the rise of politico-military organizations and strong popular demand for land redistribution. Progressive peasant organizations emerged despite the legal proscription. Restrictions on legalized trade unions and two successive fraudulent general elections further reduced the credibility of the political system.

At the same time, on the external side, the Sandinistas had ousted the very conservative Somoza regime in Nicaragua, which lead to an international fear of communist takeovers in the rest of Central America. The United States' Kissinger plan and the Socialist and Christian Democrat Internationals advocated structural changes in the region. In El Salvador a US-backed coup of 'young' military officers deposed the landlord-related government and gave way to a reformist state with a certain degree of autonomy from the landholding classes. More structural reasons for increasing state autonomy in El Salvador were the expanding control of the state in the economy and the rising influence of non-landholding classes and the army. Internally, the new government had the support of the middle-class-based Christian Democrats, the state bureaucracy, an important faction of the military and reformist trade unions. The programs for agrarian reform introduced by the government a few months later had both an anti-landlord and anti-communist character.

The Taiwanese reform of the 1950s had similar characteristics, although for different reasons. Structurally, it was basically the tenancy system that created restrictions to further agricultural growth. The communist takeover of mainland China caused the flight of about two million people to the island in 1946–9, increasing its population by 40 per cent. Among these migrants were the cadres of the Kuomintang Party, bureaucrats and a part of the nationalist army. This invasion took place after the withdrawal of the Japanese colonial authority from Taiwan. High immigration, albeit on a much smaller scale, also occurred at the end of the 1960s in El Salvador as a result of the conflict with Honduras. However, these were mainly peasants and landless rural workers that settled in the poor rural areas of the country.

The mainlanders practically took over the island of Taiwan and implemented the agrarian reform to prevent a peasant uprising after the mainland defeat. Economic motives were the need to feed the growing population of Taiwan and to eliminate restrictions for further rural development in order to finance the industrialization process. The considerable autonomy of the new Kuomintang state was based on its military power, the expropriation and state ownership of land and industrial enterprises from Japanese former owners, and the political and economic support of the United States. The US played a fundamental role in the agrarian reforms of both El Salvador and Taiwan, mostly for geopolitical reasons. USAID was the important institution that participated in the planning and implementation in the first case, while the Sino-American Joint Commission for Rural Reconstruction assisted in the second.

Design and implementation

Design

The Salvadoran reform was designed to take place in three phases to be implemented soon after the start of the process, and a fourth one followed as a result of the peace accord of 1992.

The first phase affected the property of landlords with more than 500 hectares as cooperatives of at least 25 permanent workers were formed. In principle, 476 haciendas were to be expropriated, while the original owner could retain 150 hectares plus 20 per cent if improvements were made to the property. On the basis of their tax declarations, the owners were to be compensated with 20-to 30-year bonds, to be repaid by the cooperative over 30 years. The Institute for Agrarian Transformation (ISTA) had to execute Phase I and support the cooperatives with credit, inputs, technical assistance and supervision. The affected haciendas mostly cultivated export crops (coffee, cotton and sugar) or were engaged in extensive livestock farming. Big landowners succeeded in canceling a second phase of the land reform that would have affected property of 100 to 500 hectares, mostly the profitable large export-crop estates. This phase was later replaced by the 'law of voluntary land sale', which was on a much smaller scale and did not include the expropriation of land.

Phase III consisted of a program of the land-to-the-tiller type that had been successfully implemented in Asia (including Taiwan) and was strongly supported by US advisers. The program enabled small tenants to obtain up to seven hectares of land through a hire-purchase system. To qualify they had to submit applications to a new institution, the National Office for Agricultural Finance (FINATA). Large leasehold properties for export crops like cotton were exempted from this program. The fourth phase of the reform was a result of the peace settlement between the Farabundo Marti Liberation Front (FMLN) and the government after 12 years of civil war in 1992. It was a combination of the above-mentioned law of voluntary sale of land and Phase III, where the Banco de Tierras (Land Bank), another new state institution, bought the land of big owners, cooperatives or others and sold it on easy terms to former guerrilla-members, ex-soldiers and small peasants, with a maximum of 7 hectares. Given the initial rural structure of the country, it can be seen that Phase I had a mainly efficiency and productivity-enhancing effect, while Phase III was apparently more equity-oriented. Phase IV and other 'voluntary sale' actions were a mixture of these two types of instruments and intended to extend the land market in El Salvador.

The agrarian reform of the 1950s in Taiwan was at least as interventionist as the Salvadoran reform. The first program to be implemented in 1949 was the Rent Reduction Program. Land rents were reduced by law from the usual 50 to 70 per cent of the harvest to a maximum of 37.5 per cent of the annual main crop yield. Additionally, a regulation was introduced to protect the rights of tenants from the arbitrariness of oral contracts, unjustified breach of contract, and the negative effects of change of ownership of the land.

The second program that started in 1951 was the sale of public land to its tenant cultivators, farm laborers, tenants, farmers with insufficient land and new farmers. The maximum that could be purchased was 0.48 to 1.94 hectares (0.5 to 2 chia) of paddy land or 0.97 to 3.88 hectares of dryland. Sale prices were to be two and a half times the annual yield of the main crop and had to be paid in equal parts over ten years without interest.

It should be noted that the original 1947 plan was to lease the majority of public farmland to 293 agricultural cooperatives with a minimum of 50 hectares (300 mow) and 10 families each (comparable to Phase I of the El Salvador case). The remaining unsuitable pieces were to be leased to individual families who were cultivating the land. Because of lack of interest in the cooperatives, problems with collective operations and subleasing practices of individual farmers, the cooperative scheme was abandoned (Chen, 1961: 52–3).

The third part of the Taiwanese land reform process implemented in 1953 was the land-to-the-tiller program. This included the compulsory purchase and sale of private land to tenants. Depending on the quality of the land, landlords could retain from 1.5 to 6 hectares of paddy fields (3 to 12 hectares of dry land). Purchase and sale prices were the equivalent of two and a half times the main crop yield, calculated in quantity of rice or sweet potatoes, to make it independent of price fluctuations. The price was to be paid in half-yearly installments over ten years. Landlords were compensated for 70 per cent of the price in land bonds, to be canceled in real terms (rice or sweet potatoes) with an annual interest rate of 4 per cent. 30 per cent of the debt was paid with stocks in government-owned corporations.

If we look at the Taiwanese reform, the strong equity bias of the instruments is clear, which may be related to its political objectives. Obviously, it also contained the efficiency-increasing regulation of tenancy practice. One remarkable aspect is the design of a redistribution mechanism of rural income by the price intervention of the Rent Reduction Program and other measures that gave tenants the opportunity to buy land through the other programs or on the general land market. Direct equity-promoting measures were absent in the Salvadoran design. Only in Phase IV was some financial support given by the state to small farmers to operate on the land market.

Implementation

The implementation of the different programs of the Salvadoran agrarian reform was of a top-down nature and accompanied by military operations. A civil war continued throughout the 1980s. Phase I was carried out through the occupation of the haciendas and the expulsion of members of peasant organizations by the army. This instrument differed radically from the income redistribution measure used in Taiwan to meet the political goals in the first place. The agrarian cooperatives of El Salvador were closely monitored and controlled by the state institute ISTA, while technical and financial assistance came from USAID. In the 1980s the US had spent about $800 million on the land reform, though a significant part was used to repair infrastructural damage caused by the civil war and to compensate big landowners.

Large and medium landowners who were potentially affected by Phase III of the reform used death-squads and other paramilitary gangs to expel tenants who might qualify for land purchase. A large number of refugees and displaced persons appeared in the 1980s.

As a consequence of the application of these programs, both landowners and popular organizations opposed the land reform. The civil war that raged during its twelve-year course cost 30 000 lives and more than 1 million refugees, a fifth of the population. As a result of the peace agreement in 1992, Phase IV was introduced, distributing land previously purchased from owners to demobilized *guerrilleros*, soldiers, and squatters who had occupied the properties in the war. This phase progressed slowly and in 1999 still had not ended.

In general, all Salvadoran programs were plagued by inefficiencies, slow bureaucratic procedures and sometimes even sabotage. ISTA, FINATA and Banco de Tierras staff were scarce and insufficiently trained. The design of Phase III was primarily conceived by US advisers and criticized by peasant organizations and state officials (Simons and Stephens, 1981: 44–63). In all phases, participation of the beneficiaries was almost nonexistent. The formal assignment of land and cooperative rights was time-consuming and increased uncertainty in rural areas. Big landowners pressed successfully for regressive changes in the reform legislation, which resulted in the abolition of Phase II, an increase of land ceilings to 245 hectares, and other measures in their favor. As a consequence of increasing rural risk and uncertainty, investments in agriculture declined considerably and landed properties were subdivided either for sale or for delivery to figureheads.

The Taiwanese land reform implementation was also safeguarded by military actions. Before the reform, the Kuomintang government suppressed a rebellion to loosen the ties with China in 1947 at the cost of 20 000 lives (Amsden, 1988: 151). The support of the leading army general had been of fundamental importance for the reform's success. Its top-down nature was evidenced by the frequent use of decrees rather than parliamentary legislation. However, important changes in the 'rules of the game' were not a result of landlord pressure, but more a consequence of efficiency and equity arguments. The case of replacement of the leasehold cooperative model by the individual sale of public land is a clear example of this. Before the start of the reform, the landlord class was already weakened by both the expropriation of large Japanese landholdings and the absence of a strong relationship between the Taiwanese landlords and the new Kuomintang regime.

The authority behind the execution of the rent reduction program was the official Land Bureau. However, it was complemented by private supervisory agencies at village and township levels, which became the Farm Tenancy Committees composed of tenant representatives, owner-farmers, landlords and local government leaders. The Committees had an important role in the implementation process and the solution of disputes (Chen 1961: 23–6). About 4000 promoters were mobilized to introduce the new-style tenancy contracts and within a few months almost half of the farm holdings were covered (Wang Rong 1992: 11). As we will see later, the rent reduction program resulted in a significant redistribution of rural income that greatly increased the purchasing power of poor tenants. The second program was that of the sale of public land. The new owners received government assistance in the form of loans, extension services, periodic inspection and other aids.

There were also some restrictions on ownership rights to prevent reconcentration. Transfer of the land was allowed only in the case of inheritance and could be sold only to the government, which would resell it to another farmer. Within one year, a record number of 300 000 plots of public land were sold. Applications for purchases were screened by local Committees for Establishment of Owner-Farmers, composed by representatives of local governments and assemblies, farmers' associations and the local branch of the Land Bank of Taiwan. It should be noted that the program was implemented to show the landlords that the government was determined to redistribute land. Other goals were to acquire experience for the land-to-the-tiller program and to accumulate resources for the next steps of reform (Hsieh 1989: 7).

The third program could be considered the final step in the Taiwanese reform process towards the generalization of private small ownership in agriculture, intended to replace the traditional tenancy structure. During this process, the government was still protecting some of the economic interests of the landlords, despite their weak position. Care was taken to give reasonable compensation and the possibility of retaining 2.9 hectares of medium-grade land. The purchase price and repayment conditions were the same as in the case of the sale of public land (Hsieh 1989: 10). Besides its political aims, the program had the purpose of stimulating the participation of landlords in industrialization and the privatization of state corporations.

The implementation of this program was preceded by fifteen months of general ownership registration and classification. The Sino-American Joint Commission on Rural Reconstruction provided technical assistance and financial support. Most of the rechecking of the registration and the compulsory purchase of all tenant-cultivated land by the government and its resale to cultivators was completed between May and December 1953.

In these months, more than 32 000 promoters and assistants were mobilized at the national and local levels to execute these tasks, which comprised 2.1 million plots of farm land and 800 000 families of tenants, owners and farm laborers (Chen, 1961: 74–4). About 106 000 (mostly small) landowners were affected, to the benefit of about 195 000 tenants. Compensation of the landowners was completed in 1954.

To prevent reconcentration, the government introduced some follow-up measures, including the annual survey of farm households, restrictions on the resale of land to third parties and special loans of the Land Bank to land-to-the-tiller purchasers. With the implementation of different reform programs, thousands of field workers participated in land registration to complete the cadastre, assisted in the transactions and in the estimation of the quality and price of the land, and made the compulsory sale of the land effective. Examining the implementation of the three programs of the Taiwanese reform, one may say that, compared with El Salvador, the execution of each was much more integrated and better prepared. Policy changes were made for reasons of efficiency rather than politics, while the process was closely monitored and controlled by state institutions with considerable investments in financial and human resources. In both countries implementation was influenced by cyclical economic and political developments.

The impact of reform

Redistributive

The achievements of both land reforms in terms of affected farmland and families that benefited are given in Table 2.2. This contains both absolute figures and the weights in the total area of farmland and number of rural families. Most of the data presented reflect the results within a decade of implementation of the reform in the two countries. An exception is the figure concerning the (planned) redistribution ensuing from the peace accord in El Salvador, because it comprises the area already occupied by squatters in the civil war period.

The relative importance of the total reformed area was more or less the same in both countries. After one decade of land reform most of

Table 2.2 Achievements of land reform in El Salvador and Taiwan (ten years)

Program	Area (1000 hectares)		Beneficiaries (1000 families)	
	ES	Taiwan	ES	Taiwan
Rent reduction	—	257 (29%)	—	296 (36%)
Cooperatives	206 (14%)	—	30 (8%)	—
Sale public land[a]		70 (8%)		140 (17%)
Land-to-the-tiller	72 (5%)	139 (16%)	47 (13%)	195 (24%)
Voluntary sale[b]	17 (1%)	40 (4%)	12 (3%)	78 (9%)
Peace settlement	79 (5%)	—	39 (11%)	—
Total reformed	374 (25%)	249 (29%)	128 (35%)	413 (50%)
Non-reformed (% landless)	1 094 (75%)	624 (71%)	242 (65%) (31%)	406 (50%) (8%)
Total farmland	1 468 (100%)	873 (100%)	370 (100%)	819 (100%)

Sources:
Pelupessy, (1997: 145); FMLN – Coordinación Nacional Sector Campesino (1995: 12); Hsieh (1989: 4–10); Ho (1966: 52); Thorbecke (1992: 22); Chen (1961: 5–91, 308).

Notes:
[a] Cumulative sales of public land in Taiwan in 1976: 287 000 tenants bought 139 000 hectares.
[b] Cumulative voluntary sales in Taiwan in 1986: 157 000 tenants with 79 000 hectares.

the land still belonged to the non-reformed sector. For El Salvador it consisted of 300 000 hectares in the smallholder sector and about 800 000 hectares of commercial landholdings. Approximately one-third of the smallholder area remained under tenancy.

In Taiwan, 110 000 hectares (18 per cent) of the non-reformed sector was still public land at that time and the rest was cultivated by small owners and tenants. In 1976, only 40 000 hectares of public land were left, while an additional 70 000 hectares were available for sale to about 150 000 new small owners (Hsieh, 1989).

In Taiwan, both the land-to-the-tiller and the voluntary sales areas as well as the number of owners were much more important than in El Salvador. As we have seen, the Salvadorean program was greatly stimulated by government implementation measures, while the Taiwanese was also a result of the rent reduction program that affected almost 30 per cent of the total cultivated area and 40 per cent of rural families. A total income redistribution of 18 per cent of the rice pro-duction in 1948 went to the tenants and increased their net real family income by 43 per cent (Hsieh 1989: 15–18), which created additional purchasing power to buy land. Because of this and other reform pro-grams, the value of the land belonging to landlords declined and they became more willing to offer land for sale voluntarily.

This type of income redistribution did not occur at all in El Salvador, so tenants and other smallholders remained entirely dependent on land redistribution measures and government subsidies. Because of the civil war land value declined, but since there was no appropriate land market small farmers and landless could not benefit. In terms of beneficiaries, the Taiwan reform included 50 per cent of rural families, while in El Salvador the proportion was 35 per cent and as low as 24 per cent if the peace settlement of 1992 is not taken into account. More than 30 per cent of the rural families in El Salvador were landless, while in Taiwan this figure was less than 10 per cent. In terms of beneficiaries, the cooperativization program of El Salvador had rela-tively the smallest effect, especially when compared with the public land sale program of Taiwan, which favored a two times greater pro-portion of rural families.

The unequal nature of the Salvadoran reform can also be deduced by looking at the number of hectares allocated per family. While the total reformed area gives an average of 2.8 hectares per family, the individ-ual programs varied between 1.4 and 1.5 for land-to-the-tiller or volun-tary sale and 6.9 hectares for the agrarian cooperatives. The Taiwanese average of 0.6 hectares per family gave a variation of 0.5 to 0.7 hectares (land-to-the-tiller). The non-reform sector in El Salvador had an average extension that is up to twice as high if the landless are excluded. This average masks the high concentration in Salvadoran non-reformed agriculture, where the smallholder sector is 2.9 hectares per family and the commercial sector averages more than 50 hectares.

Before and after the reform, agricultural tenancy relations declined in both countries, although not for exactly the same reasons. In El Salvador, landowners generally tried to cancel tenancy contracts or agreements to prevent future application of the land-to-the-tiller program, even when owners of 7 hectares or less were not to be affected. In 1971, 60 per cent of the landholding and 24 per cent of the farmland came under tenancy contracts.[2] These proportions fell to 32 per cent and 7 per cent respectively in 1991, indicating that in post-reform El Salvador the tenancy land market maintained its importance only for smallholders. For Taiwan in 1949, about 40 per cent of the landholdings with approximately the same proportion of total cultivated area was reduced to 15 per cent for both categories immediately after reform, and had declined to 5 per cent thirty years later in 1987.[3] This was a logical result of the small owner stimulating land reform and agrarian policy afterwards.

Productive growth

The productive consequences may be observed in the average growth rates of agriculture and of individual crops in the respective reform periods (Table 2.3).

El Salvador showed negative growth in agriculture and stagnation in the livestock sector. This was a result of a strong negative output growth of the main export crops, coffee and cotton, and small or very small growth rates for the other crops. The yields per hectare stagnated and decreased for coffee, cotton and the food crop beans. In general, there was a decrease in harvested land for each crop with the exception of beans.

The strongly positive growth rates of Taiwanese agriculture are based on both output and productivity growth of all its main crops. Sugar, tea and bananas were to some extent replaced by soybeans and peanuts. It is interesting to compare the absolute yields of the two crops both countries have in common: rice and sugarcane.[4] In the 1980s the average yield of rice in El Salvador fluctuated between 2.9 and 4.2 metric tonnes per hectare (t/ha) and for sugar cane between 72.8 and 84.7 t/ha. The Taiwan figures for rice were 2.7 t/ha after ten years of reform implementation and a maximum yield of 3.9 t/ha in

Table 2.3 Agricultural average annual growth rates (%) in the reform period in El Salvador and Taiwan

	El Salvador 1980–9		Taiwan 1952–62	
Agriculture	–3.3		3.7	
Livestock	0.4		7.3	
Total	–1.5		4.8	
Main crops	*Production*	*Yield*	*Production*	*Yield*
Coffee	–4.7	0.3		
Maize	1.2	1.8		
Cotton	–21.5	–1.5		
Sugar	0.1	0.8		
Beans	1.4	–2.7		
Rice	0.5	1.4		
Sorghum	0.8	0.7		
Rice			3.0	2.9
Sweet potatoes			4.0	3.9
Sugar			2.5	3.0
Peanuts			4.7	3.0
Tea			5.4	6.0
Soybean			13.7	4.8
Bananas			2.8	3.3

Sources: Montoya (1991: 21, 30, 45); Wang Rong (1992: 18, 19).

the 1980s (Thorbecke, 1992: 40). For sugar cane, 65.7 t/ha was registered (Wang Rong, 1992: 19). This means that the absolute level of physical land productivity during the reform was higher in El Salvador than in Taiwan.[5] However, the productivity growth rates were higher for Taiwan.

El Salvador's seven principal crops lost 20 per cent of their collective weight in real GDP. The virtual disappearance of cotton and the decline in the coffee area were responsible for this and were insufficiently neutralized by the increases of the areas for sugar cane, maize and beans (Pelupessy, 1997: 271). The four principal Taiwanese crops, rice, sweet potatoes, sugar cane and peanuts, also dropped from 80 per cent to 72 per cent of the total cropland between 1951 and 1964, owing mainly to the decline in the rice area.[6] The proportion of rice in the GDP of total agriculture dropped from 50.5 per cent to 30.1 per cent in the period from 1953/5 to 1966/8 and a further fall to 11.8 per cent was recorded in 1986/8[7] (Thorbecke, 1992: 20). However,

GDP growth rates were much higher in Taiwan than in El Salvador in these periods, owing to accelerating growth of the non-agriculture sectors.

In the first stage of agricultural development, yields are normally explained by the increase in labor and input intensities. For the first five years of the Salvadoran reform, we have a more or less consistent data set to estimate growth rates for the cultivated area of total agriculture and the corresponding demand for labor. The area grew by 1.4 per cent per year and labor demand in man-days showed a 0.8 per cent growth (Montoya 1992). For the period 1954–67 in Taiwan, these annual rates were 0.2 per cent and 1.72 per cent respectively (Thorbecke 1992). This indicates a higher intensification of the use of productive labor in agriculture in this country, while El Salvador showed a relative decline. Positive annual growth rates of the multiple crop index (0.7 per cent) and especially the use of chemical fertilizers (5.3 per cent) and fixed capital (2.7 per cent) confirmed that the reform boosted a labor-using and input-intensive modernization process in Taiwan.

The scant information about agricultural technology in the 1980s indicates the persistence of under-utilization of land in El Salvador in both large private estates and reformed cooperatives (Pelupessy 1997). In the 1960s and 1970s, agriculture experienced a sharp increase in the use of improved seeds and modern inputs. Its use of NPK fertilizer became the highest in the Americas. However, use in Taiwan, which before reform was 20 per cent lower, was more than 50 per cent higher than El Salvador at the end of the 1960s. Modernization trends had also been evident in the sources of energy use in Taiwan. Before reform, 67 per cent of energy used in agriculture came from human labor and 33 per cent from animal labor. In 1975, human sources counted for 35 per cent and animal labor 7 per cent, while mechanical energy contributed 58 per cent (Thorbecke, 1992: 25).

The direct impact of the first-round implementation of land reform had similar weights for the proportion of affected to non-reformed farm land in both countries. However, the range of beneficiaries was greater in Taiwan, stimulated by a significant redistribution of rural income. A labor-using technology change enhanced agricultural productivity and production in Taiwan, while growth stagnated in the Salvadoran case. The preservation of large-scale private commercial estates did not prevent agricultural decline in El Salvador, and neither did the introduction of new agrarian cooperatives.

The future of reform

The long-term success of land reform should be judged by its role in accelerating the agrarian transformation process. To make an assessment of this aspect, it is necessary to extend the study of the direct impacts discussed in the preceding section to the (indirect) effects of the reform on institutions including rural class structure, rural markets, resource transfer mechanisms to and from the rest of the economy, and the assurance of an appropriate macroeconomic policy framework. Only a part of this analysis will be done here because, for a more complete view, the effects of agrarian reform policies complementary to the land reform must also be considered. In the forthcoming discussion, we will start with the Taiwanese development because its long-term effects and trends are already known.

Changes in class structure

The landlords were a class in decay in pre-reform Taiwan. Land ownership was not as extensive and concentrated as in Latin América; ownership rights were difficult to exercise because of the complicated subtenancy system. Agricultural growth stagnated, and landlords had only a weak relationship with the new Kuomintang regime and its bureaucracy with mainland origin. The reform achieved a quick real expropriation of the farmland in favor of its tenants, estimated the compensation for land as a function of its productive capacity, and channelled part of this fund into productive activities outside agriculture. For 30 per cent of their face value, landlords were given stocks in the government-owned Manufacturing and Mining Corporation, Taiwan Paper Corporation, Agricultural and Forestry Corporation and the Taiwan Cement Corporation. However, most of these stocks were quickly resold at low prices owing to the lack of confidence of the owners, and only a small part of the money received was reinvested in productive activities (Yang, 1967: 231). A small group of former big landowners ended up as the final buyers of most of these stocks and became the principal stockholders of the four large enterprises, which later became very profitable (Yang, 1967: 239).

Although part of the resources went to stockholding in industrial enterprises, the majority of the ex-landlords have not become members of the entrepreneur class in Taiwan.

In the Salvadoran reform, no explicit consideration was given to a productive role of landlords in or outside agriculture, nor did it lead to the disappearance of the landholding class. Landowners and the related oligarchy became powerful opposition leaders to the reform and retained much of the control over agriculture and especially agro-industrial activities. Small and medium-sized farmers remained under their influence. After a decade of problematic application of the reform, the oligarchy succeeded in recovering power and tried to redress the effects of the process (Pelupessy, 1997). The sale of public land, land-to-the-tiller programs, and voluntary sales by landowners, did transform most of the tenants into small owner-farmers in Taiwan. It remains to be seen whether the changes mentioned in the previous section of this chapter will guarantee sustainable incomes and living conditions for these farmers, taking into account the trend of decreasing farm sizes that continued long after the reform was implemented there.

Table 2.4   Pre- and post-reform distribution of landholdings in El Salvador and Taiwan

El Salvador (number)			Taiwan (number)		
Size	1971	1987	Size	1952	1960
<1.4 ha	70.3	62.3	<0.97 ha	70.6	66.6
1.4 to 3.5 ha	16.0	15.6	0.97 to 1.94 ha	16.9	15.3
3.5 to 7.0 ha	5.8	9.5	1.94 to 2.91 ha	5.7	14.8
7.0 to 14.0 ha	3.4	5.6	2.91 to 4.85 ha	3.9	2.7
>14.0 ha	4.1	7.0	>4.85 ha	3.4	0.6
Total	100	100	Total	100	100
(1000)	270	286	(1000)	593	698

El Salvador (area)			Taiwan (area)		
Size	1971	1987	Size	1952	1960
<1.4 ha	10.4	8.2	<0.97 ha	25.0	35.6
1.4 to 3.5 ha	9.1	6.9	0.97 to 1.94 ha	21.1	19.3
3.5 to 7.0 ha	7.6	9.5	1.94 to 2.91 ha	12.3	30.3
7.0 to 14.0 ha	8.7	11.0	2.91 to 4.85 ha	13.2	10.2
>14.0 ha	64.3	64.3	>4.85 ha	28.4	4.6
Total	100	100	Total	100	100
(1000 ha)	1 452	1 335	(1000 ha)	661	853
Average		5.4 ha	4.7 ha	Average	1.1 ha	1.2 ha

Sources: Montoya (1991: 52); Acevedo *et al.* (1995: 2159); Wang Rong (1992: 14).

The impact of land reform on the overall distribution of landhold-ings gives a more detailed view of the structural change in agriculture. In the presentation of the data we have used different size categories in order to account for the differences in scale between the two countries (the average farm in El Salvador is four to five times larger than in Taiwan). There seems to be some similarity between the respective pat-terns of distribution of the farms in the pre-reform periods of the two countries. However, the distribution of farmland is not exactly the same: in El Salvador the class of farms with 14 hectares or more took up 64.3 per cent of the area of land and in Taiwan the class of 4.85 hectares or more accounted for only 28.4 percent of the area. After reform, concentration decreased in both countries, but the decline was sharper in Taiwan. The size of the average farm remained about the same for the two countries, but decreased after 1960 in Taiwan. In the first decade of implementation both the agricultural area and the number of landholdings increased considerably in Taiwan, while this did not happen in El Salvador. Land reform brought a further significant deconcentration in the landholding structure in Taiwan, while concentration persisted in El Salvador (Table 2.4).

Productivity and income

In the first period of the implementation of the Taiwanese land reform, land productivity increased considerably because of the higher labor and input use intensity, while application of multiple cropping tech-niques and increasing working days per worker also enhanced labor productivity.

On the other hand, the reform in El Salvador because of the com-bined effects of the decrease in both land productivity and labor inten-sity resulted in stagnating labor productivity in the crop and other agricultural sectors.[8] The effects of this development on farm families' income growth and distribution gives an indication of the sustainabil-ity of the reform model in both countries. Taiwan showed a per capita farm family income growth rate of 8.8 per cent in the period 1954–64 and 5.7 per cent for 1964–70 (Amsden, 1988: 160). In the first stage of the reform the net real income growth per family was already 7.8 per cent annually for 1948–59 (Chen, 1961: 313). In this figure are included the effects of both the rent reduction program and the land-to-the-tiller program that converted the tenant to owner. This meant that net real disposable income increased with the reduction in farm land rental rates from 55 per cent to 37.5 per cent in 1949. In 1953, there was a jump because of the elimination of the land rental and its replacement by a land tax of 15 per cent of the real rental value. After the mid 1960s, income growth was still considerable, but slowing down. Non-agricultural activities counted for an increasing part of farmers' incomes. Rural non-agricultural employment participation increased from 29.3 per cent in 1956 to 48.8 per cent of total rural employment in 1966 (Ranis and Stewart, 1987: 176).

The contribution of off-farm work to farmers' income rose from 29 per cent in 1962 to 55 per cent in 1972 (Amsden, 1988: 159). Another source reported a proportion for non-agricultural income of 40.7 per cent in 1965–9, increasing to 66.2 per cent in 1980–4 and decreasing later to 62.8 per cent in 1985–9 (Huang, 1993: 46). In any case, it is clear that after considerable income growth from on-farm activities during the first decade of reform, off-farm activities provided important additional income to farm households. This was also a consequence of the policy to strengthen rural linkages in Taiwan (Ranis and Stewart, 1987: 140–91). After 15 years of reform, income distribution of farm families gave Gini coefficients fluctuating from 0.28 to 0.33 (period 1966–87; source: Calkins *et al.*, 1992: 117).

In El Salvador, the growth rate of average rural family income in current prices was 5.8 per cent between 1977 and 1985 (Montoya 1992: 76). The current income growth rates of members of the cooperative and land-to-the-tiller programs were 5.9 per cent and 3.2 per cent per annum respectively (Montoya, 1992: 78–9; assuming their average incomes for 1977 were the same as the rural average). As a price deflator, one could apply the general, consumer food and rural basic food basket price indexes. The growth rates of these were 12.5, 15.5 and 10.2 per cent per annum respectively. This implies that all previously mentioned indicators gave negative real income growth rates for the Salvadoran farmers. Legal minimum agricultural wages also declined by 12.8 per cent in real terms each year in this period.

The Gini coefficient for rural income decreased from 0.54 in 1978 to 0.44 in 1985, indicating a tendency toward a more equal rural family income distribution. However, the inequality should be higher because the upper rural income classes, like, for instance, absentee landlords and oligarchy, are registered as urban residents, while the significant figure for rural unemployed is also not included (Montoya, 1992: 77). The Gini coefficients for families in the two Salvadoran reform programs mentioned earlier were, in 1985, 0.30 for the cooperatives and 0.38 for land-to-the-tiller. Off-farm income and outside rented land may have caused the slightly higher inequality in the latter group. In any case, income distribution for the reformed sector is less skewed than for the rural sector as a whole. The skewedness of income distribution of the cooperative reform beneficiaries of El Salvador seems to be comparable to that of total agriculture in Taiwan.

The Taiwanese land reform and the increased linkages with off-farm employment created higher and more equally distributed real income growth rates for farm families than in El Salvador. If these tendencies persist, one could question the efficiency of the reform process for future agricultural development of El Salvador, let alone that the sector could be a viable provider of resources for industrialization. The more or less equitable and positive growth rates of Taiwanese agriculture meant that the sector could generate resources for industrialization, which in its first stage had an import substitution nature. Between 1956 and 1960 there was a considerable outflow of resources from agriculture composed of net taxes, land rents, private investments and the net terms of trade effect (Karshenas, 1992). This outflow seems to be higher than the significant inflowing income stream of off-farm labor activities. Taiwan was one of the few cases in Asia where the net resource outflow contributed significantly to the national savings ratio (Karshenas, 1992).

Apparent and real constraints of the Salvadoran land reform

What were the institutional failures in the Salvadoran land reform, given the lessons from Taiwan? First, it is useful to mention four important issues that are normally considered as heavily restrictive, but in fact were not.

First, the decision to introduce a radical and interventionist reform process was correct. Just as in the case of Taiwan, agrarian development had stagnated, perhaps more in terms of equity than growth criteria. In both cases, temporal downturns obliged relatively autonomous states to intervene, at least to do some crisis management. Second, pre-reform institutional restrictions were present for the bimodal as well as the unimodal development case. The overconcentration of land and increasing landlessness restricted Salvadoran growth, while the tenancy system and extreme land fragmentation were among the principal constraints in Taiwan. Both countries suffered from (relative) rural overpopulation. Third, land reform need not be purely market oriented; widespread and autonomous state intervention may be even seen as a condition for successful reform. Finally, political objectives are not necessarily detrimental to reform. An anti-communist or politically otherwise oriented land reform could be successful if the political goals have their correct place in the decision-making process, if its economic costs are calculated correctly and if politics does not contradict economic decisions.

The first real error in El Salvador was the absence of actions to change the economic role of the land-controlling class, the oligarchy, within or outside agriculture. The omission was even worse when one takes into account the century-long economic and political influences of this class and its relationship with the army, which were much stronger than in Taiwan. Generally, the knowledge of the Salvadoran authorities about rural social structure was biased or incomplete and no consideration was given in the reform process to, for instance, the inexactness of the rural property registration system.

A second big mistake was the exclusion of popular organizations in the design and implementation of the land reform. Added to the incapacity in quantity and quality of human resources working at the reform institutions – ISTA, FINATA, and MAG – this turned out to be a serious problem. The tenants of the land-to-the-tiller program in El Salvador were left to the mercy of landowners and death-squads in the struggle to register as potential beneficiaries and there was nothing comparable to the tens of thousands of trained promoters and their assistants in Taiwan. Apparently, state autonomy was not strong enough in El Salvador to redistribute income and power from landowning and related classes to beneficiaries of the reform and the landless.

A third point refers to the design of the reform, where programs were planned in isolation and not articulated to each other. The role of the advisers from USAID was also not clearly specified; they acted independently of those Salvadorans responsible for the execution of the reform, and their contribution cannot be compared to the solid and integrated work of the Sino-American Joint Rural Reconstruction Commission. Financial resources from the United States were not always directed to productive investments in agriculture as in Taiwan. In El Salvador external agents may have enhanced state autonomy, but their actions did not necessarily strengthen the reform process.

Fourth, the insufficient extension of the Salvadoran reform and its slowness are often criticized because these augmented uncertainty in the countryside, resulting in a lack of new investment in agriculture and even in a decrease in investments – as, for instance, in the case of cotton. This does not however seem to be a conclusive point. When we talk about the affected area, the scope was comparable to the

Taiwanese case, but the beneficiaries of the measures were relatively fewer. In this sense, the Phase I cooperative program was too exclusive. El Salvador had nothing comparable to the Taiwanese rent reduction program, which also benefitted a lot of small tenants outside the reformed areas. Land reform should be concerned with the redistribution not only of land but also of rural income. Increasing rural uncertainty was also present in Taiwan, but was reduced in time by consistent measures and follow-up activities. On the other hand, civil war continued for more than a decade in El Salvador, which obviously did not help stimulate the mechanisms for resource flows toward rural areas.

This brings us to the fifth flaw in the Salvadoran process. After the change of the Christian Democratic government and ten years of implementation, the reform was considered finished. With the peace settlement, two years later, a new program was introduced. Land reform without a follow-up tends to fail. As the Taiwan experience showed, less than five years of swift implementation of reform programs were followed by thirty years of follow-up policies by newly established institutions, during which the results were widened and deepened. In effect, after more than forty years, there is still a need for some adjustment to enhance rural productive capacity and efficiency in the 1990s (Huang, 1993: 43–65).

A sixth serious constraint is that reform policies in El Salvador neglected the resource transfers into and from agriculture. There was and is an almost total absence of institutions for investment-generating measures, nor was anything done to prevent the capital flight out of agriculture. Landowners had economic and political arguments to transfer capital to other sectors. Government economic policy did not consider the terms of trade of agriculture with the rest of the economy, the exchange rate was over-valued and tax and subsidy measures did not favor agriculture. Macro policy, in general, contradicted the goals of the sectoral reform.[9]

Notes

1. Most of the data come from Pelupessy (1997) (El Salvador), and Chen (1961) and Ho (1966) (Taiwan).
2. There are no reliable figures for the immediate pre-reform period, so part of the change should be attributed to the development in the 1970s. (Sources: Montoya, 1991: 52–3; Acevedo *et al.* 1995: 7.)
3. Partial owners are considered to be in the owner category. (Source: Hsieh, 1989: 14.)
4. El Salvador has dryland and Taiwan wetland rice.

5. Agricultural practices of two crops of rice a year made the final result of Taiwan higher: in 1955, 4.4 t for each cultivated hectare, and 1964, 6.0 t.
6. The decline in cultivated land should be bigger because the multiple cropping technique of rice increased its registered cropping area.
7. Total agriculture includes crops, livestock, forestry and fishery.
8. Livestock, forestry and fishery. (Source: Montoya, 1992: 11, 18, 37.)
9. This issue has not been discussed explicitly in this chapter, see Pelupessy (1997: 139–72) for a detailed treatment.

3

Comparative Advantage of Food Crops Under Structural Adjustment in Nicaragua

Richard Eberlin

Introduction

In most Latin American countries the agricultural sector plays a major economic role, not only producing food for domestic consumption but often also as the main source of hard currency through its production for export. Moreover, agriculture provides a large share of employment and is an important source of capital for the rest of the economy. Owing to major economic difficulties, since the 1980s most Latin American countries have had to implement structural adjustment programs (SAPs) led by the International Monetary Fund (IMF) and the World Bank.

Many of these countries also received technical and financial assistance from the Swiss Development Cooperation (SDC). Within the controversial topic of structural adjustment, SDC had a particular interest in its impact on the agricultural sector. In order to intensify its support for Nicaragua, particularly in the agricultural sector, SDC mandated the Department of Agricultural Economics (DAE) of the Swiss Federal Institute for Technology in Zurich to analyze the effects of structural adjustment on the income of agricultural enterprises in Nicaragua. Recommendations were to be made on policy measures to increase agricultural production of selected products for domestic consumption as well as for export. Furthermore, the research project made an analysis of which agricultural products from Nicaragua have a comparative advantage on the Central American market.

Considering the available literature on the subject of structural adjustment and the specific Nicaraguan situation, the following general hypothesis was formulated: 'A structural adjustment program has positive impacts on the agricultural sector only if the institutional framework and the infrastructure are developed accordingly.'

This perception of the background and the identification of the problems suggested a number of specific research questions. In order to provide a sound decision basis for SDC towards the agricultural sector of Nicaragua, the following issues were addressed:

1. the actual situation and the development potential of the agricultural sector in Nicaragua under the current conditions of political and economical change;
2. the impact of the structural adjustment measures on agricultural incomes and specifically on different types of farms;
3. the competitiveness and the comparative advantage of the Nicaraguan agricultural sector at national and international level;
4. possible measures for the promotion of agricultural production under current conditions.

In order to facilitate the discussion on structural adjustment, three different levels for economic policy analysis can be distinguished (World Bank, 1991: 4ff.; Demery *et al.*, 1993: 85ff.). Economic theory is usually divided into macroeconomics dealing with aggregate variables affecting demand and supply, and microeconomics dealing with decision-making behavior of individual economic units. However, the link between macroeconomic variables and individual reactions has so far no clear theoretical basis. Households do not react directly to macroeconomic changes (like exchange rates), but rather to changes at the mesoeconomic level that are driven by the macro level (for example: domestic prices of tradable inputs and outputs).

Figure 3.1 sheds some light on the possible linking mechanisms and vehicles. Therefore the 'meso level' is introduced, which can bridge the gap between macro- and microeconomics. The meso level consists basically of the markets, which ensure the exchange of goods, factors and services, and the endowments in social and physical infrastructure and public services, such as health care, education, transport and communication, which form the framework for the individual's economic activities.

As illustrated in Figure 3.1, the macro level consists of economic policy measures affecting different macroeconomic variables like the exchange rate and interest rate, price relations between tradables and non-tradables, or government spending. These can be divided into monetary, fiscal, trade, sectoral and social policies. The meso level converts these variables through markets and infrastructure into price signals, whereby the endowments in infrastructure basically influence

Figure 3.1   Macro, meso and micro levels of economic policy measures and analysis

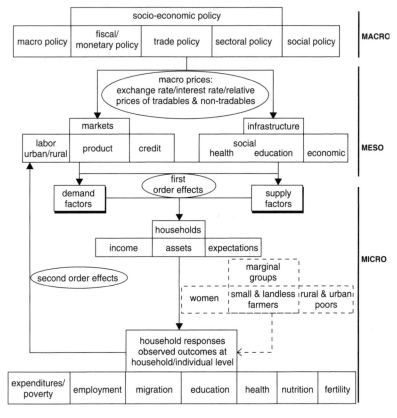

(Adapted from World Bank, 1991, p. 86 and Demery *et al.*, 1993: p. 5)

the transaction-cost part of the prices in all its facets. In other words, supply and demand factors affect a household's reaction, depending on income, asset endowment and expectations, which again influences the markets (second-order effects). This reaction can be observed in a variety of measurable variables at household level, and can serve as an indicator for the impact of policy measures at the macro level. In the following section the different structural adjustment policies as applied in Nicaragua will be discussed, on the basis of this theoretical framework.

Structural adjustment in Nicaragua

The government of Violeta Chamorro (1990–6) implemented a structural adjustment program to correct the economic failures of its Sandinista predecessor. The so-called 'Lacayo Plan' was introduced in 1990, with the following set of measures (in chronological order) implemented under the guidance and funding of the World Bank and the IMF Enhanced Structural Adjustment Facility (ESAF):

1. August 1990:
   — monetary reform and first devaluation (1 US dollar (US$) = (1 Nicaraguan Córdoba (C$)).
2. March 1991:
   — second devaluation to 1 US$ = 5 C$ (400 per cent);
   — credit restriction for the public sector;
   — reduction of the refinancing rate of the private banks;
   — reduction of government spending and increase in government revenues;
   — reform of the credit system;
   — privatization and deregulation of the public sector (National Development Bank (BANADES), state enterprises, state grain marketing board (ENABAS), etc.);
   — liberalization of domestic trade (abolition of state marketing structures and of most price controls);
   — liberalization of external trade;
   — adjustment of the interest rate.
3. January 1993:
   — third devaluation to 1 US$ = 6 C$ (20 per cent);
   — implementation of a 'crawling peg' exchange rate regime;
   — further reduction of government spending and increasing revenues;
   — repeated adaptation of credit and monetary policies.

The impact of these three main packages of the structural adjustment program can be summarized by assessing the macro, meso and micro levels of economic policy-making as defined in the previous section.

Macro level

Devaluation

After the devaluations, the overvaluation of the córdoba still oscillated around 15 per cent (in relation to base year 1991, see FIDEG, 1993;

BCN, 1994a and b). For the determination of the overvaluation rate, the applied methodology and base year are decisive. Other estimates place the overvaluation at over 50 per cent in comparison with 1988 (Clemens, 1994: 9ff.). It is therefore very difficult to estimate the precise impact of the devaluation measures. Taking the FIDEG numbers as the 'best estimate', the overvaluation in January 1997 was around 14 per cent (FIDEG, 1997).

Inflation

The hyperinflation of 13 500 per cent in 1990 descended to 10 per cent in 1992 and then oscillated between 15 and 26 per cent, according to different estimates from government sources and FIDEG. This means that the measures implemented have effectively controlled inflation.

Trade balance

The impact on the agricultural export sector was initially limited, since other measures (i.e. deregulation of the financial sector) and external factors (like trends in international commodity prices) did offset the initial price signals or incentives. On the other hand, imports increased instead of decreasing, because the effect of liberalization on external trade was transmitted faster to the consumers than the price signals to the producers, and because domestic production could not follow the increase in demand. The liberalization of trade (abolition of price controls, reduction of tariffs, etc.) brought about an easier availability of commodities at a cheaper price, especially for those products that were rationed before and only available at high prices on the black market. In the first period after adjustment imported goods were mostly consumer goods (in 1992 and 1993 approximately half were consumer goods and fuels), while demand for intermediary and capital goods was low due to gloomy economic perspectives. The maintenance or increase of imports was possible thanks to the external funding which formed part of the structural adjustment program, and through donations and loans (World Bank, 1993: 7ff.), making the Nicaraguan government extremely dependent on external aid.

Improvement of the trade balance was difficult to attain because the development of international commodity prices (with the exception of coffee after 1994) was not favorable to Nicaragua. Terms of trade decreased from 87 points in 1990 (1987 = 100) to 62 points in 1992 (World Bank, 1993: 9). The fall was due mainly to unfavorable cotton and coffee prices (Clemens, 1994: 9).

Government budget reform

The budget deficit decreased from 36 per cent of GDP in 1990 to five per cent of GDP in 1992 (Corbo and Bruno, 1993: 12; FIDEG, 1993). These cuttings endangered or even destroyed many of the achievements of the Sandinista period in the health and education sectors.[1] To prevent further conflicts with labor unions, the government created a system of premiums for employees who left voluntarily, and initially at least 15 000 persons (20 per cent of the labor force) took this opportunity. The main motive to leave was the extremely low salaries. The normal state worker's salary was sufficient to purchase only one-third of the *canasta básica*, the minimum food and basic needs basket. Of these workers, however, 95 per cent never found a new job in the formal sector. The resulting unemployment rate and the growing living costs mainly affected urban areas. However, the abolition of direct and indirect subsidies to the agricultural sector resulted in a spread of poverty also to the rural areas.

Meso level

Reform of the credit system

Financial system reforms mostly affected small farmers and farmers located in remote areas who were dependent on credit from the national development bank (BANADES). The number of credits granted to farmers in 1991 declined to one third of the 1990 level. Credits granted to other sectors were also substantially reduced. Many farmers could not afford to buy inputs and had to sell their property (mostly received by the agrarian reform during the Sandinista government or during the transition period), thus favoring a new concentration of land ownership. The extent of this reconcentration is difficult to assess. However, there are some clear indications of growing inequality from the reactivated colonization of the new agrarian frontier or the change in the distribution of land ownership according to farm size classes (Clemens, 1994: 6). In urban areas, reduced credit supply mostly affected medium and small enterprises, but also big enterprises producing consumer goods.

Privatization and deregulation of the public sector

The greatest impact from deregulation, as argued before, was the privatization of BANADES. The bank had principally to reform its credit policy in favor of more commercially oriented rules (strict security rules, positive real interest rates, credit solvency, etc.), away from the soft, 'rural development' – oriented credit policies (soft loans, low or even negative real interest rate, no punishment for defaulting, etc.) set by the former government. The majority of the state enterprises had to be privatized and a special institution (CORNAP) was founded to implement this task. The IMF stopped its ESAF assistance in 1994 because of the slow progress in these deregulation measures – which were crucial for the 'Bretton Woods' institutions – and the consequent non-achievement of the proposed fiscal benchmarks.[2]

The privatization was contested by the labor unions and after protests and a so-called 'concertation' process (an economic and social pact), the workers (i.e. the unions) were guaranteed up to one-third of the shares of the enterprises (World Bank, 1993: 2; Corbo and Bruno, 1993: 16). The current government is now trying to revert some of these privatizations in favor of the original pre-Sandinista owners (mostly ex-Somozistas), risking social unrest again.

Liberalization of domestic trade

Liberalization of domestic trade and the abolition of the state marketing structures in the input and output markets (for example ENABAS for agricultural output) completely changed market access for medium and small farmers. They had to switch from a sole marketing agent with guaranteed and fixed prices to confront a newly established oligopolistic trading structure with a completely non-transparent pricing structure.[3]

Liberalization of external trade

The overall average nominal protection rate decreased from 43 per cent in January 1990 to 19 per cent in August 1993. For the agricultural sector, specifically food, it decreased from between 30 and 50 per cent to between 21- and 31 per cent (Corbo and Bruno, 1993: 14–15; Clemens, 1994: 11). Despite the liberalization not being complete, the domestic industrial sector could not compete with the imports even after devaluation, and had to downsize or close down with the respective consequences for the workers.

Micro level

Relative prices of tradables and non-tradables

The improvement of relative prices took some time, and therefore the devaluation did not yield the expected results. Furthermore, if any improvement happened at all (though not visible from available data), the price incentive would not have reached the farmer because of the many intervening factors, like bottlenecks in infrastructure and marketing, credit restrictions, lack of appropriate extension messages and technology, lack of market information, etc.

Marketing and processing

As mentioned before, the oligopolistic market structure prevented price incentives reaching the producers. Furthermore the agro-industrial processing structure, for example for milk and meat, was obsolete and deficient, while the necessary investments could not be realized because of credit restrictions (Clemens, 1994: 19).

Land ownership

The most important problem restricting an accelerated and substantial development in the agricultural sector was probably the insecurity in ownership. Though not directly caused by the structural adjustment program, the property rights issue affected the impact of different deregulation measures (privatization, credit restriction, etc.), in the sense that measures that in principle were positive took a negative turn.

The policy analysis matrix

For the analysis of structural adjustment programs, a methodology is required to measure the total policy impacts and to give insights into the factors influencing individual efficiency (profitability) and social efficiency (welfare). This implies that we ought to assess the factors that influence the competitiveness and the comparative advantage of certain commodities.[4] For this we used the method known as policy analysis matrix (PAM). The ideas behind the PAM can be traced back to the discussion on the applicability of economic theory with respect to real-world situations. According to economic theory, perfect competition leads to a 'Pareto optimum' where the resources are allocated efficiently in the production of goods demanded (market equilibrium). Furthermore, assuming an open economy, trade leads to higher welfare if production concentrates on the goods for which a comparative advantage exists.

The basic problem is that economic theory is often very far from reality. The normal situation is marked by inefficient allocation of resources through distorted markets bearing no relation to Pareto optimality. The reasons for the distortions can be so-called market failures, as well as state failures and policies that do not correct the effects of such failures. In short, there are different factors that are distorting the economic process, which can be analyzed under the scope of economic efficiency and optimal resource allocation. For measuring these distorting effects, different methodologies and success criteria are available (e.g. cost–benefit analysis, general and partial equilibrium models, input-output matrix; see Tsakok, 1990; Timmer *et al.*, 1985). The 'policy analysis matrix' as developed by Monke and Pearson (1989, 1991) is a recent methodology having its predecessors in cost–benefit analysis and the theory of international trade.

Structure of the PAM

The PAM (see Table 3.1) consists of a simple production budget, where net benefits are the result of revenues minus costs. There are three particular elements that distinguish this method from others. First, *two budgets* are estimated, one calculated with *market prices* (also called financial or private prices), the other calculated with *shadow prices* (also called economic or social prices). Secondly, the production costs or inputs are composed of *tradable* and *non-tradable* goods. Goods or services are tradable if they can be traded on the world markets. Non-tradable goods are those that, by their physical nature (land) or other conditions (like mobility), cannot be traded internationally (capital, labor, services). In practice, inputs that are not purely tradable or non-tradable have to be divided into their tradable and non-tradable components (for example fertilizers produced in the country with imported raw materials). The third and most important element are the **transfers**, the difference between the budget at market prices and the budget at social prices (third line of the matrix), which offer a measure of the divergence – caused by market

Table 3.1   Policy analysis matrix

| | Revenues | Production costs | | Profits |
		Tradables	Non-tradables	
Market prices	A	B	C	D
Shadow prices	E	F	G	H
Transfers	I	J	K	L

Private profit (market prices):	$D = A - B - C$
Social profit (shadow prices):	$H = E - F - G$
Effects of policy measures and market/state failures (transfers):	
Product transfers:	$I = A - E$
Input transfers on tradables:	$J = B - F$
Input transfers on non-tradables:	$K = C - G$
Net transfers:	$L = D - H$ resp. $L = I - J - K$

failures, state failures or corrections – between the whole economy (social prices) and the production sector (market prices).

The PAM allows an analysis of the distorting or correcting effects of economic policy measures and the impact of state or market failures on private profitability (efficient production system) and on social profitability (efficient use of abundant and scarce resources). The private profit D is the net benefit above the normal returns of the activity, hence it indicates the competitiveness under given economic conditions. The social profit H is the net benefit for the society of a given activity and indicates the profits to be made if markets are not distorted or have no failures. It indicates comparative or absolute advantage and efficient allocation of the available resources.

Figure 3.2 Nicaragua: agricultural cycles of beans and maize

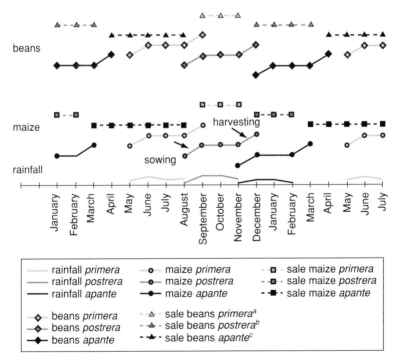

Source: Vargas 1996.
Notes:
[a]primera: first harvest
[b]postrera: second harvest
[c]apante: third harvest

Even more interesting are the transfers on different markets. When the product transfers are positive ($I > 0$) then the producer is receiving an implicit or explicit subsidy, whereas in the case of negative values production is being taxed. If the input transfers (on tradables or non-tradables) are positive (J or $K > 0$) then the factor in question is being taxed, either explicitly with a levy or implicitly through, for example, the exchange rate. In the negative case it means that a subsidy is given.

The net transfers are the sum of the transfers through all markets (product, tradable and non-tradable inputs) or the difference between private profit and social profit. In the positive case ($L > 0$) the net transfer indicates the welfare loss that the economy is incurring by producing this particular commodity. On the other hand, for the producer it implies the increasing amount earned with respect to an undistorted situation (implicit or explicit subsidy). If the net transfer is negative ($L < 0$) then gains or savings in resource use are realized. However, whether for the producer it is an implicit or explicit taxation, resources are transferred from the respective producing sector toward the economy. If the value of L is near zero (0) then there are no distortions at all, or the policies on different markets are neutralizing each other. By confronting private and social profit (D and H), we can compare production systems with identical commodities inside a country or between countries. However, if we like to compare production systems producing different commodities, we need to calculate some indicators with common coefficients. The following coefficients can be calculated using the PAM:

Private cost ratio	PCR = $C/(A–B)$
Domestic resource cost ratio	DRC = $G/(E–F)$
Effective protection coefficient:	EPC = $(A–B)/(E–F)$
Subsidy ratio to producers	SRP = L/E

The *private cost ratio* (PCR) is an indicator for profitability of the production system under the current conditions. In comparison with other commodity systems or with other countries, it indicates competitiveness.

PCR < 1 means *private profitability* and competitiveness.

PCR > 1 means loss for the producer.

The *domestic resource cost ratio* (DRC) indicates the *economically efficient* use of the domestic (non-tradable) resources. In comparison with other commodity systems or with other countries it indicates comparative advantage, or in other words competitiveness on international markets.

DRC < 1 means efficient production and comparative advantage.

DRC > 1 means that the economy is incurring welfare losses.

The *effective protection coefficient* (EPC) indicates the relative incentives which producers are receiving through policies or failures in product and/or tradable input markets, giving a measure of positive (subsidy or protection) or negative (taxation) support.

> EPC < 1 means transfers from the producing sector to the economy (for example taxation through the tradable markets).
>
> EPC > 1 implies transfers from the economy to the producing sector (for example subsidy through the tradable markets).
>
> The closer to 1 the EPC is, the less distortion are present on these markets.

The *subsidy ratio to producers* (SRP) indicates the net transfers of the whole system and therefore also the incentives that producers are receiving. It shows the extent to which all policies are subsidizing (or taxing) the commodity in question.

> SRP < 0 means that the producer is being taxed by policy interventions.
>
> SRP > 0 means that the production is being subsidized.
>
> The closer to zero SRP is, the less distorting are the economic policies.

Summarizing, the PAM allows us to analyze the effects of the measures of the structural adjustment policy on the agricultural sector, by comparing the private profitability (budget at market prices) with the economic efficiency (budget at social prices), which, in principle, represents the situation that structural adjustment programs want to attain.[5] Additionally the development of the coefficients of the production systems can be compared with the situation before starting the structural adjustment program in order to assess whether a real improvement in efficiency has been realized.[6]

Empirical application

The PAM starts with the construction of a production budget comprising the two budgets calculated with market prices and with social prices, and including the division of the production costs into tradable and non-tradable inputs. Table 3.2 shows the basic structure with the main elements for the calculation of the PAM for a hypothetical example (adapted from Monke and Pearson, 1989: 146).

The figures for the production budget at private prices are derived from survey data or other secondary sources. However, the economic side of the budget has to be adapted as well as possible from the

Table 3.2 Basic structure of the PAM

Budget with market prices (Non-tradables: Labor Unskilled, Labor Skilled, Capital, Land, Total non-trad; Tradables; Total; Cost per unit) — Budget with shadow prices (Non-tradables: Labor Unskilled, Labor Skilled, Capital, Land, Total non-trad; Tradables; Total)

Costs	Quantity	Unit	Cost per unit	Unskilled	Skilled	Capital	Land	Total non-trad	Tradables	Total	Cost per unit	Unskilled	Skilled	Capital	Land	Total non-trad	Tradables	Total
I. Fixed inputs	1	C$	20			18		18	2	20	25			23		23	2	25
II. Direct labour	20	day	10	180	20			200		200	8	144	20			164		164
III. Intermediate inputs																		
A. Machinery/contracted	5	hour	50		135			135	115	250	56		135			135	144	279
B. Inputs	5	qq	100		165			165	335	500	117		165			165	419	584
IV. Commodity in process										$Z1$								$Z2$
				180	320	18	0	518	452	970		144	320	23	0	487	565	1,052
				$C1$	$C2$	$C3$	$C4$	C	B			$G1$	$G2$	$G3$	$G4$	G	F	
								$C = C1 + C2 + C3 + C4$								$G = G1 + G2 + G3 + G4$		
Revenues											130							
V. Output	10	qq	100							1,000								1,300
										A								E
VI. Profit										30								249
										D								H

$$D = A - B - C - Z1 \qquad H = E - F - G - Z2$$

PAM	Revenues	Production costs		Profits
	Revenues	Tradables	Non-tradables	Profits
Market prices	1,000 / A	452 / B	518 / C	30 / D
Shadow prices	1,300 / E	565 / F	487 / G	248 / H
Transfers	-300 / I	-113 / J	31 / K	-218 / L

Indicators:

PCR	$C/(A - B)$		0.95
DRC	$G/(E - F)$		0.66
NPCO	A/E		0.77
EPC	$(A - B)/(E - F)$		0.75
PC	D/H		0.12
PCB	$(B + C)/A$		0.97
SCB	$(F + G)/E$		0.81
NPCI	B/F		0.80
SRP	L/E		-0.17
CSI	DRC/SCB		0.82

Source: adapted from Monke and Pearson (1989: 146).

Figure 3.3   Prices of white maize in Nicaragua 1991–96.

Maiz blanco

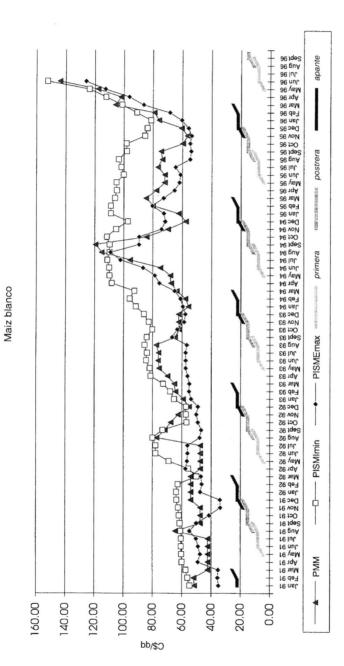

Source: Demery *et al.*, 1993; FIDEG, 1997.
Notes:
PMM, domestic market price; PISMImin, import-parity price; PISMEmax, export parity price; *primera, postrera, apante,* cropping seasons

available information. The following steps were required to adjust private prices to social or economic prices:[7]

1. Classify all items into tradables and non-tradables.
2. For tradable items the social price is the price on the world market adjusted for the transaction costs (transport, handling, etc.); this is also called import (or export) parity price.

    For a good that is an import substitute the import parity price is:
    $$P_b = P_w + T_d - C_d \qquad\qquad (P_w = CIF)$$
    For an exported good the export parity price is:
    $$P_b = P_w - T_d - C_d \qquad\qquad (P_w = FOB)$$

    where:

    > P_b: parity price;
    > P_w: world market price (CIF = FOB + T_w; P_w = CIF in the case of imports, FOB in the case of exports);
    > T_w: international transport costs (sea freight and insurance);
    > T_d: handling, transport and marketing costs from the harbor to the market;
    > C_d: transport, processing and marketing costs from the farm gate to the market.

3. Convert the price of all tradables into local currency using the real exchange rate which represents the opportunity cost of foreign currency.
4. The private prices of non-tradables have to be converted into social prices mainly using the 'opportunity cost' approach:
    — social valuation of labor (real salary);
    — social valuation of land;
    — social valuation of capital (interest rates).

Basic grains production in Nicaragua

Data collection on production costs and structure for the major cropping seasons was done in seven municipalities located in two representative regions (Table 3.3). The survey concentrated on production cost data for maize and beans. The areas and crops were selected because of the availability of survey data from studies done before the structural adjustment program started (see Aguilar and Espinoza, 1994; Clemens and Simán, 1993; Saborio and Clemens, 1992; Paniaga *et al.*, 1992; Tijerino, 1993).

A sample of 300 farms (50 for each region and cropping season) was taken and the survey was stratified according to the production

Table 3.3   Nicaragua: regional distribution of maize and beans samples

Region	Department	Municipality
Region I	Nueva Segovia	El Jicara, Jalapa
Region IV	Granada	Nandaime
	Masaya	Diria, Diriomo
	Rivas	Rivas, Tola Belén

Source: see text.

structure, taking into account total area, cultivated area of the specific crop, use of family or hired labor, integration into the markets and the technology level. Since no clear relation between farm size and level of technology could be found, the sample was finally stratified according to level of technology used. However, the assumption could be made, but not proven with the sample at hand, that a relation exists between farm size and technology.

Three levels of technology were distinguished and defined as separate farm types: high technology (use of machinery and external inputs), intermediate technology (use of oxen and external inputs) and low technology (traditional use of hand hoes and low use of external inputs). The survey data were complemented with information provided by the national development bank (BANADES, 1993–6) and other sources (Barquero, 1995; CONCAFE, 1994; MAG, 1993 and 1994; Mendoza, 1992a and b; Siu and Rose, 1994; Vargas 1996).

In order to show changes in the production structure as a consequence of the impact of the structural adjustment, it was decided to compare the situation prior to the program with the situation afterwards. For the empirical study, however, this 'before and after' approach had to be approximated because of lack of appropriate data and time limitations. Therefore, the period of the cropping season 1991–2, where data were available, was regarded as being the 'preadjustment' period, because one can assume that the adjustment measures could not yet have had their impact in the sector. Secondly, the cropping season 1994–5 was regarded as the 'post-adjustment' period for the analysis. While the adjustment process is still not completed, external support for the program is now officially 'suspended'.[8] Nevertheless, it was assumed that most important adjustment measures have had their impact on the sector.

Maize and beans were treated as importables as well as exportables. The varieties and qualities of maize and beans produced in Nicaragua do not appear in international grain markets, though these specific varieties are traded within the Central American region. Therefore, the following procedure has been used for calculation of the import- and export-parity prices. First, the main trading partners for these commodities were determined. It was found that for black beans the neighboring countries Honduras, El Salvador and Costa Rica maintained some trade relations, whereas for maize no important trade flows could be found. However, as the variety in question (white maize for tortilla making) is also produced and consumed in these countries, they would be potential trading partners; it was thus decided to include them also in the case of maize. To define the import-parity price the monthly average wholesale price of the respective country was taken from statistics and the transport and marketing costs to bring it into the wholesale market of Nicaragua were added.[9] Second, from the resulting prices of the three countries the lowest one was taken to get the reference price.[10] Third, for use in the PAM, the monthly average reference price and the domestic market price were weighted according to the selling pattern of the farmers. The selling pattern was found in the survey and refined for use in the calculations. Thus it was postulated that, on average, farmers were selling part of their harvest immediately in the first month after harvest, another part in the following month, and so on up to the harvest of the next crop. Table 3.4 indicates the percentages used in this study.

The yields, nominal salaries and production costs at private prices were taken from the results of the survey (averages of the technology level). The percentage division between tradables and non-tradables of

Table 3.4 Weights of sale of harvest of maize and beans in Nicaragua (percentage of harvest sold)

		Month after harvest/cropping season					
		1	*2*	*3*	*4*	*5*	*6*
1. *Primera*	Maize	50%	30%	20%			
	Beans	50%	30%	20%			
2. *Postrera*	Maize	50%	30%	20%			
	Beans	40%	30%	20%	10%		
3. *Apante*	Maize	50%	30%	5%	5%	5%	5%
	Beans	50%	25%	15%	5%	5%	

Source: see text.

61

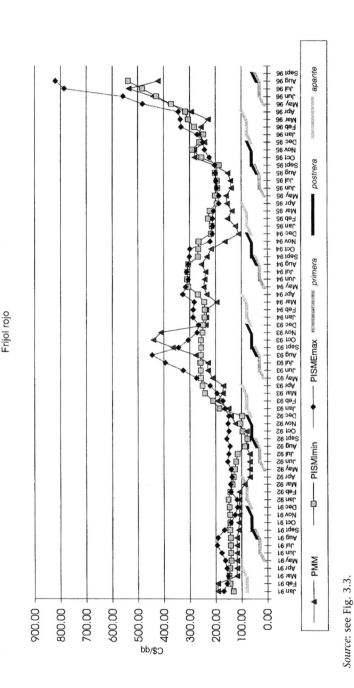

Figure 3.4 Prices of beans in Nicaragua 1991–96.

Frijol rojo

Source: see Fig. 3.3.
Notes:
PMM, domestic market price; PISMImin, import-parity price; PISMEmax, export parity price; *primera, postrera, apante,* cropping seasons

the intermediate inputs was derived from the literature (USAID, 1991, 1992) and supplemented with own estimates.[11] The real salary was defined with the help of the concept of a 'minimum reservation price for labor', which is the cost of a minimum consumer basket for survival. The real interest rate was determined by taking nominal interest adjusted by the inflation rate and by the planned devaluation (crawling peg) for the private prices and the real devaluation for the social prices, respectively (see BCN, 1994a and b). Land as a cost factor was not used in the calculations because it was not possible to find reliable data on land prices and rental values. This is due to the confused situation concerning property rights on land and the deficient land registration system. Therefore all benefits also include the rent of land as a production factor. The real exchange rate was calculated using the purchasing power parity model with data provided from the Central Bank (BCN, 1994a and b; Edwards, 1992).

The cropping systems diagram (Figure 3.2) indicates the approximate timing and duration of the rainy season and the resulting cropping calendar in the studied regions in Nicaragua.

Results

We focus attention on a detailed discussion of the results from the bean crop as an exportable and from the maize crop as an importable.[12] For bean production, export was becoming an important outlet of national production, mainly owing to the low price in comparison to the neighboring countries. Second, the low bean production in these countries, due to climatic conditions, increased the demand for this variety of bean, which was not available from other sources. On the other hand, trade statistics show that the white maize for tortillas was exported only in minimal quantities, whereas there was some import, specifically from neighboring countries. However, for both crops, prospects as exportables as well as importables were calculated to address all potential trading opportunities.

Beans as exportable

Table 3.5 shows most important indicators for the bean crop in the two regions. In region I the data for the 1991–2 crop was insufficient to be included and in region IV the technology levels for the *primera* season could not be fully distinguished.[13] In the following page or so the PAM-related indicators are discussed and a summarizing evaluation is made.

Table 3.5 Beans as exportable in Nicaragua

| | Region IV | | | Region I | | |
| | *Average sample* | | | | | |
Year *PAM coefficients*	*91/92* *Postrera*	*94/95* *Primera*	*94/95* *Postrera*	*91/92* *Postrera*	*94/95* *Primera*	*94/95* *Postrera*
PCR	1.73	0.38	0.73	n.a.	0.32	0.55
DRC	0.83	0.26	0.37	n.a.	0.23	0.29
EPC	0.50	0.73	0.56	n.a.	0.74	0.58
SRP	−0.28	−0.21	−0.35	n.a.	−0.23	−0.35
	Intermediate technology					
PCR	1.82	n.a.	0.71	n.a.	0.34	0.63
DRC	0.83	n.a.	0.36	n.a.	0.25	0.33
EPC	0.47	n.a.	0.56	n.a.	0.74	0.57
SRP	−0.28	n.a.	−0.35	n.a.	−0.21	−0.35
	Low technology					
PCR	0.91	n.a.	0.52	n.a.	0.29	0.37
DRC	0.51	n.a.	0.27	n.a.	0.20	0.20
EPC	0.59	n.a.	0.59	n.a.	0.74	0.60
SRP	−0.29	n.a.	−0.38	n.a.	−0.24	−0.37

Source: Own fieldwork.
Notes:
PAM: indicators estimated from PAM.
n.a.: insufficient data available.

PCR   The private cost ratio (PCR: 1.73) for the pre-adjustment period shows that beans production for export would not have been a profitable enterprise, except for those using low-level technologies. This picture changed for the post-adjustment period, where in the 1994–5 season the high prices improved the results (PCR: 0.38) and the 1994–5 *postrera* season also showed good but somewhat lower results (PCR: 0.73), owing mainly to the lower domestic price level in the main production season for beans. This indicates that farmers benefitted from policies implemented so far.[14]

The better results of the *primera* season in 1994–5 can be explained by the fact that because of climatic conditions the farmers of this region preferred to produce maize in the *primera* season and beans in the *postrera* season. Therefore overall production in the *primera* is low, hence the price is higher. This is valid for region I and for different levels of technology.

In region I the better prices of the *primera* season allowed a good level of profitability; however the main production season was the *postrera*. The better results compared with region IV are due to the generally higher yield observed in the latter. The lower-level technology performed better in both periods and regions. This can be explained by the fact that it operates with nearly no external or purchased inputs and therefore production costs are much lower compared with those for higher technology levels.

DRC   The improvement of the domestic resource cost ratio (DRC) for region IV again confirms the tendencies of an improving profitability coefficient over time as discussed above. However, it would have been economically even more profitable to export without distortions. For all levels of technology in region IV an improvement can be observed from the pre-adjustment period to the post adjustment period. The figures indicate that the potential export of beans was and is an economically efficient enterprise and the economy as well as the producers would have benefitted.

EPC   The effective protection of beans is lower than unity, in other words it is implicitly taxed on the tradable markets. The implicit taxation was more pronounced during the pre-adjustment period for the intermediate technologies and equal for the low technologies in region IV (depending on the use of tradable inputs). In region I the high prices in the 1994–5 *primera* meant a lower implicit taxation.

SRP   The subsidy ratio to producers (SRP) reflected the growing implicit taxation of the policies, as well as the existing bottlenecks in the market, which mostly affected the low-level technologies. Generally in the pre-adjustment period the taxation was less accentuated than in the post-adjustment periods, because the implicit taxation by the product price was compensated partly by the implicit subsidy in the input market. However, in the more recent period all implicit subsidies disappeared and the implicit taxation through the still overvalued exchange rate increased therefore its influence.

The results show the improvement in the private profitability (PCR) and economic efficiency (DRC) indicators from the pre-adjustment period to the post-adjustment period. This improvement can be interpreted — at least partly — as being the positive result of the structural adjustment measures. Furthermore, the export of beans was and continues to be a good potential for the production sector and the economy. This is confirmed by the actual trade of beans with the neighboring countries. In 1994 and 1995 Nicaragua was a net exporter of between 17 and 20 per cent of its national production, mainly to El Salvador where 65 per cent of its exports were sold (MAG, 1994; Vargas, 1996). However, the other indicators (EPC, SRP) clearly show that the positive (high-price) situation in the reference markets for Nicaragua did not reach the farmers. In other words, the price signals from abroad were not transferred into the domestic markets. The implicit taxation observed, owing to a still overvalued exchange rate, was hindering an improvement of the production sector, and consequently delayed or even constrained the expansion of production. On the other hand, bottlenecks in infrastructure and marketing were clearly hampering the success of the export potential.

White maize as importable

In Table 3.6 the indicators for the maize crop considered as an importable commodity are presented.[15] The following conclusions can be drawn:

PCR The private cost ratio (PCR) for the pre-adjustment period indicated profit for the intermediate technology level but none for the low technologies, whereas the latter performed better in the post-adjustment period (*primera* of 1994–5). The difference in the post-adjustment period between *primera* and *postrera* season was due to higher input costs and lower prices.[16]

The difference between *primera* and *postrera* in both regions is due to market factors. However, in the *postrera* season the intermediate technologies showed better results compared with the lower level of technology, whereas in the *primera* season it was the contrary. This is due to the lower yield reported for this season (30 qq/mz in *primera*, 20 qq/mz in *postrera*) whereas the price difference is less important. Compared with region IV, all values in region I were better (i.e. lower); this is explained by better yields reported for the latter region.

DRC The domestic resource cost ratio for region IV shows the best results with respect to the price development for the 1994–5 *primera* season. In the pre-adjustment period as well as in the post-adjustment period the domestic maize production compared with possible imports of maize was economically efficient. The change in the DRC ranking sequence between intermediate and low technology from pre- to

Table 3.6 Maize as importable in Nicaragua

	Region IV			Region I		
	Average sample					
Year	91/92	94/95	94/95	91/92	94/95	94/95
PAM coefficients	Postrera	Primera	Postrera	Postrera	Primera	Postrera
PCR	0.65	0.58	0.84	n.a.	0.36	0.54
DRC	0.43	0.35	0.45	n.a.	0.22	0.31
EPC	0.70	0.66	0.58	n.a.	0.67	0.60
SRP	−0.23	−0.28	−0.32	n.a.	−0.29	−0.31
	High technology					
PCR	n.a.	n.a.	1.24	n.a.	n.a.	0.49
DRC	n.a.	n.a.	0.62	n.a.	n.a.	0.28
EPC	n.a.	n.a.	0.53	n.a.	n.a.	0.60
SRP	n.a.	n.a.	−0.28	n.a.	n.a.	−0.30
	Intermediate technology					
PCR	0.47	0.63	0.70	n.a.	0.37	0.41
DRC	0.32	0.38	0.38	n.a.	0.23	0.24
EPC	0.71	0.65	0.59	n.a.	0.67	0.61
SRP	−0.22	−0.27	−0.32	n.a.	−0.28	−0.32
	Low technology					
PCR	1.36	0.35	0.59	n.a.	0.34	0.77
DRC	0.81	0.20	0.32	n.a.	0.21	0.40
EPC	0.64	0.68	0.62	n.a.	0.68	0.61
SRP	−0.25	−0.30	−0.35	n.a.	−0.30	−0.35

Source: Own fieldwork.
Notes:
PAM: indicators estimated from PAM.
n.a.: insufficient data available.

post-adjustment period is notable. This indicates the preference in price policies during the post-adjustment period for the use of non-tradable factors.

The DRC values for region I show the same tendencies as for region IV. The intermediate technology in the 1994–5 *postrera* season was performing best because of the relatively better yields compared with the low technology.

EPC   The indicator for effective protection (EPC) shows that policies in all periods, for all technologies and all regions were of a disincentive nature. This is less the case in the pre-adjustment period and more in the 1994–5 season for both regions. In other words, though the production was profitable, the producer was implicitly taxed by the price structure. The relation of the values between the technologies and periods indicate that the low-level technology is favored over the higher levels in the post-adjustment period.

SRP   The subsidy ratio to producers (SRP) in all cases, with increasing negative values over the periods, gives the percentage of implicit taxation of the producer. However, it is less in the pre-adjustment period than in the post-adjustment period, and lower for higher-level technologies. This means that policies in general in both periods favored the higher use of tradables, whereas the results of the DRC suggests that the low and medium levels of technology were economically more efficient.

The results show that in the pre-adjustment period the production of maize was less profitable for the low-level technology, but better for the high-level technology than in the post-adjustment period. This is due to the different price relations between product and input costs in the adjustment period. Furthermore, the economic indicators show that in the post-adjustment period price policies favored low or intermediate technologies. This is a first indication of the change in relative prices for tradables and non-tradables as a consequence of the structural adjustment measures. When tradables become more expensive, technologies that use less tradable inputs (like fertilizers, pesticides and mechanization) show better results. This observed improvement of the situation is due also to the fact that the farmers adapted their production system to the new price relations between tradables and non-tradables by substituting tradable inputs with non-tradables (i.e. labor, but also land by expanding the area). However, the implicit taxation (due to an overvalued exchange rate, market bottlenecks, etc.) indicates an impediment for the farmers to profit from their efficient production which also hinders expansion. Comparing private indicators (PCR) with social indicators (DRC), it shows that, with respect to maize as an importable crop, structural adjustment measures were far from being realized at the 'farmers' level. In other words, the positive price signal could not reach the farmers because of the already mentioned market imperfections, the bottlenecks in infrastructure and the institutional set-up. Based on the above-mentioned factors, only the overvaluation of the exchange rate is more or less directly observable; the other factors can merely be determined qualitatively. Finally, the conclusion can be drawn that the domestic production of maize compared with its import from the countries of the region in all cases not only was profitable, but also showed a high economic efficiency.

Conclusions

The economic situation of the maize production in region IV as well as in region I showed an improvement, partly owing to an improvement of the relative prices because of the structural adjustment program, but also because the producers managed to adapt their production system to the new situation despite structural bottlenecks. The maize production for domestic consumption (maize regarded as importable) showed a good private profitability and was economically efficient. In the periods considered as post-adjustment, exports would even have been profitable for the producers as well as for the economy as a whole. With respect to the impacts of the structural adjustment program on producers and consumers, it can be concluded that they were less favorable for the first group but favorable for the second, in so far as the opportunity costs for the consumers (social price) would be higher. In other words in a situation of a completely open economy, producers would have been better off.

The bean production started from a much less favorable situation in the pre-adjustment period in comparison with maize. However, it also reached a profitable and efficient level in the period regarded as post-adjustment. The reasons are basically the same as for maize. Bean production does not enjoy such high protection as maize and as such is implicitly taxed. Bean production is economically efficient and it is considered to have a production potential that could be developed with appropriate measures, like fostering real devaluation and improving the export infrastructure. With respect to consumer and producer groups, the same holds for beans as for maize.

The following conclusions are related to the outlined macro–meso–micro analytical framework (see Figure 3.1). They are also based on an extensive review of secondary literature on the case of Nicaragua (see Alfsen *et al.*, 1996; Clemens, 1993 and 1994; Edwards, 1992, Evans, 1996; Gómez, 1994; Mendoza, 1992a and b; Norton, 1993; Vargas, 1996).

Perspectives for agricultural development

At the macroeconomic level, an important role for the development of the agricultural sector in Nicaragua can be seen against the background of the situation of relative stagnation, in which the country remained during a long period. Though the agricultural sector was the only sector with a positive growth rate for many years, various structural elements were not satisfied for its development. Failures in infrastructure for marketing – specifically for storage and transport, restricted access to credit in rural areas, restricted availability of extension services, and extension messages that do not take into account actual price relations – as well as the still unresolved issue of property rights, strongly limit rural development.

The measures of fiscal and monetary policies and the reform of the financial system led to credit restrictions for the agricultural sector, affecting mainly small and medium producers. As there is practically no self-financing capacity, this had serious negative effects on agricultural production. However, there are some signs that alternative credit systems are developing that could alleviate this situation.

At the meso level, the marketing and commercialization process is still very inefficient and distorted, despite the virtual disappearance of the state marketing board for basic grains (ENABAS). The problems in the marketing sector have not been resolved, because of the absence of real competition. For individual producers, who normally sell their harvest at the farm gate, this implies that a state monopoly was replaced by a private one.

A further problem – the shortage of credit for the agricultural sector – is twofold. First, credit is granted under purely commercial criteria as opposed to the development (in effect 'gift') criteria used during the Sandinista period. This implies that farmers have to be up to date with the amortization of outstanding credits, have to present a collateral (like a land title) and face positive and high real interest rates. The second problem is that lack of proper land titles prevents most small and medium farmers, who obtained their land through the Sandinista land reform without a proper legal land titling process, to apply for credits. There are some attempts being made to overcome these problems by creating alternative rural financing channels, which for example work with group solidarity and which have lower (subsidized) interest rates.

Precisely in this situation the functioning of an agricultural extension system would be of paramount importance. It could foster technologies and production systems which are less dependent on external production factors (purchased inputs), and thus require less finance for the production season. However, the existing extension system lacks extension messages and programs adapted to the small and medium farmers' actual situation.

The question of the property rights has several causes and antecedents. First there is the so-called *piñata*, where during the transition period some Sandinista government officials granted themselves private houses, shares of enterprises or large agricultural estates. Some of the confiscations made during the Sandinista period were later questioned as not being justified. These cases were brought to court by former owners for revision. Although the Chamorro government had managed to resolve a large number of these cases in litigation, the position of the actual government is less transparent with respect to this question. It is not clear if the objective is a 'counter' land reform (giving back the lands to the pre-Sandinista owners) or just a redistribution of lands dishonestly acquired (*la piñata*).

Structural adjustment, agricultural income and farm differentiation

An important objective of the structural adjustment program is to improve the structure of the economy in such a way that the price signals can effectively guide the allocation of resources. In other words, the market should be able to transfer price signals from consumers to producers. In general, the proper transmission of price signals depends on a correctly valued exchange rate, the absence of rent seeking mechanisms (for example by oligopolistic structures) and low transaction costs (by good infrastructure). However, the price signals often do not reach the producers, owing to the lack of rehabilitation and reconstruction of the road infrastructure to rural areas, the insufficiency of the transport system and other infrastructure services. In some remote areas these problems are aggravated further by the periodical assaults of armed groups on the rural population. The market distortions are twofold. First, rent seeking activities are still present because farmers in remote areas are dependent on middlemen and small traders for the commercialization of their goods at the farm gate. These middlemen can exert their market power mainly because of imperfect information available to the farmer. Second, transaction costs are high for marketing owing to bad infrastructure or the difficult availability of credit related to a reduced number of banking entities in rural areas. In some remote areas this leads to an increasing tendency towards subsistence production. However, in areas where conditions are more favorable, the results from the survey suggest that the change in relative prices was helpful to improve the situation of private profitability and economic efficiency.

Furthermore, negative and positive effects of the structural adjustment program can be distinguished. The measures with negative impact, as

Figure 3.5 Exchange rates, Nicaragua 1991–96.

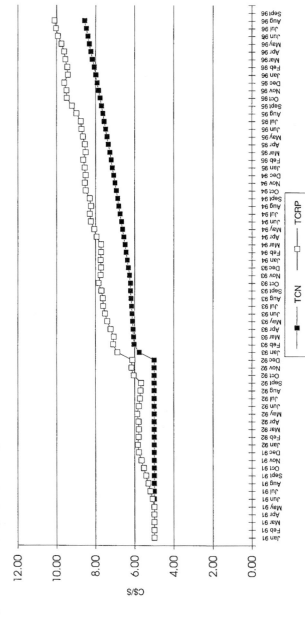

C$/$

Source: BCN, 1994a,b; FIDEG 1997.

Notes:

TCN, nominal exchange rate (official); TCRP, real exchange rate (purchasing power parity)

already mentioned, are the credit restrictions, the deregulation of the state sector mainly regarding credit and marketing, and the liberalization of external and domestic trade. The impact of these measures on the agricultural sector and specifically on the production structure was negative because of the imperfections in the transmission mechanism for the price signals towards the farmers. Instead of a desired easing of the production conditions, these have been further aggravated. For example, the credit restrictions affect the farmers who either were previously able to obtain production credit by belonging to a cooperative, or belonged to a cooperative that received credit as a whole.

On the positive side, the adjustment in relative prices related to the adaptation of the exchange rate has led to a modification in production systems, resulting in an increased private profitability and economic efficiency as could be measured in the PAM analysis. This was clearly linked to a decrease in the use of purchased inputs like fertilizers and pesticides. However, this led also to a decrease in yields, which in some areas could not be compensated for by increasing the cultivated area. The negative impact in the production systems is most evident in situations where the property rights issue is still unresolved.

With regard to the ecological impact of structural adjustment, observations on positive as well as on negative effects can be made, without being able to quantify it in any way. On the positive side, the reduced application of chemical fertilizers and pesticides has to be mentioned. On the negative side, the reduced use of external inputs leads to decreasing yields; hence land use becomes less intensive with possible negative effects on erosion and soil fertility.

Comparative advantage of the Nicaraguan agricultural sector

The interplay of the different adjustment measures has sent contradicting price signals. On the one hand, the relation of relative prices of tradables and non-tradables has improved, thanks to the devaluation of the national currency, among other measures. On the other hand, the institutional framework has not developed accordingly. The attempt to close the gap still existing between nominal and real exchange rates with the help of a crawling peg mechanism is constrained by several factors. One factor is the so-called 'dollarization', which means that certain economic sectors or branches are able to raise their domestic prices according to the devaluation of their currency relative to the US dollar by indexed prices. Cases are the nominal interest rate augmented with the rate of devaluation and the prices of fuels and other imported goods that are adapted regularly, or even daily. Some industries producing domestic goods with a strong oligopolistic power and/or high dependence on imported raw materials (like detergents, edible oils and wheat flour milling) are able to adapt their consumer prices according to the devaluation index. If, for any reason (for example a fall in production) other domestic prices rise, the domestic inflation rate will rise faster than the international rate (in this case the US-inflation rate), hence the overvaluation of the currency will increase.

Another factor is the planned chronological sequence of the adjustment measures, which was not strictly followed in the beginning. This has led to a situation where effects were contrary to the desired goals. The liberalization of external trade in conjunction with devaluation is a clear example. While prices of imports increased through devaluation, the decrease through the abolition of tariffs and duties was larger, and in the end imported goods were cheaper than before. This is mainly valid for some goods that were cheap but were rationed in supply, and only available at a high price on the black market.

The empirical study, however, revealed that the producers adapted their production system to the new relative prices of tradables and non-tradables. They changed from a relatively higher technology level in the pre-adjustment period to a lower technology level, mainly increasing the use of labor (intensification) and to a lesser extent bringing more land under cultivation (extensification). This effect can be observed especially in the newly increasing areas of shifting cultivation in the eastern lowlands of the country.

Policy implications

The following policy implications and recommendations can be derived from the preceding discussions:

Further real devaluation

This measure is of primary importance for the agricultural sector. First, the exportables sector could improve its situation substantially. The importables sector (maize) could also benefit from increased protection against its main substitute in consumption, namely imported wheat. However, problems could occur in the other sectors, while the structure of the economy makes real devaluations rather difficult.

Development of infrastructure for marketing and export

This enables the revealed export potential for beans and also maize to be turned into a growth factor for the agricultural sector. Furthermore, as these crops are predominantly grown by small and medium farms, this would also improve the aspects of distribution of economic welfare, and increase the economic contribution from the rural areas.

Institutional development

Various deregulation measures of the structural adjustment program left institutional gaps in some areas. According to the theoretical foundations of the orthodox structural adjustment programs, the market is better suited to fulfill many of the tasks the state sector was performing. However, in some cases the market or the private sector is not prepared or willing to provide the necessary services. Therefore, the dismantling of such services by the state has to be accompanied by a program of gradual handing over or even creation of new institutions, either commercial or non-profit community organizations.

Reorientation of extension and research policies

The analysis has shown that under changing relative prices the possible use of externally bought inputs is a restricting factor for production. Therefore, an efficient use of these inputs and other alternatives has to be fostered. This could be implemented through the extension system as well as with the adaptive research capacities of the country. There already exist many technical possibilities, such as integrated pest management, sustainable agricultural systems and organic production. These should be implemented in close cooperation and participation with the research system (universities), the extension institutions (INTA, NGOs) and the farmers' organizations (like UNAG). Analyses of such low-external-input production systems in other countries have shown their private profitability and economic efficiency in the use of available resources, hence they also improve the comparative advantage of the systems in question.

These recommendations fit into the macro–meso–micro framework presented at the beginning of this chapter (see Figure 3.1). Devaluation would improve the positive signals from the macro-level prices; the development of infrastructure and institutions might improve the performance at the meso level, and finally the adapted research and extension messages would improve the profitability and efficiency of the household production at the micro level.

Acknowledgments

The research funded by SDC was carried out during the period 1993–6. It was implemented in close cooperation with the CIES/ESECA-UNAN

(Centro de Investigaciones Económicas y Sociales; Escuela de Economía Agrícola de la Universidad Nacional Autónoma de Nicaragua). Special thanks are owed to Orlando Mendoza and Gustavo Siles, who were the driving forces in the field work and data collection in Nicaragua.

Notes

1. According to Evans (1996: 11), the health budget of around US$200 million in the mid 1980s was cut down to around US$80 million in 1992.
2. However, the World Bank retracted recently from this extreme liberal position as documented in the *World Development Report* (cited in NZZ, no. 145, 1997: 19).
3. In the meantime the Ministry of Agriculture has set up an agricultural information and dissemination system with price bulletins etc.
4. In this chapter competitiveness is synonymous with individual efficiency or profitability, while comparative advantage is synonymous with social or economic efficiency. See Monke and Pearson (1989: 17ff.).
5. A market without internal distortions and fully integrated into the world market.
6. It has to be mentioned that this approach does not follow the classical 'contra-factual' analysis used in other studies. However, considering the objectives of the study and the limitations of data availability, the PAM was regarded as the most useful methodology.
7. Adapted from Monke and Pearson (1989: 160ff. and 188ff.); also Tsakok (1990: 107ff.).
8. Because of non-completion of certain key requirements the support from IMF and WB was suspended (FIDEG).
9. For the export parity price these costs have to be subtracted.
10. Assuming that importers can choose from the cheapest supply. For the export parity price it would be the highest price.
11. For a detailed description of the assumptions and the calculation procedure used see Eberlin (1998).
12. A detailed discussion of all the results can be found in Eberlin (1998). This also includes an analysis for coffee production.
13. *Primera* and *Postrera*: see Figure 3.2 for an approximate representation of timing and duration.
14. In the case of beans, emphasis for the interpretation lies in the results of the *postrera* season, which is the main cropping season for beans.
15. The data for the 1991–2 *primera* season were insufficient and only in the 1994–5 *postrera* season could a high technology level be distinguished in the sample.
16. In the case of maize the emphasis for the interpretation is laid on the results for the *primera* season, which is the main cropping season for maize.

4
Agrarian Policy Responsiveness of Small Farmers in Costa Rica

Peter C. Roebeling, Fernando Saenz, Edmundo Castro and Gerardo Barrantes

Introduction

Decisions on resource use are taken by primary producers, guided by a variety of objectives and subject to specific household characteristics. In order to analyze farm household behavior, while taking into account sustainability considerations, an analytical framework is required that addresses technical possibilities and limitations for land use given existing farm household characteristics, and possible adjustments in the farm households' production structure due to modifications in the market and institutional environment (Hengsdijk and Kruseman, 1992: 2–4). A recursive linear programming and farm household modeling approach is presented in order to analyze response reactions of farm households in the short and medium term (one to five years), which result from well-defined changes in production conditions.

The integrated modeling approach is used to analyze the potential effect of a specific Costa Rican government policy program (Productive Reconversion Program for the Agricultural Sector). This program attempts to stimulate rural development and transformation of the national agricultural sector, by means of promoting modern and vertical production processes and improving market integration of small and medium peasant farmers. This study is confined to small farm households (< 20 ha) in the Atlantic Zone of Costa Rica. Trade-offs between welfare and agro-ecological sustainability criteria are addressed at the farm level, and permit concession of both objectives. Integration of both aspects generates information to improve policy formulation with respect to suitable incentives to simultaneously foster small farm household income-utility objectives and sustainable land use in the Atlantic Zone.

Development objectives identified by the Costa Rican government for the Atlantic Zone include improved competitiveness of the agricultural sector under trade liberalization, while at the same time improving natural resource management. Resource degradation control is also considered necessary to secure long-term agricultural production potentials. Agro-ecological sustainability issues in the Atlantic Zone include soil nutrient mining (nitrogen, phosphorus and potassium) and leaching of chemical fertilizers and biocides (measured in active ingredient content) to ground and surface water (Kruseman *et al.*, 1994: 31–5). The effects of biocide and fertilizer use on the environment depend on farm-level decisions with respect to choice of land use types and technologies.

The present chapter analyzes the potential effect of the Productive Reconversion Program (which includes structural and price policies) on small farm households in the Atlantic Zone. Central questions to be answered include: (1) What is the effect of the Productive Reconversion Program on farm household utility and income levels? (2) Does it result in increased production of (non-) traditional export crops? (3) What would be the effect on soil nutrient depletion and active ingredient use? These questions are analyzed at the farm household level, as decisions are made by the primary producers who are faced by an altered decision environment.

The chapter is structured along the following lines. The next section gives a description of the agrarian production structure and farm stratification in the Atlantic Zone of Costa Rica. In the following section, a description of the modeling framework is given, followed by a review of the major agricultural government policies in Costa Rica over the last fifty years (1950–97), and finally a scenario definition is presented. The section after that describes the base run situation as well as the farm household's responsiveness towards different policy instruments as defined by the Productive Reconversion Program. Finally, in the last section the main conclusions with respect to the methodology applied and results generated are presented.

The Atlantic Zone's agrarian production structure

The Atlantic Zone is located in the eastern part of Costa Rica, coinciding with the province of Limón and encompassing 918 316 ha (18.1 per cent of the of the Costa Rican territory). The population in 1992 was 226 264 with an annual growth rate of about 3.3 per cent (DGEC, 1992). Agricultural production is based on annual food crops (maize and beans), perennial crops (banana, plantain, palm heart, cassava and some pineapple) and livestock focused on meat production. Depending on the location in the zone, average annual rainfall is between 3500 mm and 5000 mm without dry months, with an average daily temperature of 25°C (De Bruin, 1992: 2–4). Soil types are classified into three types (De Bruin, 1992: 27–37): young fertile poorly-drained volcanic soils; young fertile alluvial well-drained volcanic soils; and old infertile well-drained soils, developed on fluvio-laharic sediments.

Over the period 1963–73 the number of farms in the Atlantic Zone hardly varied, while the agricultural area increased by 17.5 per cent, largely through colonization of forest areas. Mean farm size increased from 39.4 ha in 1963 to 46.2 ha in 1973. Over the period 1973–84 the number of farms increased by 76.1 per cent, while the agricultural area increased only by 16.7 per cent, resulting in a decline in average farm size to 30.6 ha in 1984. Population growth was 5.3 per cent per year over the period 1963–73, which far exceeded the national average of 2.3 per cent per year, mainly because of substantial immigration from other zones in Costa Rica. Although population growth declined to 3.5 per cent per year over the period 1973–84, it was still above the national average of 2.6 per cent per year (DGEC, 1966, 1976, 1987).

Table 4.1 shows the agricultural production structure and importance of a variety of production activities in the Atlantic Zone for the year 1984. In terms of land use, livestock and banana production were the dominant types, followed by basic grains (maize and rice) and plantain. Added value data of 1984 however show that livestock activities contributed only 3.6 per cent to total value added in the zone, while banana production accounted for 84 per cent. Basic grains as well as plantain accounted for about 4 per cent of total value added. In terms of importance to total national agricultural production, the Atlantic Zone was the main producer of bananas and plantain while also basic grains and cassava accounted for respectively 29.6 per cent and 18.4 per cent of total national production.

From 1984 to 1991 regional land use underwent major modifications. The pasture area in the Atlantic Zone more than doubled (Stoorvogel and Eppink, 1995: 66–73), while the banana area also increased considerably, by 45.2 per cent to 32 988 ha in 1991 and to about 50 000 ha in 1994. On the other hand, the area under basic grains (rice, maize and beans) decreased by 72.4 per cent to 3505 ha in 1991.

Within the Atlantic Zone different farm types can be identified according to their land use types and related farming systems, resource

Table 4.1 Cultivated area and production in the Atlantic Zone of Costa Rica

Activity	Crop area		Production		Added value[a]		
	(ha)	(% total)	(× 10³ kg)		(× 10⁶ ¢)	(% total)	(% national)
Pasture/livestock	106 206	61.2	147 885.0	(no. of cattle)	275.6	3.6	7.2
Banana	22 713	13.1	800 484.7		6 343.3	84.0	76.0
Plantain	4 684	2.7	30 991.5	(unit)	309.8	4.1	50.5
Pineapple	200	0.1	10.9	(unit)	n.a.	n.a.	8.1
Palm heart	1 050	0.6	4 200.0		n.a.	n.a.	n.a.
Beans	724	0.4	280.2		11.0	0.2	1.6
Maize	8 842	5.1	10 931.9		227.5	3.0	21.8
Rice	7 243	4.2	17 376.4		101.4	1.3	7.8
Cassava	775	0.5	6 059.5		3.1	0.1	18.4
Other crops	21 037	12.1	—		276.7	3.7	—
Total crop area	173 474	100.0			7 548.4	100.0	

Source: DGEC (1987); MIDEPLAN (1991).
Notes:
[a] Added value calculations based on BCCR National Accounts.
¢: Costa Rican Colon.
n.a.: not available.

Table 4.2 Farm stratification in the Atlantic Zone of Costa Rica (1984)

			Farm type			Total	
		Small	Medium	Hacienda	Banana		Atlantic
	Unit	*0 to 20 ha*	*20 to 50 ha*	*>50 ha*	*>100 ha*	*Sample*	*zone*
Number of farms		6 480	1 690	803	83	9 056	9 316
Agricultural area[a]	ha	46 255	48 472	86 991	18 780	200 498	285 315
Farm area (av.)	ha	7.1	28.7	108.3	226.3	22.1	30.6
Farming system		Mixed	Mixed	Livestock	Bananas		
Objectives		Utility and full income		Quasi-rent	Profit		

Source: DLV calculations based on DGEC (1987).

Notes:

[a] The agricultural area includes wildlands located on farms, the totals thus exceeding the total crop area presented in table 4.1.

av: average.

availability, main production activities and objectives. Table 4.2 shows the farm stratification resulting from the 1984 agrarian census, and results in the identification of small and medium peasant farms, banana plantations and extensive haciendas (Kruseman *et al.*, 1994: 37–9). The stratification covers 97 per cent of all farms and 70 per cent of the agricultural area in the region.

Extensive haciendas and banana plantations cover about 37.1 per cent of the total agricultural area, while representing only 9.5 per cent of all farms in the Zone (see Table 4.2). Extensive haciendas are led by a quasi-rent objective, therefore valuing not only returns obtained from livestock fattening but also expected returns from investments in land, while profit maximization is the main objective of banana plantations (Kruseman *et al.*, 1994: 43–8). Small and medium farms represent 69.6 per cent and 18.1 per cent respectively of all farms in the Zone, while covering 16.2 per cent and 16.9 per cent of the total agricultural area respectively. They are characterized by a mixed farming system as well as utility and full-income objectives (Kruseman *et al.*, 1994: 41–3). Utility is thereby defined as the capacity of a good or service to satisfy a necessity or desire (Miller, 1991: 151–2), while full income is defined as the difference between net revenue and the monetary value of nutrient losses (Kruseman *et al.*: 1996: 8). Agricultural activities of small farm households are mainly oriented towards basic grain production, cassava, plantain and some banana, in combination with cash crops like palm heart, papaya and pineapple. Livestock activities are oriented towards meat as well as milk production (dual-purpose). Production is mainly for the market, although food security in basic grains, milk, cassava and fruits is attained largely through own production (Castro *et al.*, 1996: 25–32).

In order to obtain more recent data on the identified farm types (DGEC data are about 15 years old!), additional information from a study by Castro *et al.* (1996) in the Atlantic Zone of Costa Rica was used for the determination of the actual farm households' resource base (yearly availability of agricultural land, labor, savings, cattle and capital inputs). Table 4.3 shows that the average small farm's cultivable area equals 8.9 ha, which is distributed over the three soil types identified earlier. Average family size of five persons results in a labor supply of about 41 labor days per month, while labor can also be hired in at the current wage rate. In terms of capital availability, the small farm type is rather poorly endowed. Available own savings are extremely low, while bank credit accessibility is also restricted because of inflexible and rigid collateral requirements. Informal credit is more

Table 4.3 Average annual resource endowment for small farm type in the Atlantic Zone of Costa Rica

Farm area[a] (hectares)	Labor (days)	Savings (colones)	Cattle (units)	Equipment (units)	Sprayers (units)	Vehicles (units)
8.9	491.9	5.1×10^4	4.1	0.9	1.1	0.2

Source: DLV calculations based on Castro *et al.* (1996).
Notes:
[a] The farm area differs from that presented in Table 4.2, since the calculation is based on the sample by Castro *et al.* (1996).

widely used, although the involved costs may be very high (Quiros *et al.*, 1997: 48). Land preparation is almost completely mechanized and done mainly by contract workers, while sowing and fertilizer application are done mainly by hand. Herbicides, insecticides and fungicides are applied by manual backpack sprayers. Farmers in the Atlantic Zone have considerable problems with marketing their products at remunerative prices, owing to several constraints (Jansen *et al.*, 1996: 90–1), which include few alternative sales outlets, limited market power of farmers, high transport costs and unfair bargaining practices of transporters when there are shortages of this service.

Methodological framework

Description of the farm household model

The methodology used is a combination of two approaches (Kruseman *et al.*, 1996: 7): a multiple-goal linear programming (MGLP) framework is utilized for the analysis of the production side in order to determine crop and technology choice, while the consumption side is analyzed using an econometrically derived (non-linear) utility function. The results is a farm-household-modeling (FHM) approach that links the econometrically specified behavioral expenditure part with the linear programming optimization procedure of the production structure (Ruben *et al.*, 1994: 5–10). This is done in order to appraise the impact of modifications in prices on farm profits and utility, factor allocation and land use. The model is based on the traditional farm-household-modeling approach (Singh *et al.*, 1986: 17–47), with the major adaptation of the inclusion of a direct utility function in order to ensure non-separability (Kruseman, 1996: 5–9).[1]

Selection of production activities takes place in a stepwise optimization procedure, while objective functions are based on a utility function and on a full-income concept (Kruseman *et al.*, 1996: 7–9). First, investment decisions are taken on the basis of expected prices and maximizing full income, subject to a cash and credit constraint, production technology, minimum consumption requirements and initial farm characteristics.[2] Subsequently, consumption decisions are taken on the basis of actual prices and maximizing utility, subject to the net farm income, time constraint and the farm resource availability adjusted in the first step. A goal weight generator is used to attach weights to these different objective functions, in this way solving the non-separable model and thus allowing for non-recursive relations between the production and consumption part of the farm household model (Kruseman *et al.*, 1996: 31–3). Investment and production/consumption decisions are modeled separately, in order to differentiate between medium- and short-term considerations, respectively. The investment model permits the analysis of household behavior with respect to the allocation of savings and credit among operation costs and investments, and in fact reflects the existence of capital market imperfections. The consumption model permits the analysis of farm household consumption preferences and of how these preferences determine crop choices.

Economic science makes use of a so-called 'positive analysis', which is strictly limited to making affirmative descriptions or scientific predictions of *what is* (Miller, 1991: 14–15). On the other hand there is also the 'normative analysis', which takes into account personal values and judgments making affirmative descriptions of *what should be*. Many mathematical programming models have a somewhat normative structure, as behavioral relationships are incorporated into the model. Relationships between variables in the present farm household model are, however, parametrized using econometric techniques and based on actual (observed) behavior. As a consequence, the model can be characterized as a positive model while the selection of analyzed agrarian policies is purely normative.

Figure 4.1 provides a schematic presentation of the farm household model, thereby identifying the farm household's restrictions, possibilities and objectives. Farm household *restrictions* are given by their initial resource endowment, while the attitude towards savings (expressed in a savings coefficient) and future considerations (expressed in a time discount rate) also determine the optimal solution. Resources available to the household include land, labor, savings, cattle and fixed capital

Figure 4.1   Schematic presentation of the farm household model

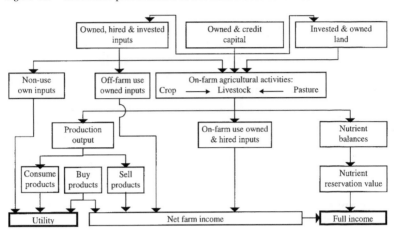

inputs, as determined by the farm household survey performed by Castro *et al.* (1996) and presented earlier in Table 4.3. Moreover, soil nutrient availability is considered an important resource, changes in which are reflected in nutrient balances.

The small farm household's time discount rate is set at 7.5 per cent per year (Zuñiga, 1996: 6), while savings available for the financing of operation costs and investments are a proportion of net farm income obtained in the previous year, consumption being the remainder (Bade *et al.*, 1997: 14–15).[3] The savings coefficient for the small farm household is set at 25 per cent of the net farm income. Operation costs are defined as costs related to the use of hired labor, inputs and feed supplements, and can be financed out of earnings from off-farm employment, available own savings and formal and informal credit capital sources. Investments refer to the establishment of perennial crops and purchase of equipment and cattle, which can be financed out of available own savings and formal credit. While formal credit is limited to a fraction of the farm household's land value (25 per cent), informal credit is limited to a fraction (10 per cent) of the expected marketed crop production value. Annual real interest rates for the use of formal and informal credit capital sources are 12.0 per cent (Zuñiga, 1996: 6) and 47.3 per cent (Quiros *et al.*, 1997: 48) respectively.

Farm household *possibilities* are provided by on- and off-farm production activities. On-farm production activities are defined for crop, pasture and livestock activities, while off-farm production activities refer to off-farm employment possibilities for family laborers. Production technologies are defined for crop, pasture and livestock activities (Bouman *et al.*: 1998), in the form of well-defined input and output coefficients (Hengsdijk *et al.*: 1998). Input requirements are defined in terms of land, labor, equipment, fertilizers, agro-chemicals and seeds. Output is defined in terms of harvested yield for human and animal consumption, crop residues for animal consumption, soil nutrient balances and active ingredient use levels. Inputs as well as outputs are defined per hectare per year, apart from labor, which is defined per hectare per month in order to account for peak periods. Crop activities are defined for maize, beans, pineapple, bananas, plantain, palm heart and cassava; livestock activities refer to cattle for fattening and/or milk production, and pasture activities are defined for natural and improved pasture types. A distinction is made between actual and alternative production techniques, where actual production techniques refer to currently practised production systems and alternative production techniques to sustainable (in terms of nutrient use) production systems that are not yet commonly used in the region. Fallow is assumed to leave nutrient balances unaffected.

Optimization takes place for utility and full-income *objectives*. Utility can be obtained through consumption of on-farm production and leisure Q_j^{cons} or market purchased products Q_j^{buy}, and is maximized subject to the net farm income, which is defined as returns from sold production Q_j^{sold} and off-farm employment O^{off}, net of the costs related to the use of fixed and variable inputs I_i, capital sources C_b, and consumption. The net farm income NFI is given by:

$$\text{NFI} = \left\{ \sum_j p_j Q_j^{sold} + wO^{off} \right\} - \left\{ \sum_i p_i I_i + \sum_b p_b C_b + \sum_j p_j \left(Q_j^{cons} + Q_j^{buy} \right) \right\} \qquad (1)$$

where p refers to the prices related to commodities j, fixed and variable inputs i and capital sources b, and w the off-farm wage rate. Utility functions are derived from the 1987–8 National Household Income and Expenditure Survey (DGEC, 1988, 1990), using a negative exponential utility function for basic food crops (characterized by decreasing marginal utility that asymptotically reaches a maximum) and an exponential utility function for other food products, non-food and leisure (characterized by decreasing marginal utility without maximum). Since utility is additive separable, the objective utility function Z_1 is given by:

$$Z_1 = \text{UTIL} = \sum_j U_j^{\max}\left\{1 - \exp\left[-\rho_j\left(Q_j^{\text{cons}} + Q_j^{\text{buy}}\right)\right]\right\}$$

$$+ \sum_j \rho_j\left(Q_j^{\text{cons}} + Q_j^{\text{buy}}\right)^{\sigma_j} \tag{2}$$

where $U_j^{\max}$ is the maximum attainable utility with commodity j, ρ_j the conversion factor of consumption to utility, and σ_j the exponent of consumption commodity j.

The full-income objective is defined as the net farm income corrected for the expected monetary value of nutrient losses (van der Pol, 1993: 14–15), thereby using the farm household's nutrient reserve price for the valuation of current nutrient gains or losses as reflected in the nutrient balance B_n. The full-income objective Z_2 is given by:

$$Z_2 = \text{Full Income} = \text{NFI} - \sum_n p_n B_n \tag{3}$$

where p_n is the reserve price related to nutrient. The investment and consumption components of the model are calibrated separately, and final model results are obtained by their weighted sum (Bade *et al.*, 1997: 15–16). Calibration of the model with relative goal weights of 60 per cent for utility and 40 per cent for full income provides a reasonably good fit.

Expected as well as actual market prices are used for model optimization, while transaction costs are taken into account for the determination of these prices at the farm gate level. The model makes use of expected prices as medium-term investment decisions are taken, while actual market prices are used for short-term consumption decisions. Expected prices are based on a weighted average of market prices over the last three years, with coefficients of expectation set at 0.5 for year (t-1) and 0.25 for years (t-2) and (t-3). Transaction costs are defined as a margin between market and farm gate prices, which result from transport costs, marketing margins and imperfect market information.

Review of agrarian policies in Costa Rica

The last fifty years of agrarian policy in Costa Rica can be divided in two main periods, before and after the crisis in 1980. Development policies applied during each of these periods are quite contradictory. During the period before 1980, state control and protection of the agricultural sector were high, while the period after 1980 is characterized mainly by a trade liberalization policy (SEPSA, 1997: 1).

Before 1980 agrarian policies were directed towards the production of traditional export crops like coffee, banana, sugar cane, cacao and meat, as well as basic food grains like rice, sorghum, maize and beans (Gonzales, 1994: 5). Basic food crop production was promoted in order to meet internal consumption requirements. Policies applied to foster the production of traditional export crops and basic food grains included (Cartín and Piszk, 1980: 26–9): (1) the regulation of input and output prices, (2) investment in infrastructure, (3) technical assistance, (4) credit facilities and (5) import and export market regulation.

Regulation of imports and exports, as well as input and output prices, were oriented mainly towards basic food grains (Cartín and Piszk, 1980: 27–9). The marketing process was regulated by the state through the Consejo Nacional de la Producción (CNP), in order to stabilize internal food crop prices. The CNP was the main buyer and seller of these food grains, and guaranteed the purchase of the total national basic food crop production. Purchase prices to local producers were thereby higher than sales prices to local consumers, in this way providing incentives for basic food crop production while keeping the costs of living low. When the national basic food grain supply was guaranteed, the CNP exported these crops to Central America and the Caribbean, while import of basic food grains was approved only in cases of shortages caused by natural phenomena (Guardia *et al.*, 1987: 45–51). On the other hand the import of inputs (like fertilizers, pesticides and machinery) was taxed (Mora *et al.*, 1994: 19), and provided an incentive for basic food crop production, because these crops are characterized by relatively low input requirements as compared with cash crops.

Investments in infrastructure were performed not only by the national government through the construction of roads and bridges, but also by the CNP, the Ministerio de Agricultura y Ganadería (MAG) and the Instituto de Desarrollo Agrario (IDA) (Cartín and Piszk, 1980: 25–7). The CNP made investments in purchase centers and storing facilities for basic food grains, as well as small sales centers for these crops throughout the country. The MAG made wide investments in regional offices, vehicles, research stations and extension programs, in order to facilitate their technical assistance program. Finally, the IDA focused on the organization and establishment of small and medium farm settlements.

Technical assistance was provided by the MAG, and focused on the introduction of high-yielding varieties, which required the adoption of new, higher-input-demanding production techniques in order to raise productivity levels of basic food grains and traditional export crops. Assistance was not aimed towards specific producers, but was supplied to every kind of producer that demanded assistance. It was supplied in the form of courses, excursions to field research stations, experimental plots and free supply of variety samples. (Cartín and Piszk, 1980: 26–7).

Credit facilities were provided by the public bank system. In order to facilitate credit accessibility, the CNP provided guarantees to all agricultural producers that focused on basic food crop production (Cartín and Piszk, 1980: 29). This policy did not have the desired effect. In the first place, credit services were often allocated and renegotiated under political circumstances, with high costs and losses for the capital provider. Secondly, the credit guarantee was supplied to producers of all sizes and thus mainly benefitted large producers. As a consequence there was only a limited supply of credit capital to the small and medium producers (Cartín and Piszk, 1980: 29).

The period before 1980 was characterized by distorted markets, dependency on just a few export products (banana, coffee, sugar cane and cacao) for the generation of foreign currency, high levels of internal consumption accompanied by low levels of internal savings and growing levels of external indebtedness. Moreover, the state bureaucracy grew rapidly and inefficiently. This situation led to a general crisis that brought the economy down and resulted in a reduction of the real income. As a consequence, the development model of high state control and protection was abandoned (SEPSA, 1997: 1).

Although many of the policies oriented to the promotion of basic food crop production were supposed to benefit small and medium producers, experience showed that it were mainly large producers with political contacts who benefitted most. For example, the CNP did not perform an important role in the maize and beans market where small and medium farmers operate, while it performed a satisfactory role in the rice market with mainly large farmers (Cartín and Piszk, 1980: 29).

After 1980 agrarian policy changed abruptly. The Costa Rican government adopted three different structural adjustment programs (PAEs) that were designed by the International Monetary Fund (IMF) and the World Bank. These programs were supposed to: (1) correct fiscal and monetary distortions, (2) improve state services, (3) promote the privatization process of state enterprises,[4] and (4) insert the national economy into the global economy (SEPSA, 1997: 1). The main consequence of these

PAEs for the agricultural sector was its increasing incorporation into the open-market economy. Agricultural export crops were promoted through a 100 per cent reduction in export taxes to new markets, a 100 per cent reduction in import taxes for inputs like pesticides, fertilizers and equipment, and by favorable interest rates for credits directed towards agricultural export activities (Mora *et al.*, 1994: 19). As a consequence, the importance of traditional export crops (coffee, banana and sugar cane) was further strengthened, while non-traditional export crops (pineapple, flowers, ornament plants, root and tuber crops, and fresh fish) were also promoted (Gonzales, 1994: 65-6).

Promotion of agricultural export production was favored, while protection by the state was practically eliminated. Moreover, a monetary devaluation process started after 1980 in order to increase the productivity as well as the competitiveness of the agricultural sector (Mora *et al.*, 1994: 15). On the other hand, farmers producing for the local market were affected negatively as they faced higher production costs as prices of imported inputs rose while not being compensated by higher product prices.

As noted above, it is possible to make a distinction between small and medium farms oriented towards basic food crop production for the local market on the one hand, and plantations and livestock haciendas oriented towards export production and with substantial capital sources and guarantees on the other hand. The new economic strategy led to a crisis for small and medium farmers, as the process of privatization and less state participation reduced their profitable opportunities. The abolition of the regulation in output prices, in combination with technical assistance and credit oriented towards cash crops, favored non-traditional export production. Small and medium farmers were not prepared for this great change because they faced volatile markets, lacked the proper infrastructure for trading their own production, faced poor market information and were confronted by a limited capital availability, which restricted the possibility of capital-intensive cash crop production (Mora *et al.*, 1994: 24-8).

Many small and medium farmers suffered economic exclusion and poverty (Mora *et al.*, 1994: 37).[5] Moreover, the new policies had negative effects on the quality of the natural resource base (land, water and forest). The newly introduced cash crops were characterized by high productivity as well as high input use levels, leading to substantial soil nutrient depletion as well as pollution of soil and water resources respectively (Kruseman *et al.*, 1994: 31-5). Also, many of the excluded peasants were displaced from their farms as they had to sell their land to banana companies. This displacement caused social problems because peasants had to move either to the cities, thereby contributing to urban poverty, or to newly colonized land, thereby increasing the pressure on the natural resource base.

After 1990 the concern for this increased rural poverty and the deterioration of the natural resource base led to a search for a new development strategy that would balance economic growth with protection of natural resources and social welfare (SEPSA, 1995: 3–4). This was why 'sustainable development' became one of the government's policy objectives. A number of actions were planned for transformations in the agricultural sector in Costa Rica which required changes in production systems as well as in environmental management. The role of the state was transformed from direct producer into stimulator.

For the period 1994–8, agricultural policies were defined to achieve a continuous rise in rural income and welfare with the following three specific objectives (SEPSA, 1995: 17–21): (1) improvement of the competitiveness of agricultural production, which implies an increasing peasant added value participation in the market; (2) conservation of the natural resource base; and (3) increased participation of small and medium producers in the definition of agricultural policies for sustainable development. The role of the state was established by means of the Productive Reconversion Program, which was approved by law in December 1997 by the Costa Rican Assembly. This plan has an annual budget of 3000 million colones, and the main objective is to improve the integration of small and medium farmers into the globalization process (SEPSA, 1995: 17–21; SEPSA, 1997: 4; *La Gaceta*, 1998: 1–4).[6] The policy scenarios developed in the next section are based on this program.

Scenario definition

Regional development objectives emphasized for the Atlantic Zone are improvement of the competitiveness of agricultural production under trade liberalization as well as improved natural resource management (Kruseman *et al.*, 1994: 15–17).

In this context the Productive Reconversion Program focuses specifically on improved market integration of small and medium farmers (*La Gaceta*, 1998: 1–4). However, control on resource degradation is also necessary to maintain medium- and long-term agricultural production potentials (Ruben *et al.*, 1994: 3). The program focuses on state support for farmers' organizations in the areas of infrastructure, credit and marketing of inputs and outputs. The plan attempts to recover the importance of sectoral policies, which were used to influence the socioeconomic environment of the agricultural sector.

In this study an analysis is made of the potential effects of the Productive Reconversion Program on small farm households in the Atlantic Zone of Costa Rica. What is the impact on farm household utility and income levels? Does it result in an increased production of (non-) traditional export crops? What will the effect be on soil nutrient depletion and active ingredient use? These central questions result in the definition of the following two scenarios.

The first considers the small farm household base run situation, which describes the situation before policy intervention and is used for the calculation of the potential effect of different policy measures. Base run results are calculated for the small farm household that is guided by full-income and utility objectives for optimization, while facing on-farm production possibilities in the form of actual as well as alternative crop, pasture and livestock activities. Optimization takes place subject to expected prices when taking investment decisions and to current prices when taking consumption decisions, and resource use is limited by the initial farm household resource availability. Base run model results are presented in absolute values for the identified objectives, production structure, sustainability indicators and resource use balances.

The second scenario considers the effect of different agricultural policies proposed by the Productive Reconversion Program, thereby comparing the base run situation with the specific policy run situation. This information is used for the calculation of supply response reactions at the farm household level, and will give insight into the effect of the program in terms of farm household income and utility objectives, the chosen production plan and resource use, and also sustainability of land use. Agricultural policies considered and as reflected by the Productive Reconversion Program include:[7] (1) a 20 per cent decrease in the transaction costs of the marketing of products, (2) a 20 per cent decrease in transaction costs of the purchase of inputs, (3) a 20 per cent increase in the access to formal credit sources, and (4) a 20 per cent rise in cash crop prices. Moreover, combined policies include: (5) a general 20 per cent decline in transaction costs of inputs as well as outputs and (6) the same general 20 per cent decline in transaction costs in combination with a 20 per cent increase in the access to formal credit sources. Agrarian policy simulation results are presented in the form of response multipliers, indicating a percentage change in factor allocation as compared with the base run situation determined in the first scenario and induced by the different policies.

A reduction in transaction costs has an impact on the input as well as the output side, resulting in lower and higher farm gate input and output prices respectively (Antle, 1983: 182–4) and thus influencing directly the cost–benefit relations of agricultural activities. Government investments in infrastructure and collective services are important for the development of local factor and product markets. The development of local markets, education, extension services and financial institutions has a strong impact on production and investment decisions by shifting the production frontier or by increasing the rate of return to private investments (Binswanger *et al.*, 1993: 350). The Productive Reconversion Program attempts to encourage the organization of small and medium producers, as well as coordination and cooperation among them and the institutions involved in the agricultural sector (*La Gaceta*, 1998: arts 4 and 6). Organized farm groups can lower the transaction costs related to the purchase of inputs as well as the sale of outputs by lending or leasing the CNP's infrastructure, also by buying inputs at wholesale prices (*La Gaceta*, 1998: art. 5).

Increased credit accessibility widens production as well as investment possibilities, as capital availability is increased. De Groot (1996: 213) argues that credit constraints reduce incentives for investments in soil conservation, because the shift from annual to perennial, agroforestry or silvopastoral production systems is difficult without proper credit provisions. The Productive Reconversion Program enables the CNP to give trustworthy guarantees in favor of the organized farm groups, in this way acquiring access to loans at the public bank system. Assets acquired through these public loans will however be kept as a guarantee by the CNP, while at the same time it keeps control over the use of this public loan (*La Gaceta*, 1998: art. 7).

An increase in cash crop prices directly influences cost–benefit relations of agricultural activities, and may lead to an increasing importance of cash crops in the production structure. As discussed by Hayami and Ruttan (1985), adjustments of farming systems and the adoption of new technologies based on the more intensive use of land, labor or capital take place only when factor proportions are constrained. As market and/or institutional failures are widely apparent, the success of government efforts to accelerate the process of intensification is generally low (De Janvry, *et al.*, 1991: 1401–3). The organization of farm groups, as proposed by the Productive Reconversion Program, may result in higher farm gate cash crops prices through the improved bargaining position in relation to export intermediaries. Moreover, peasant groups may increase pressure towards the government for better export conditions, such as reduction in export taxes. On the other hand, the Productive Reconversion Program includes a component of quality certification for export products, as well as the development and transference of modern agro-industrial technology. This may result in a higher added value proportion of export products, as a consequence of better market prices (*La Gaceta*, 1998: art. 22–8).

Small farm households in the Atlantic Zone: model results

Small farm household base run description

The actual production plan as well as base run indicators for the small farm household are shown in Table 4.4. The actual production plan reflects the current land use pattern of small farm households in the Atlantic Zone as obtained from the farm survey by Castro *et al.* (1996), while base run results are calculated for the small farm household that is guided by the identified objectives for optimization under expected (investment decisions) and current (consumption decisions) market prices, initial resource availability, and actual as well as alternative activities. Differences in actual and base run production plans are determined mainly by the fact that actual (in practice executed) as well as alternative (potential) activities are offered to the model in the base run situation.

In the actual as well as the base run situation about 64 per cent of the agricultural area is dedicated to pasture and fallow, and the remaining 36 per cent to cereal, root and tuber and cash crop production. Production in the base run is however oriented far more towards cash crop production as compared with the actual situation (about 35 per cent and 21 per cent of the agricultural area in the base run and initial situation respectively). While base run cash crop production is oriented mainly towards the cultivation of plantain and pineapple, in the actual situation it is oriented mainly towards plantain and banana production. Food crop production for on-farm consumption is oriented towards maize, beans and cassava in the actual as well as the base run situation, although the area dedicated to these crops is far smaller in the base run situation (about 1 per cent against 15 per cent in the initial situation). Since cattle in the base run situation are held purely for meat and milk consumption while in actual practice they may also be held for savings purposes, the cattle stock in the base run situation is far lower than in the actual situation (1.2 animal units against 4.1).

Table 4.4   Actual and base run indicators for the small farm household in the Atlantic Zone of Costa Rica

Indicator	Unit	Actual situation		Base run	
		Level	*%*	*Level*	*%*
Objectives:					
Utility	Units	—	—	2 670	—
Full income	Colones	—	—	3 163 782	—
Savings	Colones	—	—	450 770	—
Production structure:					
Cereals	ha	0.44	4.9	0.04	0.4
Cash crops	ha	1.86	20.9	3.13	35.0
Root and tuber crops	ha	0.89	10.0	0.02	0.2
Pasture	ha	5.71	64.2	0.95	10.6
Fallow	ha	—[d]	—[d]	4.81	53.7
Livestock	Cattle	4.10	—	1.22	—
Sustainability indicators:					
N-Balance	kg/ha	—	—	–108.1	—
Active ingredient use	kg AI/ha	—	—	15.1	—
Resource use:					
Land balance[a]	%	—	—	46.3	—
Labor balance[b]	%	—	—	87.4	—
Capital balance[c]	%	—	—	11.0	—

Source: actual situation obtained from Castro *et al.* (1996).
Notes:
[a]   Percentage of own land used for production.
[b]   Percentage of own labor applied on-farm.
[c]   Percentage of total capital use met by own sources.
[d]   The data provided by Castro *et al.* 1996 refers only to the pasture area, though in practice this may also be fallow.

In the base run situation plantain and pineapple are the main crops in terms of land use, since they show the highest net margin on the fertile, poorly and well-drained soil types respectively. A considerable part of the land is not used because of the establishment costs (plantain) that are to be met by the limited capital availability, as well as the limited amount of available own labor. Since land is not a constraining factor, food crops (maize and cassava) for on-farm consumption are cultivated on the most productive, fertile, well-drained soil type. Initially owned cattle are held for the production of meat and milk that is partially marketed and partially consumed, while being completely fed by feed obtained from on-farm pasture production.

The selected actual plantain cash crop activity not only occupies the major part (50 per cent) of the cultivated area, but also is characterized by highly negative nitrogen balances (about 200 kilograms nitrogen loss per hectare per year). In combination with the far less nitrogen-depletive pineapple, pasture, cereal and root and tuber crop activities (25 per cent, 23 per cent, 1.5 per cent and 0.5 per cent of the cultivated area respectively), this results in an average annual nitrogen loss of about 108 kilograms per hectare. For this same reason, the annual use of active ingredients in the production process is on average 15.1 kilograms of active ingredient per hectare.

Resource use indicators show that not even 50 per cent of the cultivable area is used in the production process, while own labor and capital sources are fully utilized. Put differently, the limited labor and capital availability constrain the full use of the land resource. The major part of the small farm household's own labor availability is used on-farm, while about 13 per cent is used for off-farm employment in order to generate income as well as capital for the finance of production costs and on-farm investments. Nevertheless, only 11 per cent of the total capital requirements are met by own capital sources (savings and earnings from off-farm employment), the remaining capital requirements being met by formal and informal credit capital sources.

Small farm household agricultural policy responsiveness

Response multipliers for the partial agricultural policies as well as combinations of them are given in Table 4.5, thereby comparing base and six policy run results. Partial and combined policy response reactions are calculated for: 20 per cent changes in different categories of transaction costs, output prices, and access to credit markets as formulated in above under 'Scenario Definition'.

Objective values all show positive response reactions with respect to the identified agricultural policies, though at the expense of soil fertility and also at increasing levels of active ingredient use. Combined policies are far more effective in raising objective values as compared with the partial policies, since a combination of utility and income-stimulating effects is received. An interesting effect in terms of sustainability occurs, however. While relatively elastic positive response reactions in objective values are accompanied by relatively elastic negative effects on sustainability in the partial policies, the combined policies show relatively elastic positive response reactions in objective values in combination with relatively inelastic negative effects on

Table 4.5 Farm household response multipliers for different agricultural policies in Costa Rica

	Partial policies				Combined policies	
	(1)	(2)	(3)	(4)	(5)	(6)
	Transaction costs		Formal credit	Price cash		
Indicator	Product − 20%	Input − 20%	Access + 20%	Crops + 20%	(1) & (2)	(1) & (2) & (3)
Objectives:						
Utility	4.8	0.2	1.6	4.8	6.3	7.4
Full income	2.0	0.1	0.5	2.0	2.5	3.2
Savings	1.0	0.1	0.5	1.9	2.6	3.3
Production plan:						
Cereals	-1.6	-0.6	-0.6	-1.6	-1.8	-1.8
Cash crops	0.5	0.1	0.5	0.5	0.7	1.3
Root and tuber crops	0.0	0.0	0.0	0.0	0.2	0.2
Pasture	-3.7	-0.1	-0.1	-3.8	-3.8	-3.8
Fallow	0.4	0.0	-0.3	0.4	0.3	-0.1
Livestock	-3.6	-0.1	-0.1	-3.6	-3.6	-3.7
Sustainability indicators:						
N-balance[a]	-1.3	-0.1	-0.4	-1.3	-0.2	-0.6
Active ingredient use	1.4	0.1	0.3	1.4	0.7	1.0
Resource use:						
Land balance[b]	-0.5	0.0	0.4	-0.5	-0.4	0.1
Labor balance[c]	0.4	0.1	0.6	0.4	0.1	0.6
Capital balance[d]	-1.6	-0.2	-2.5	-1.6	-0.9	-3.0

Source: model runs.

Notes:

Response multipliers are given for a one per cent change in prices or goal indicators. The response multiplier is given by (Sadoulet and de Janvry, 1995: 72–82) the division of the percentage change dependent variable Y and the percentage change in independent variable X .

[a] A negative response multiplier refers to a detoriating N-balance.

[b] Percentage of own land used for production.

[c] Percentage of own labour applied on-farm.

[d] Percentage of total capital use met by own capital sources.

sustainability. Put differently, marginal returns obtained per unit of lost nitrogen and per unit of applied active ingredient are far larger for combined policies than for partial policies.

Within the partial policy runs, the 20 per cent decline in product transaction costs and the 20 per cent rise in cash crop prices show almost identical relatively elastic results. In both cases, farm gate output prices rise and result in equal farm gate cash crop prices, and, in turn, further increases in the profitability of cash crop production, while food crop production remains important only for on-farm consumption. The 20 per cent decline in input transaction costs as well as the 20 per cent increase in formal credit accessibility show relatively inelastic response reactions. Transaction costs involved in the purchase of inputs are relatively small (10 per cent of the input price). Releasing the capital constraint has also a relatively inelastic effect because of the existing labor constraint, which limits the full benefit of the extra capital availability.

All analyzed partial policies lead to a rise in the cash crop area (plantain), at the expense of the cereal (maize) and pasture area and as a consequence, also of the cattle stock. Capital is more profitably invested in cash crops, because net marginal returns from cash crop production show the highest absolute rise as an effect of lowered input costs, or increased output prices.[8] In combination with the higher capital requirements of the cash crops and the limited capital availability, this results in a more intensive land use as reflected in the land balance. Only when capital availability increases is land use extended, because cost–benefit relations of agricultural activities are not altered. The extra capital availability allows for an increase in the area dedicated to the most productive crop plantain, although the extra labor demand is partly met by a decrease in the pineapple and food crop area, as well as in the hiring of labor.

Partial policy runs that have the highest negative effect on pasture and livestock production are those that affect output prices. Livestock and pasture production are highly related, because livestock feed requirements are met mainly by pasture and to a minor extent by crop residues. Benefit–cost relations of agricultural activities are altered in favor of cash crop production, while livestock production remains important only for on-farm consumption purposes. Reduced farm gate input prices and increased formal credit accessibility do not have this effect, because benefit–cost relations are not (sufficiently) affected and thus meat and milk production remains an important source of consumption as well as income.

Apart from the increased formal credit accessibility run, on-farm labor productivity is increased by all of the analyzed partial policy runs because net margins rise due to lower input costs and/or higher production values. Labor is thus more profitably applied on-farm, which results in a lower level of off-farm employment as reflected in the labor balance. As a consequence, the part of the total capital requirements met by own capital sources (savings and earnings from off-farm employment) also diminishes, as reflected in the capital balance. Again the effect is largest when output prices are altered. In the case of the increased formal credit accessibility, off-farm labor for the generation of own capital becomes less important. The capital constraint is relaxed (and therefore makes own capital generation through off-farm employment less important) and allows for an increase in the area of the most productive crop (plantain), resulting in increased on-farm labor requirements that are now met not only by family labor but also by wage laborers.

All analyzed partial policies result in diminished soil nutrient stocks, while the use of active ingredients in the production process also increases. This effect is explained by the increased relative importance of plantain production, at the expense of (relatively sustainable in terms of nutrient and active ingredient use) food crop and pineapple production. Plantain production is characterized not only by high levels of nutrient depletion, but also by high use of active ingredients.

In terms of the production plan, the combined policies show a cumulative effect of the partial policies. While objective values show a synergetic increase, sustainability and resource use indicators show a dampened effect of the partial runs that constitute the combined policy run. In the partial runs the plantain cash crop area is increased at expense of the pineapple cash crop, cereal and pasture area. Food crop, meat and milk production are maintained only in order to meet minimum consumption requirements. In the combined policy runs, which all include lowered input costs in combination with a rise in output prices, not only plantain but also especially pineapple production increases because of the altered benefit–cost relations.[9] Contrary to plantain production, pineapple production is characterized by relatively low levels of nutrient depletion as well as active ingredient use. The increasing relative importance of pineapple production in the production plan results therefore in lower levels of nutrient depletion as well as active ingredient use, as compared with the cumulated partial runs. However, sustainability indicators deteriorate as compared with the base run, owing to the increased focus on cash crop production, which is characterized by relatively high active ingredient and nutrient use levels.

When the general decline in transaction costs is accompanied by an increase in formal credit accessibility, objective values show a further rise, as compared with the general decline in transaction costs, while sustainability indicators worsen more strongly. The increased capital availability allows for an increase in the area dedicated to the most productive crop plantain, while the resulting extra labor demand is met by a slight decrease in the pineapple area (as compared with the general 20 per cent decline in transaction costs). As a consequence, the relative importance of the unsustainable plantain production system increases and therefore results in higher levels of nutrient depletion and active ingredient use.

Contrary to the general decline in transaction costs in combination with an increased access to formal credit, the general decline in transaction costs results now in an intensification of land use. While altered cost–benefit relations allow only for a redistribution of the limited resources (labor and capital) dedicated to the more labor and capital intensive cash crops, the increased capital availability also allows for an increase in the use of the land resource as the capital constraint is relaxed. In both cases, the use of own labor applied on-farm increases, since labor is more profitably applied in this way. In the case of the increased formal credit accessibility, this effect is stronger, as the importance of off-farm labor for the generation of own work capital is reduced. This effect is also reflected by the decreasing importance of own capital sources in total capital use.

Conclusions

The farm household modeling approach presented offers a new perspective in analyzing farm household responsiveness towards changes in its decision environment resulting from agricultural policies, thereby taking into account sustainability considerations. The model considers farm household utility and medium-term income objectives, subject to farm-household-specific resource restrictions and production possibilities. The modeling framework integrates crop, pasture and livestock activities at the farm level within the household's market environment for inputs and commodities.

Competitiveness of small and medium farm households in the agricultural sector is considered a problem by the Costa Rican government. Therefore the government designed the Productive Reconversion

Program, which attempts to improve the competitiveness of small and medium farm households under trade liberalization, while improving natural resource management. Furthermore, control of resource degradation is considered important to secure agricultural production potentials in the long run.

For small farm households in the Atlantic Zone of Costa Rica it is shown here that the Productive Reconversion Program could result in a rise in fulfillment of utility and income objectives as well as a further orientation towards cash crop production, although at the expense of soil nutrient fertility and an increased use of active ingredients in the production process. Furthermore, it is shown that combined policy measures have a larger positive effect on utility and income objectives as compared with the sum of partial policy measures, while at the same time leading to lower nutrient depletion and active ingredient use levels.

At the farm household level, outcomes show that more than half of the agricultural area is not used for production purposes (fallow), while the remaining area is dedicated to pasture, cash and food crop production. Food crop production for on-farm consumption requires only a minor part of the agricultural area, since it is maintained purely to meet minimum consumption requirements. Cash crop production will be orientated towards plantain and to a minor extent pineapple crops, as these show the highest net marginal returns. Cattle are held for commercialization as well as on-farm consumption purposes. Plantain production especially is accompanied by high nutrient depletion and active ingredient use levels, which may seriously affect future production potentials and will be accompanied by pollution in the private and public domain properties. Limited capital and labor availability restrict further use of the land resource.

The analyzed partial policy instruments included in the Productive Reconversion Program (a decline in transaction costs of the marketing of products and the purchase of inputs and rises in the access to formal credit and in cash crop prices) all have a positive effect on farm household objective values. Objective values and orientation towards cash crop production are stimulated mostly by price policies, as the increasing marginal returns from cash crop production allow for a redistribution of resources in favor of these crops. The decline in input transaction costs has a far lower impact, because transaction costs involved in the purchase of inputs are relatively small, while benefiting most the high-input-demanding cash crop activities. The full effect of the increased formal credit capital availability is limited by the labor constraint, while it allows for an extension of the area dedicated to the most productive crop (plantain).

All of the partial policy instruments foster plantain cash crop production, at the expense of pineapple, food crop and pasture production. Increasing returns obtained from cash crop production allow for the (partial) purchase of food crops as well as meat and milk at the market, instead of producing it on-farm. In this way, capital and labor resources are liberated for cash crop production. Higher returns allow for a larger use of credit sources, while off-farm labor for the generation of own work capital becomes less important as own labor is more profitably applied on-farm. The increased importance of plantain production results in deteriorating soil nutrient balances as well as an increased use of active ingredients.

Analyzed combined policies (a general decline in transaction costs, either in combination or not with an increased access to formal credit) show a reinforced positive effect on objective values and a dampened negative effect on sustainability indicators, as compared with the cumulative partial policies that compose the combined policy. The simultaneous decrease in transaction costs of marketing, as well as the purchase of inputs, results in an increase of the pineapple and to a minor extent the plantain area, owing to altered cost–benefit relations. Since pineapple production is far less nutrient-depletive and ingredient-demanding than plantain production, the negative effects on sustainability indicators are less.

This chapter has shown that the Productive Reconversion Program could be effective in raising income and utility levels for small farm households, while export production may also be stimulated. This is accompanied however by relatively high soil nutrient losses and active ingredient use levels. Partial policies are far less effective than combined policies in raising income and utility levels as well as promoting export production. Moreover, combined policies result in lower levels of nutrient depletion and active ingredient use.

Acknowledgements

The DLV research project is financed by the Bilateral Agreement of Sustainable Development Costa Rica – The Netherlands, through the Dutch Embassy. The research represents a cooperative effort of Wageningen Agricultural University in The Netherlands, and the Universidad Nacional Autónoma in Costa Rica. The REPOSA field research station and H. Hengsdijk are greatly acknowledged for their collaboration with respect to the development of the technical coefficient generator and for their professional recommendations and comments, as well as the facilities offered at all times.

Notes

1. Separability or recursiveness of a model implies that production decisions are taken independently of consumption and labor supply decisions (Singh *et al.*, 1986: 7), and only holds when assuming fixed-price markets (Delforce, 1994: 166). The recursive property does not hold when:(1) any of the prices in the model is affected by production decisions, (2) imperfections in the market exist, and (3) risk and risk aversion are recognized (Delforce, 1994: 166).
2. Farm characteristics refer to the farm household's resource base (available land, labor, savings, cattle and capital inputs), time discount rate and savings coefficient.
3. The amount of income that is set aside for savings depends on (1) the time discount rate as it values future and present consumption, and (2) the degree to which savings can generate future income (Kruseman *et al.*, 1996: 45–6).
4. Privatization refers to the process in which government enterprises are taken over by commercial private ones.
5. Economic exclusion refers to diminished access to product and factor markets.
6. Globalization refers to the reduction in communication and transportation costs of international trade in goods and services, cross-border flows of capital as well as exchanges of technology (Van den Noord, 1996: 195).
7. Policy scenarios are defined for 20 per cent changes in parameter values and do not reflect the changes proposed in the Productive Reconversion Program. The 20 per cent level proved to be the minimum level for significant policy response reactions.
8. It must be noted that cash crops are characterized by high levels of input demand, and therefore benefit most from a decline in farm gate input prices.
9. Note that plantain production is concentrated on the fertile, poorly drained soil type, while pineapple production is concentrated on the fertile, well-drained soil type.

5

Towards Sustainable Land Use at the Agrarian Frontier in Nicaragua

Jan P. de Groot

Introduction

This chapter deals with settlements in the humid tropics. The question it raises is: what are the conditions for a transition to more productive and sustainable land use systems? What is the *motivation* for settlers to change technologies and to invest in recovering and maintaining soil fertility? What is their capacity to implement such strategies? The first sections refer to colonization in the Central American context and include a general treatment of the relevant issues. Afterwards, a case of the Nueva Guinea colonization area in Nicaragua is presented.

In the next section the process of settlement in the humid tropics of Central America is characterized as being unsustainable and of low productivity, as the possibilities for forest fallow are soon exhausted. On-migration to the new agrarian frontier is one of the options to escape from this low productivity trap. But on-migration or repeated migration, as Schneider (1995: 5) states, can also arise from a different situation: higher land prices and improved land tenure security. The determinants of on-migration and related policy options to reduce it are discussed next. Following this, three types of agrarian frontiers that are relevant for policies to enhance sustainability are defined: the maturing, the older and the new. The Nueva Guinea colonization area is next described; the case study of this chapter. It is characterized as an older agrarian frontier: aging, but without much economic dynamism. However, there is an incipient export demand for a number of crops and livestock products that can offer a base for the development of more productive and sustainable land use systems in the area. The next section analyses two cases of export opportunities that motivate producers to adopt higher-input technologies, which also help to maintain soil fertility. The section after this discusses the case of low-cost, low-external-input technologies to restore the degraded soils, and the one following analyses pasture improvement. In the final section, concluding remarks are formulated.

This chapter is based on various sources. Use is made of a survey among 349 settlers by PRODES in 1992–3. An update of this survey was organized by the author and ESECA among 54 settlers selected by a sample of the earlier survey and revisited in 1995. Case studies of cost of production were made by ESECA and PRODES in the period 1992–6.

Colonization in the humid tropics of Central America: low levels of productivity and sustainability

The indigenous land use system in the rain forest of Central America is shifting cultivation. After two or three crops on a cleared plot, a forest fallow is observed that permits the regeneration of a secondary forest. In humid and semi-humid climates the main storage of nutrients is often not the soil but the standing vegetation. Regeneration of the vegetative cover implies restoration of the productive capacity of the land. At the end of a fallow period – between ten and twenty years – agriculture is taken up again. This system is usually ecologically stable and sustainable (Ruthenberg, 1976; Leonard, 1987).

The interior and the Pacific Coast of Central America are the traditional agricultural production zones. The peasant economy in these zones has been greatly affected – particularly since the 1950s – by market incorporation of agriculture, by the development of the agro-export sector and by cattle ranching. Peasants have been drawn increasingly into the market economy and forced to rely on either the intensification of their land use systems or else to migrate to the agrarian frontier (Williams, 1986; Utting, 1991). The low labor/land ratio in cattle ranching in comparison with crop production pushed more peasants into colonization areas (Howard-Borjas, 1992).

Limited access to land and unemployment in the traditional production zones cause the agrarian frontier to extend to the humid tropics of the isthmus. Settlers coming from other climatic conditions have to adapt to the ecosystem of the rain forest. Most of them promptly face land degradation. As the vegetative cover decreases, productive capacity declines. The rapid depletion of soil fertility forces them to cut down the remaining forest in their claim. As most settlers convert their land to pasture, no forest fallow is applied and the productive capacity of the soil is not restored.

Socio-economic factors are important in explaining this prevailing land use system in the agrarian frontier. Colonists do not operate – as in the indigenous farming system – a closed economic system. They are partly integrated into the market economy, but most markets for land, credit, inputs and products are incomplete or imperfect. Arriving without any capital, the settlers initiate an extractive type of agriculture with relative high yields, at low inputs. However, this lasts only as long as they can cut down the remaining forest. As soils become exhausted and weed control gets more difficult, productivity declines. Pressing subsistence needs and uncertain markets for commercial crops make investment in restoring soil fertility (the use of fertilizers) or in weed control (an improved land preparation) unattractive. Credit for such inputs is hardly available.

Settlers get locked into a low-productivity trap (Bakker, 1993). As soil fertility declines, yields decrease, and an increasing acreage is needed for subsistence crops. Labor productivity also declines, and less time is available for other income-generating activities or investment in land improvement. Land left fallow is invaded by natural pastures of low nutritional value; sometimes pastures are sown in. Cattle ranching is thus a logical outcome of unsustainable crop production (ibid.). In addition, it is also the consequence of imperfect or missing markets for commercial crop production, which could make soil conservation a feasible proposal.

Even when infrastructure is poor, cattle can be transported more or less easily over large distances. They can also be sold to larger ranches willing to expand their pastures in the humid tropics. Consequently, cattle raising becomes the logical option for the settler. However, as access to credit is limited, most settlers have to build up their own herd, and can only gradually invest in fences and pastures. Low soil fertility is an important constraint on grass species; only less demanding species of low nutritional value and poor palatability can be used (NRC, 1993). Even in using these species, however, grasslands commonly degrade rapidly, weeds invade the pastures and stocking capacity decreases. Cattle raising – just as subsistence cropping after the initial good harvests – has a low productivity, as factors of production are used extensively and production time, conditioned by the low quality of pastures, is long (Howard-Borjas, 1992). Notwithstanding this low productivity, settlers prefer investment in cattle to investment in soil conservation. As indicated, market outlets, lower risk, low labor requirements and the easy conversion of crop land into pastures determine this preference. These settlers' farming systems in colonization zones are hardly stable and have low levels of sustainability.

One way to escape this low-productivity trap is repeated migration (Bakker, 1993). Settlers can sell their land – now turned into pastures – and move on to deforested new frontiers. By selling land settlers can acquire working capital, thus improving their starting position in a new location. Ozorio de Almeida and Campari (1995) call this itinerant accumulation. This on-migration to a new agrarian frontier, or itinerancy, is an important threat to the Central American rain forest.

Pasture expansion, the conversion of forest to pasture, has been the most important change in land use in Central America since the 1950s. Whereas until the end of the 1970s this expansion occurred mainly in the Pacific Coast and the interior, after 1980 forest conversion increasingly affected the rain forest of the Atlantic Coast. Settlers who succeeded as ranchers expanded their pastures as a strategy of primitive accumulation. Large ranchers from the interior interested in the relatively cheap land in the humid tropics or in the more favorable distribution of rain in that zone for livestock activities, bought land converted to pastures or had the forest converted to grassland. This was made possible by landowners using temporary contracts with peasants for forest clearing with the obligation for the peasants to return the land after some years covered with pastures. Initially, property rights in the agrarian frontier were less secure than in traditional production areas, but the conversion to pastures provided a better claim than forest (Jones, 1990).

The expansion of the area under pastures in the 1980s coincided with a period of environmental degradation of grasslands and reduced pasture management. In the humid tropics, often with poor soils, pasture production declines after a few years, unless they are fertilized. Less-productive native species and weeds replace the planted grasses, and pasture quality deteriorates. Without proper management the carrying capacity of pastures also decreases: overgrazing, lack of field rotation and frequent burning result in soil compaction, erosion, lack of organic matter and in a low water retention capacity (Ibrahim, 1994). The falling profitability of cattle-raising, the lower export volumes and prices of meat, and the decreasing availability of credit have contributed to the reduction of pasture management. Ranches often prefer to deforest new areas than to recover soil fertility or weed control of degraded pastures.

On-migrating settlers sell their land to ranchers after utilizing the nutrients that are easily available shortly after cutting and burning the forest. Instead of continuing production at low levels of productivity and sustainability, they prefer migration to the new frontiers, thus starting a new cycle of deforestation. Lately it has been argued by Schneider (1995) that land degradation might not be the only reason for repeated migration to new agrarian frontiers. This argument is discussed in the next section.

Determinants of on-migration to new agrarian frontiers

Recent literature presents evidence of good economic performance of agricultural settlements and ranches for the Brazilian Amazon (Ozorio de Almeida and Campari, 1995; Schneider, 1995; Toniolo and Uhl, 1995; Trinidad de Almeida and Uhl, 1995; and Mattos and Uhl, 1994). At the same time these authors find that settlements with higher incomes also show a higher farm turnover and land abandonment. This results in on-migration to a new agrarian frontier, putting additional pressure on the remaining rain forest. Sustainable development requires this on-migration to be reduced.

The current explanation emphasizes land degradation as the main factor behind farm turnover and land abandonment (Bakker, 1993; Maldidier, 1993). After two or three subsistence crops, settlers are confronted with depletion of soil fertility and severe weed infestations. As land is abundant in the new frontier they migrate to the new agrarian frontier. Moreover, as their human capital quality is low, they have few opportunities in the urban economy and are prepared to live further out on the agrarian frontier (Schneider, 1995: 23). The land at the original location is sold as pasture to livestock producers, who make less intensive use of the land. If this mobility of settlers is explained by quick depletion of natural resources, by soil mining, the way to overcome it is to make settlers' agriculture at the original site more productive and sustainable (PRODES, 1992). The information on the Brazilian Amazon, however, suggests an explanation which goes the other way round: on-migration, as a consequence of higher incomes in the older agrarian frontier (Schneider, 1995: 15). Policy measures to strengthen incomes in this case, instead of reducing on-migration may promote farm turnover and land abandonment. Given these opposite explanations it is important to analyze the relevant determinants of on-migration.

The land degradation thesis emphasizes the economic rationality of the settlers' quick depletion of soil fertility (Bakker, 1993). With land abundant relative to other inputs it is cheaper to open up new areas than to invest in maintaining soil fertility. With high interest rates settlers face high (personal) discount rates for future net income streams, and thus are reluctant to adopt sustainable techniques, those techniques characterized by high costs in the present and benefits in the future. The present worth of future income streams using such techniques is determined by the rate of yield decrease, caused by soil degradation, and by the discount rate. In the humid tropics yields decline rapidly, but as the settlers' discount rates are also high, their present high income from resource mining compensates for the fall in future income from yield decreases. Sustainable techniques or production practices may be more attractive only if the additional cost to conserve resources is relatively small or yields relatively higher, and if the discount rate stays within certain margins. The initial (undiscounted) net income from sustainable techniques relative to unsustainable practices must be substantial to motivate producers to use the first (Schneider, 1995: 21).

The alternative thesis does not link farm turnover and land abandonment to degradation of the agricultural resource base, but to higher land prices and improved land tenure security (Schneider, 1995: 23). As the agrarian frontier matures, as infrastructure and communications improve, and as transport costs diminish, future net income streams are perceived to increase and consequently the reservation price for land goes up. Land prices also increase in response to speculative demand from urban-based buyers interested in holding land in times of inflation as a store of value (Ozorio de Almeida and Campari, 1995: 1) or in taking advantage of future price increases. As the potential buyers – producers and speculators, partly urban-based – have access to capital markets, their discount rate is lower than that of the early settlers. Therefore, their perceived present value of future net income streams from production and speculation is also higher, and they can easily bid the settlers off the land (Schneider, 1995: 23). As economic rent is bid away, land becomes more expensive relative to other inputs, inducing more sustainable techniques and practices. Producers buying the land have higher opportunity costs than the early settlers, but as the frontier matures they perceive that now they can farm profitably at this location; speculators, however, find that land ownership can cover their opportunity costs. When formal government is established in the maturing frontier, physical occupation of the land is no longer necessary – as was the case of the early settlers – to secure and protect property rights. Speculation becomes possible without homesteading, which explains land abandonment under conditions of rising land prices (Schneider: 33).

The policy prescriptions to reduce on-migration to the new agrarian frontier in this analysis differ from those responding to the land degradation thesis. Intensification – more productive and sustainable land use – is not the prescription, but is the result of the increase in land prices. Early settlers are selling their land not because their productivity has decreased, but because a later generation of producers/speculators has better access to capital and to government services (extension, protection of property rights), and is more capable in using these resources. The first settlers capitalize the increase in land prices by selling their land. To prevent the early settlers from on-migration, their discount rate must decline and their capacity to use government services must be enhanced.

Schneider (1995: 31) concludes that giving initial property rights to first settlers would improve efficiency and equity. Physical occupation of the land, as is the case with early settlers, makes government protection of property rights less demanding. Moreover, giving title to the first settlers would favor a most marginal group, not only when they start clearing the rain forest, but also when they sell the land to new buyers. Formal land titles can improve access to credit, affecting the discount rate. The author also states that to increase the opportunity costs for such marginal groups as these early settlers would require that they have better access to education.

Three types of frontiers

As can be deduced from this analysis, it is important for the discussion of policies aimed at enhancing sustainable production techniques in colonization areas, and at reducing on-migration to new frontiers, to distinguish relevant types of frontiers and the stage of development characterizing them. In a schematic overview, three types are discussed: the *maturing* frontier, the *older* and the *new* frontier. Each starts with a short characterization, the rationality of the use of sustainable or unsustainable techniques, the motivation and capacity for a transition to a more productive and sustainable production system and the question of farm turnover and land abandonment.

The maturing frontier, MF, is characterized mainly by its incorporation into the market economy; as infrastructure has developed, including the internal road network, communications have improved, and government services increased, the regional economy is diversifying and the demand for agricultural produce is expanding. Agriculture is switching from subsistence production to production for the market; commercial, higher-value crops are introduced. Such intensification and specialization are found also in livestock production, where small farmers specialize in dairy and calf production and larger ranchers in fattening. Land prices increase as a consequence of demand by new producers and speculators.

As land prices increase there is an incentive to invest in soil conservation. With the intensification and commercialization of agricultural production, income increases and farmers can pay for maintaining soil fertility. The perceived net income from sustainable techniques Y_s increases relative to income from unsustainable techniques Y_u. The present worth of the discounted, future, net income stream Y_s will exceed the present value of the income stream Y_u, in particular because the new producers, with more urban connections, have access to credit and thus have a lower discount rate than the first settlers. As socio-economic conditions change, producers switch over to more productive and sustainable techniques. Speculators will leave part of the land idle; forest fallow will contribute to restore soil fertility of this abandoned land.

The transition process of investment and innovation in land use systems (De Groot, 1996) is motivated by the increase in land prices the new opportunities for market production and the access to capital markets and is thus induced by external factors. The capacity to make this transition is based on access to credit and to government services, on internal factors, on non-farm income sources and, eventually, on small-scale exploitation of some remaining forest.

On-migration of the early settlers to new agrarian frontiers occurs as they are bid off the land by new producers and speculators with better access to credit and government services. This form of itinerant accumulation cannot be reduced without providing these settlers with better access both to these services and to education to increase their opportunity cost in the labor market.

The older frontier, OF, differs from the *MF* not so much in age but in economic dynamism. This zone is not well incorporated into the market economy, either because infrastructure and communications are poorly developed, or because the wider economic environment is not favorable. Land, including both cropland and pastures, is degraded. Nutrient mining no longer provides good yields. Yields have stabilized at low levels of productivity. Degraded land is cheap; as the socio-economic situation is depressed, there is no incentive to intensify production and to invest in soil conservation.

Perceived Y_s is lower than when use of external inputs (fertilizer, land preparation and pesticides) is considered. Settlers are locked in into a low-productivity trap, which makes it difficult to adopt sustainable techniques.

Perceived Y_s, however, can increase when low-cost external inputs are used to restore soil fertility such as bean fertilizer, pasture improvement and agro-forestry practices. That is, when yield increases are substantial and costs of soil conservation relatively low. The perceived present worth of the discounted, net, future income stream Y_s may exceed the present value of the income stream Y_u when yields increase rapidly and when the discount rate is low. This last condition is not reached easily in the *OF*, as settlers have little access to capital markets. Part of the degraded land is abandoned; forest fallow contributes to the recovery of soil fertility.

The motivation for transition can come from evidence that the current farming system is a failure and from external factors like demonstration and instruction on sustainable techniques also from securing property rights to settlers, from access to credit and from expanding opportunities for market production. Capacity to implement a transition process can be based on access to credit, on the provision of planting materials and internal factors and on mobilizing family labor for investment in soil conservation and, eventually, small-scale exploitation of some remaining forest.

On-migration to new frontiers is an escape from the low-productivity trap resulting from land degradation and the stagnating socio-economic situation. Policies to reduce on-migration are the same as those to enhance sustainable techniques: motivate and assist settlers in adopting more productive and sustainable practices, improve external and internal infrastructure and extend government services – not only to increase the opportunity cost of settlers, but also to make living in the *OF* more attractive than far out on the new frontier.

The new frontier, NF, is characterized by its isolation and the abundance of available land. Land is free or cheap: production levels can be maintained as long as land under forest can be cleared. There is little incentive to invest in soil conservation; the use of unsustainable techniques is rational. Perceived Y_u is higher than perceived Y_s, because in the short run the unsustainable technique provides high yields through nutrient mining, whereas no costs are made for soil conservation. The discounted, net, future income stream Y_u exceeds the income stream Y_s, because, although yield decline in the unsustainable technique is high, the discount rate of settlers in the NF is also high. Part of the land in the NF is untouched; settlers consider this as a reserve.

Settlers are not very motivated to make a transition to more sustainable land use; their motivation can be strengthened by external factors: by providing them with a title to the land; by extension at low-cost –

low-external-input practices of soil conservation and by limiting the possibilities for further migration in the future. These settlers have the capacity for a transition process, by providing them with planting materials and through internal factors and through small-scale forest exploitation and mobilizing family labor.

The older frontier in the humid tropics of Nicaragua

Nueva Guinea is a colonization area on the older frontier of Nicaragua's humid tropics. The country has some 5.2 million ha of humid tropical land on its Atlantic Coast, over 40 per cent of its territory (Jones, 1990: 62). Rainfall in the Nueva Guinea area ranges from 2300 to 3100 mm annually, and declines moving inland. There is a brief dry season of two to three months. Temperatures are between 23° and 26° C (Acuña *et al.*, 1990: 5).

In the 1930s extraction of rubber, ipecac (*raicilla*), and hardwood became of some importance in the area, but colonization did not start until the 1960s when the first groups of peasant colonists arrived. Official colonization, implemented by the Nicaraguan Land Reform Institute (MIDINRA), started in 1965 (Clercx, 1990). In a first phase the Institute only gave orientation to a process of spontaneous colonization, providing settlers with a legal title to the land. By 1969 1400 families had settled in the area and seven colonies had been founded. In a second phase colonization was planned. In the 1970s the state settled more than 5000 families, but spontaneous colonization also continued. In 1985 the military conflict brought a temporary end to the

Table 5.1   Nicaragua: Nueva Guinea colonization area – number of farms and farm size distribution, 1990

Farm size	Farms		Area		Average size
(ha)	(no.)	(%)	(ha)	(%)	(ha)
<17.5	1 035	15.1	7 062	2.8	6.8
17.6 to 35.0	4 005	58.6	128 193	51.0	32.0
35.1 to 70.0	1 448	21.8	79 891	31.8	55.2
70.1 to 105.0	190	2.8	17 702	7.1	93.2
>105.0	116	1.7	18 436	7.3	158.9
	6 794	100.0	251 284	100.0	37.0

Source: Based on Clercx (1990: tables 9 and 12B), estimated with data from MIDINRA (Land Reform Institute).

influx of settlers, but after 1990 the colonization process started again. In 1990 the area had over 12 600 families, and a total population of about 76 000. There were 7300 families on 6800 farms (see Table 5.1), 3000 families of landless peasants and 2300 families (18 per cent) with non-agrarian activities.

The distribution of land in the area was substantially influenced by the official land reform program of the 1970s, which assigned settlers plots of about 35 ha. In Table 5.1, which shows the size distribution of farms in 1990, this starting position can still be observed. However, the table also shows the effect of the process of social differentiation going on in the area: landless peasants entering in search of land, some settlers losing (part of) their land, others expanding in particular in livestock activities and a number of ranchers from outside buying land which is still considered cheap. Some of the original settlers have on-migrated to the new frontier. From a survey in 1992 among 340 farmers, PRODES distinguishes five types of farmers (Table 5.2).

Nueva Guinea can be defined as an older frontier. Colonization started over thirty years ago, and the area is an aging frontier; but economic dynamism so far is limited. Less than 20 per cent of the active population is non-agrarian, and consequently internal demand for agricultural produce is limited. Current internal resources of the area do not present a basis for rapid economic growth. Much valuable hardwood had already been cut down even before colonization started; later, much of the forest was burned down in the process of land clearing; and in 1988 a hurricane destroyed a large part of the remaining trees. Some larger scale plantation agriculture was tried on the east coast (bananas in the past; African palm in the 1980s), but has not developed into lasting economic activities. In a nearby local research station there is a good collection of rubber clones, and other germ plasm (cacao, African palm, bamboo), but although conditions are promising, in particular for rubber, not much planting has been done. In the course of the years infrastructure (for example the main road to Managua) was improved, but was badly maintained. Red beans – mainly a surplus from subsistence production – and cattle for a long time have been the most important market products of the area. Both suffer from depressed price levels and decreasing land productivity. In general the Nicaraguan economy since 1990 has undergone a period of structural adjustment and contraction. Consequently, the Nueva Guinea area has encountered a stagnating demand for agricultural produce.

Farmers have few opportunities for off-farm employment; sharecroppers type (1) rent out labor to farmers with livestock activities,

Table 5.2 Nicaragua: Nueva Guinea, farm types and information on farming systems

Type of producer	Average size (ha)	Gross income (US$)	Crop production		Livestock production			Labor
			Income share	Type	Area[a] (ha)	Cattle (head)	Stock rate[c]	
1. Sharecropper	7.0	341	(72)	Subsistence	–	–[b]	–	Rent out
2. Subsistence crop	35.1	802	(54)	Subsistence	19.6	6	(3.3)	Family
3. Subsistence crop–livestock	40.3	1 346	(49)	Subsistence market	25.4	13	(2.0)	Family
4. Peasant livestock	72.1	3 389	(20)	Subsistence market	52.8	39	(1.8)	Family
5. Farmer livestock	118.0	8 133	(10)	Market	106.2	90	(1.4)	Rent in

Source: based on PRODES (1996) and Ambrogi (1995).
Notes:
[a] Not including abandoned pastures and 'forest fallow'.
[b] Only swine and poultry.
[c] If abandoned pastures are included then the stocking rate (number of hectares per animal) increases to (4.8:1) for type 2; (2.6:1) for type 3; (1.6:1) for type 4 and (1.3:1) for type 5.

type (5), mainly for weeding of pastures and some crop activities. Peasants of types 2, 3 and 4 mainly use family labor on their farms; they neither rent out much labor nor are they reported to rent in much labor. On smaller farms the proportion of cropland is somewhat higher and the proportion of pastures somewhat lower than on larger farms in order to use the family labor. Some of the larger farmers type (5) combine farming with trade activities, mainly of livestock. The current wage level is reported to be US$ 2.15 per day. Without rapidly growing local activities, and without a thriving domestic demand, the base for a transition to more productive and sustainable farming systems seems small. As land prices are not going up and demand stagnates, there is little incentive to increase production. Consequently, the motivation for diversification towards higher-value crops, and intensification, which implies restoration of soil fertility, is low. However, there are some incipient developments in the area that offer certain potential for such a transition. The first is an increasing demand for small-scale exports, and the second is a growing experience with low-cost – low-external-input methods for recovering and maintaining soil fertility.

Incipient demand for small-scale exports

Although the Nueva Guinea area is rather isolated – over 150 km from Managua along a road that is costly to maintain – there is an increasing demand from export traders looking for low-cost production zones. Products currently exported from the area are: cocoyam (*quequisque*, *Xanthosoma s.*), ginger (*jenjibre*, *Zingiber officinale*) and cheese. The *quequisque*, a tuberous crop, is bought by Costa Rican traders who pack and export the product to Costa Rica and the USA. Multinational DOLE buys ginger for export, in particular to the Caribbean. Entrepreneurs from El Salvador buy milk in the area, process it in the plant they established, and export fresh cheese to El Salvador. There are other products that are currently being successfully cultivated in very small plots in the area and offer good export potential. These include black pepper, palm heart, rubber, pineapple, cinnamon and ipecac (*raicilla*, *Cephaelis ipecacuanha*). This export demand offers opportunity for diversification and intensification, which can contribute to economic and ecological sustainability. The cases of *quequisque* and ginger indicate the potential for more productive and sustainable farming systems.

Tuberous crops such as cassava and *quequisque* adapt better to the humid climate of the area than do basic grains (PRODES, 1996). However, when the former are cultivated on a larger scale and without adequate rotation, extraction of nutrients is high. Fertilizer application is required to maintain soil fertility, to reach higher yields and to produce a larger proportion of exportable quality (certain size and weight standards). Some 700 ha are currently cultivated with *quequisque* by small producers on plots smaller than one fifth of a hectare, but also by larger producers cultivating up to two to three ha. Most of the small producers (types 2 and 3) do not use external inputs, except for some herbicides occasionally (Table 5.3). Yields, at 4.0 tonnes per hectare (t/ha), are low, and only half of the produce fulfills export standards; the rest has to be sold on the internal market at a lower price. Although the area per farm is very small, net return to the farmer is attractive, but nutrient extraction makes the crop unsustainable if it is not followed by a long fallow.

Table 5.3   Nicaragua: production costs, gross and net returns per hectare for cocoyam (*quequisque*), 1995

	Low-input crop systems (n = 95)	*High-input crop systems* (n = 4)
Total costs	US$ 192	US$ 393
Labor	97[a]	131[b]
Soil preparation	57[c]	114[d]
Inputs	20[e]	133[f]
Transport	18[g]	15[h]
(External inputs, services and labor)	(75)	(373)
Gross return/ha	488[i]	1 391[j]
Net return/ha	296	1 018
Net return/labor day	6.6	19.9

Sources: low-input systems PRODES (1996), complemented with ESECA case-studies.
Notes:
[a] 45 days × US$ 2.15 (12 soil preparation; 12 cutting seed and planting; 12 weeding and cultivation; and 9 harvesting 88 qq).
[b] 61 days (12 soil preparation; 12 cutting, disinfecting seed and planting; 9 weeding and cultivation; 3 application of fertilizers and pesticides; and 25 harvesting 250 qq).
[c] Plowing with oxen.
[d] Plowing with tractor.
[e] Seed: 6 quintals at US$ 3.40/qq.
[f] Seed: 6 quintals at US$ 3.40/qq; 400 kg NPK fertilizer at US$ 0.22/kg; 1.5 litres herbicides (Gramoxone) at US$ 8/litre; 2 lb fungicides (Furadan) at US$ 7/lb.
[g] Transport of 50 per cent of total harvest (4 000 kg) to the local market at US$ 0.20/qq.
[h] Transport of 30 per cent of total harvest (11 400 kg) to the local market at US$ 0.20/qq.
[i] 2 000 kg at US$ 169/tonne and 2 000 kg at US$ 75/tonne.
[j] 5 700 kg at US$ 169/tonne and 5 700 kg at US$ 75/tonne.

A small number of the larger producers (of types 4 and 5) use a technology with more external inputs. As can be observed in the table (*n* = 4), they have higher yields (and probably produce a larger proportion of export quality, but this effect is not shown). This cropping system not only gives a higher net return, but because of the high level of fertilizer application soil fertility is maintained. These producers have better land preparation and weed control, select and treat the seed used, and apply high levels of NPK fertilizers. These improved practices do pay off, as they have higher yields: 11.4 t/ha as against 4.0 t/ha under the low-input system. It is possible that these farmers can select a more fertile lot for the crop, but there is no indication of that. The higher operational costs (US$ 393/ha against 192/ha for the low-input technology) and the higher level of external inputs (US$ 227/ha against 57) make this cropping system inaccessible for smaller producers. The higher external input producers are larger livestock farmers with capital accumulated in cattle, which gives them access to credit sources.

Table 5.4   Nicaragua: production costs, gross and net returns per hectare in ginger (*jengibre*) in low- and high-input cropping systems, 1995

	Low-input crop systems (*n* = 14) *crop*	High-input systems (*n* = 3)
Total costs/ha	US$ 202	US$ 372
Labor	110[a]	148[b]
Inputs	92[c]	184[d]
Transport	–	40
(external inputs and labor)	(15)	(269)
Gross return/ha	1 470[e]	2 513[f]
Net return/ha	1 268	2 141
Net return/labor day	2.49	31.0

Source: see Table 5.3.
Notes:
[a] Labor 51 days (soil preparation 8; planting 6; weeding 12; harvest 15; and transport to the farm 10).
[b] Labor 69 days (soil preparation 18; seed selection, treatment and planting 6; application of fertilizers and pesticides 1; weeding 12; harvesting 29; and transport 3).
[c] Inputs: seed (32 qq at US$ 2.40/qq), packing material US$ 15.
[d] Inputs: seed (43 qq at US$ 2.40/qq), fertilizers (215 kg NPK at US$ 0.22/kg); pesticides US$ 14; and packing material US$ 20.
[e] 215 qq (60 at US$ 18.3 and 155 qq at US$ 2.4).
[f] 285 qq (115 at US$ 18.3 and 170 qq at US$ 2.4).

The acreage under ginger in the Nueva Guinea area is currently about 270 ha. Producers know this crop, because in the first half of the 1980s Costa Rican exporters were also buying ginger for export. This trade stopped in the second half of that decade, but now the activity has been reinitiated. On small parcels still under forest or under brush vegetation, small-scale plantations with low external input use are found (Table 5.4).

The harvest is about twelve months after planting. Yields on non-degraded soils are fairly high, although the proportion of export quality is sometimes low (less than 30 per cent). A small number of producers, however with higher external input technologies, produce for export and under natural or even artificial shade. These producers invest in good soil preparation, which is difficult under trees or brush vegetation; they select their seed, use a fairly high level of fertilizers and apply pesticides and fungicides. Through these practices yields are higher than under low-input use and a larger proportion of the harvest is of export quality (up to 40 per cent). This crop yields relatively high net returns under low- and higher-input systems, as net return per labor day is higher than the wage rate in both cases. As it is grown under shade it is also environmentally sustainable, in particular under the higher-input system where fertilizer application maintains soil fertility. Even small farmers with only one-fifth of a hectare under this crop have an attractive net return of US$ 254. However, low family income and risk-taking capacity are important constraints on investing in a cropping technology based on higher external input levels, even when the return to this investment is high. Market conditions permit a certain extension of the acreage under ginger, but there are not many settlers – especially small ones – with suitable land under forest or brush vegetation. Artificial shade is too expensive to use on degraded soils.

As these examples show, external demand can induce and actually does induce some intensification in the Nueva Guinea area. Intensification is an incentive for more sustainable land use, in particular for maintaining soil fertility, but intensification does not automatically lead to use of more sustainable technologies. As the case studies indicate, producers also must have access to external inputs. In the OF, settlers on larger farms and with more cattle are able to finance external inputs, while smaller settlers depend on credit, which is rather scarce in the OF. Credit programs that assist small producers of export crops can contribute to more sustainable production systems.

Low-cost technologies for recovering soil fertility

Basic grains (maize, red beans and rice) are the main subsistence crops of settlers in the Nueva Guinea area; any surpluses are sold in the market. Owing to rapid depletion of soil fertility, loss of organic matter, increase of diseases and weed infestation, yields fall rapidly. In the case of maize, yields on recently cleared land reported at two t/ha can fall to 500 kg/ha when the settlers have degraded all their land. Instead of one hectare for subsistence production of maize, they now need three or four ha. This increases the cost of production, in particular labor cost per unit of maize and makes the use of herbicides almost inevitable. Settlers also try to increase yields through the use of fertilizer, but they often lack resources for adequate applications. The use of externally bought inputs increases, but settlers have difficulties financing these inputs.

Evidently there is an urgent need for low-cost, low-external-input technologies to restore soil fertility, to redress the continuing process of soil degradation and the consequent conversion of crop land to (also low-quality) pasture. An example of such a technology is the use of a cover crop, like velvet bean or fertilizer bean (*mucuna; Mucuna deeringianum*) in rotation with maize. This is a traditional technology widely practiced by peasants in the humid tropics of the Atlantic Coast of Mexico, Honduras and Guatemala. The bean is used as a substitute for fertilizers as it fixes nitrogen from the atmosphere, suppresses weeds and when left as a mulch prevents erosion, in particular on hilly land. The mucuna bean can produce 50 t of green matter and fix up to 150 kg/ha of nitrogen; yields of the main crop (maize) can increase substantially (Bunch and López, 1995). It is, as can be observed in Table 5.5, a low-cost, low-external-input technology to raise yields in the short run; and by implication to improve soil fertility and organic matter content in the longer term. However, the rotation of mucuna – maize occupies the land for a whole crop year. In June mucuna is planted, in October it is cut and is sometimes worked into the soil or left as a cover, and in November maize is planted for harvesting in March. Such an extensive land use in many cases is not a problem in the Nueva Guinea area, where degraded land is abundant and soil restoration is much needed. However, in other areas, where land has been restored, more intensive soil use can be required, and farmers practice double-cropping while maintaining soil fertility through higher external input levels, such as high fertilizer applications. This is especially the case on flat land, where there is not much risk of soil erosion, because on hillsides cover crops have an important function in erosion control (De Groot and Pasos, 1994).

Table 5.5 Nicaragua: production costs, gross and net returns for maize without and with mucuna-maize rotation, 1995

	Without rotation	*With rotation fertilizer bean*		
		Year 1	*Year 2*	*Demo. plot*
	(n = 51)	*(n = 3)*	*(n = 3)*	*year 3*
Total costs/ha	US$ 140	US$ 164	US$ 173	US$ 204
Labor	103[a]	142[b]	150[b]	181[b]
Inputs	37[c]	22[d]	23[d]	23[d]
(External inputs)	(34)	(22)	(7)	(7)
Gross return/ha[e]	112[e]	182[e]	246[e]	381[e]
Net return/ha	−28	18	73	177
Net return/labor day	−0.6	0.3	1.0	2.1

Source: without rotation: Ambrogi, (1995); case-studies farmers with rotation: PRODES, (1996); with rotation on demonstration plots: Sanclemente *et al.*, 1994.
Notes:
[a] 48 labor days.
[b] 14 additional labor days for mucuna crop.
[c] Seed US$ 3; fertilizers US$ 15; pesticides US$ 17; packing material US$ 2.
[d] Maize seed US$ 3; mucuna seed US$ 16; no fertilizers and pesticides.
[e] Yields respectively: 715 kg/ha; 1162 kg/ha; 1571 kg/ha and 2429 kg/ha.

As can be seen in Table 5.5, maize production on degraded soils has a low productivity; yield is only 715 kg/ha and return to labor is less than the current wage level of US$ 2.15 per day. The data in Table 5.5 indicate substantial productivity increases with each round of rotation mucuna–maize and return to labor even doubles in the second round. These data represent no more than a first indication of the potential for productivity increases under low-cost technologies for recovering soil fertility. The productivity increase shown in the first round in particular seems somewhat high, because initially when mucuna is planted the population of the symbiotic bacterium which fixes the nitrogen can still be scarce. In later rounds the mucuna can improve its function. What is important is that a process of soil restoration is started. No soil analysis was made in the case of the farmers whose yields are reported in Table 5.5. However, such an analysis was made on the demonstration plots with data shown in the table. Here a small improvement of soil quality was registered with respect to chemical composition (Sanclemente *et al.*, 1994: 17). Soil restoration is a long term process; the few data presented here indicate that it is rewarding. With an investment of US$ 46 in year one (30 in labor, 16 in mucuna seed) a return of US$ 70 is obtained; in year two the investment is only

30 and the return is 134. Moreover, the level of external inputs decreases from US$ 34 (fertilizers and herbicides) in the case without rotation, to US$ 20 in year one of the rotation, and to only US$ 5 in the second year. With such a small initial investment, only 14 additional labor days and US$ 16 in mucuna seed, this technology is accessible for settlers, even for those locked in a low-productivity trap.

The mucuna – maize rotation is only one example of a technology that can start a process of recovering and maintaining soil fertility, with a rapid payoff in the short run (higher yields and labor productivity) and with favorable environmental effects in the medium and long run (increased soil fertility, erosion and weed control, and reduced acreage needed for annual crops with consequently more possibilities for tree crops). As mucuna is a climber, it is a difficult crop (because of its size) for association (intercropping) with maize and therefore can be better used in rotation. Jack bean (*Canavalia ensiformis*) is a better alternative as a soil improver, because this crop can be interplanted with maize (PRODES, 1996). That makes it possible to have a rotation of jack bean – maize in one season with red beans in the other. Land productivity in this case is higher than in the mucuna–maize rotation. Chickpea (*guandul; Cajanus cajan*) is another option for soil improvement, which also produces a valuable pulse for human or animal consumption. Both jack bean and chickpea can also be used in alley cropping and agroforestry systems, which are effective technologies for soil improvement. However, they lack the direct payoffs that make the legume cover crops technologies, discussed above, such attractive alternatives for settlers motivated to start a process of recovering soil fertility.

Intensification of livestock production

Booming export markets for beef in the 1960s and 1970s promoted pasture expansion in Nicaragua. Between 1950 and 1978 the cattle population increased from 1.1 to 2.8 million heads. Pasture expansion was one of the major factors contributing to deforestation. Deforestation in the 1970s was estimated at 120 000 ha per annum (Maldidier, 1993). However, in the 1980s, government policies increasingly affected the livestock sector. The decline of cattle exports and the military conflict greatly reduced the cattle population. The combination of weak export demand, low prices and rising costs reduced the profitability of beef production. Between 1978 and 1992 the total stock declined from 2.8 to 2.2 million heads of cattle (Holmann, 1993).

The impact of this decline on the acreage under pasture and on deforestation is ambiguous. Most of the decline in cattle population was in traditional livestock regions. Here, farmers in part found alternative uses for land and labor; but the reduction of the stock of cattle in these regions also led to the abandonment of pastures. While the cattle population in the humid tropics in the same period remained at the former level or only declined temporarily, pasture expansion and deforestation in the agrarian frontier continued, with the exception of the period of the military conflict, the years 1983 to 1989. Pastures expanded because ranchers from other zones continued to purchase farms in the agrarian frontier to take advantage of the comparatively low land prices there. But at the same time pastures were abandoned in the agrarian frontier, probably more as a consequence of land degradation than of a decline of cattle population. It is estimated that since 1978 in the agrarian frontier of the humid east coast some 900 000 ha of pastures have been abandoned and converted to forest fallow.

In the Nueva Guinea area the same general picture emerges. The cattle population decreased in the second half of the 1980s owing to the military conflict, but since then has recovered towards earlier levels of about 50 000 heads of cattle. Ranchers from outside the area again bought the relatively cheap land and brought their herds over from drier zones (and also, lately, from regions afflicted by crime). Alternatively, as these ranchers are among the few producers with access to formal credit, they expanded their herds by buying cattle. The other livestock producers (types 2, 3 and 4) can enlarge their herds only by retaining instead of selling part of their stock. Livestock production in the area is of a dual-purpose type: most settlers produce milk and meat. Small producers give preference to milk for home consumption and occasionally selling a calf. Larger producers produce milk and fresh cheese for home consumption and the market, and sell and fatten calves.

As pasture expansion continues in the area livestock production becomes more extensive. Some of the pastures, however, are so degraded that they are abandoned, and in the best case are covered by a brush vegetation. This is a long-term technology to recover soil fertility. Smaller producers have a lower stocking rate than larger farmers. Taking into account pastures only, there is one animal for 3.3 ha on type 2 farms; 2.0 ha on type 3; 1.4 ha on type 4; and there is one animal for 1.2 ha on type 5 farms. When abandoned pastures are considered in addition, the differences are even larger. Production is more extensive on smaller units: they have proportionally more abandoned pastures, and probably producers have relatively more difficulties in enlarging their herds.

The extensive way of livestock production has a low productivity and is unsustainable (NRC, 1993). As the nutritional value of pastures is low, milk production per cow is also low, even for the mainly zebu genotype, which is most common in the area. This low nutritional value of pastures also affects negatively the birth rates of the herds and results in low gains in live weight of animals fattened and in discontinuities in growth that reduce productivity. With low productivity in dairy and meat production, returns to the existing infrastructure – fences, corrals, throughways – are low. Low productivity of animal production in the zone results also from lack of care for animal health, but the main cause is the continuing degradation of pastures. After deforestation, high-yielding grasses are used, which initially produce enough forage to support two to three animals per hectare. However, if these grass species with high nutritional requirements are not fertilized, or if no legumes are planted, pasture productivity decreases rapidly. These grasses can no longer compete with native species, and weeds invade the pastures. Establishment and maintenance of productive pastures is difficult, because most pastures are located on fairly infertile soils.

As in the case of soil restoration for crop production, pasture improvement in the Nueva Guinea area must be based on a low-cost, low-external-input technology. Most producers lack the resources to maintain pure grass pastures with NPK fertilizer application; or, what would be needed in the area, to establish entirely new, pure grass pastures based on constant fertilizer application. Low-cost, low-external-input alternatives are: growing grass–legume mixtures, oversowing legumes into existing pastures and establishing protein banks.[1] The establishment of persistent grass–legume mixtures under proper management offers one of the best alternatives for improving pasture productivity and sustainability (Ibrahim, 1994).

Recently, researchers in the Amazon and Costa Rica have made important advances in identifying potential species for grass legume mixtures. These are mixtures that, when properly managed, are persistent (legumes reinforcing the grasses), increase productivity of pastures in terms of dry matter yield and protein content, and also restore and maintain soil fertility, especially the organic nitrogen content of the soil (Ibrahim, 1994).

Extension programs in the Nueva Guinea area have stimulated farmers to produce their own seed of improved grasses for upgrading pastures. There have also been some trials with grass–legume mixtures, but these were limited to observing and weighing forage; no trials under grazing conditions were implemented. Practical experiences are lacking, and so far there has been no systematic analysis of costs and benefits of grassland improvement with real increases in animal production (milk or life weight) registered.

Settlers in the area actually show less preference for improving their pastures than for increasing the productivity and sustainability of crop land.[2] Low land productivity in crop production is relatively less efficient than in grassland production, because the input of labor, seed and herbicides is higher in crop production. If soil fertility is low then the return to this input is also low. Grassland production in the area is managed with a very low input of labor and some herbicides, as cattle can be moved to other pastures. Marginal productivity of the input in grassland production is higher; soil fertility affects efficiency relatively less than in crop production. The alternative for pasture improvement is to buy pasture land and cattle, to achieve the same level of production increase as with the improvement. This alternative is greatly

Table 5.6   Production costs, and net returns in subsistence crop–livestock farms in Nueva Guinea, Nicaragua

	Type 3	Type 4
Acreage in pastures (ha)	25.2	52.8
Total costs (average acreage)	US$ 432	US$ 1 216
Labor	322[a]	868[b]
Animals bought	19[c]	43[c]
Inputs	46[d]	162[d]
Depreciation	45[e]	143[e]
Gross return (average acreage)	684	2 723
Milk, fresh cheese	341	1 646
Sale of animals	211	796
Pigs and poultry	132	281
(Production home-consumed)	28%	10%
Net return/ha	10	29
Net return/labor day	1.7	3.7

Source: elaborated on the basis of PRODES (1996), complemented by ESECA survey and case-studies in Ambrogi (1995).
Notes:
[a] 150 days milking cows, cheese-making, cutting pastures and maintaining fences.
[b] 404 days milking cows, cheese-making, cutting pastures and maintaining fences.
[c] Buying piglets.
[d] Salt, animal health and cheese making.
[e] Depreciation of fences in 15 years.

preferred by the settlers, because the risk associated with this alternative is lower. The risk of improved pasture not being as productive or persistent as expected is substantial, because of weather conditions, pests, soil deficiencies and lack of knowledge. On the contrary, land has a speculative value, and (additional) cattle – although they can die – are very easy to sell in case of emergency. As long as prices for pasture land in the area stay at the current low level of between US$ 75 and 150 per hectare, pasture improvement is relatively less attractive. A low-cost, low-external-input technology investment in pasture improvement, for example establishing a grass – legume mixture at an estimated cost of US$ 248 per hectare, is feasible, but will only become attractive at higher land prices in the area. In the meantime there is less pasture improvement than buying of pasture. From the higher stocking rates of farms of types 4 and 5, it can be deduced that, notwithstanding this preference, some improvement is going on.

Concluding remarks

As has been shown in recent studies of the Brazilian Amazon, a maturing frontier offers the best perspectives for a transition to more productive and sustainable land use systems. When economic activities – stimulated by internal and external demand and the development of infrastructure – are growing rapidly, when diversification and specialization attract a new type and generation of settlers, and when urban-based land speculators cause land prices to increase, the conditions are favorable for intensifying agricultural production and for higher investment in maintaining and restoring soil fertility. A negative aspect of this positive development is the on-migration of some of the earlier settlers to the new agrarian frontier.

The question with respect to the older frontier, where economic development is less thriving, is, whether one can find elements to start a similar type of transition process. In the Nueva Guinea area discussed in this chapter, the experience with a number of export products shows that these opportunities can motivate farmers to change technologies and to invest in upgrading and maintaining soil quality. The most important *motivation* comes from the expanding market opportunities, which increase the benefits of technology change. But as could be observed in the case studies, smaller settlers in the older frontier lack the *capacity* to translate the intensification into more sustainable land use. Credit programs in these cases can contribute to maintaining soil fertility in crop production. An alternative is the introduction of low-cost, low-external-input technologies, which enable farmers to increase productivity of crop production, and pay for investment in soil fertility from the gain in productivity. Settlers can be motivated to use low-external-input technologies by the demonstration of short-term productivity increases on degraded soils; the main requirement for the introduction of these technologies is the capacity to apply (internal) labor in their production systems. In the Nueva Guinea area the number of settlers engaged in transition processes to intensification and soil conservation is still small, but these farmers demonstrate the feasibility of these changes. Pasture improvement intensification is apparently still less attractive in grassland production than in crop production. Transition processes in livestock production come after those in agriculture. This is an aspect that must be considered in designing policies to enhance sustainability in the humid tropics.

Repeated migration from the older frontier to the new agrarian frontier is indeed related to soil degradation and low productivity. Reducing this itinerancy requires policies of the same type as those aimed at enhancing more productive and sustainable land use systems: extension, new market opportunities and access to credit resources.

Acknowledgements

The author aknowledges the help of Mario López Jiménez and Rosario Ambrogi of the *Escuela de Economía Agrícola* (ESECA), Faculty of Economics, UNAN, Managua, Nicaragua.

Notes

1. Trees with high-protein-content leaves in pastures which are bruised by cattle or cut as fodder.
2. In the PRODES program, for example, reference farmers – leaders of small extension groups – although they have agreed on and made the planning for pasture improvement, in practice have invested more in grass land acquisition than in grass land improvement or restoration.

6

Soil Conservation Practices and Farmers' Adoption Strategies in Costa Rica

Ruerd Ruben and Jos Vaessen

Introduction

Soil erosion is generally recognized as a major problem in agricultural development and therefore different soil conservation practices are now being promoted to maintain soil productivity. A wide number of programs in developing countries focus on remedies to this problem, offering a variety of incentives to the farmers. In Costa Rica, a growing number of development projects funded by government, NGOs and international institutions are stimulating the adoption of soil conservation measures at farm and regional levels. Although there is an increase in the number of projects dealing with soil conservation in Costa Rica, coverage and outreach are still quite low and unequal among farm types. Credit support and technical assistance are widely used, but how important these instruments are for farmers' adoption decisions is not generally acknowledged. Moreover, other variables may be equally important to determine the prospects of adoption of certain soil conservation practices by different types of farm households.

The design of most rural development programs addressing soil conservation is strongly based on the supply of general incentives that should enable farmers to make investments in physical soil conservation practices. In this chapter we will focus attention, however, on the demand-side, trying to determine the factors that have a significant influence on farmers' decisions concerning the adoption of certain specific soil conservation measures. Field research was carried out in the highlands of Tilarán, located in the Guanacaste Province of Costa Rica, within the framework of a soil conservation project of the Costa Rican Ministry of Agriculture (MAG) with the UN Food and

Agricultural Organization FAO. Logistic regression procedures are used to identify farm household characteristics that are relevant for the adoption decision. It is argued that this procedure can be a valuable additional tool in the diagnostic phase of soil conservation programs in order to determine potential clients and for the identification of feasible incentives and policy instruments that could induce farmers to adopt these practices.

The effectiveness of soil conservation programs could be greatly improved by giving adequate attention to the farm household characteristics that influence adoption behavior. Traditional cost–benefit analysis is generally used to assess the minimum conditions for adoption, but this procedure is not sufficient to explain differences in adoption behavior among farm households. Moreover, owing to its partial and static character, cost–benefit analysis cannot be used to identify specific incentives required to enable farmers to incorporate soil conservation practices within their farming system. Most project interventions easily rely on financial incentives as subsidized credit to improve their coverage. The effectiveness of indiscriminate supply of credit on the adoption behavior of farmers is, however, most doubtful. Initial adoption may be favored, but subsequent maintenance of the soil conservation works is not warranted. Implementation of soil conservation programs would benefit from a more adequate understanding of the factors that influence the demand for alternative technologies and the farm-household-specific incentives that favor their adoption. We relied on a comparison between adopting and non-adopting households in order to specify their responses to different types of policy incentives. With the identification of relevant factors influencing potential demand for soil conservation practices, both the outreach of rural development programs and the selectivity in the choice of incentives may be substantially improved.

The chapter is structured along the following lines. First, the growing importance of soil erosion processes and the role of soil conservation practices is reviewed. Second, the relevant factors that influence adoption behavior of soil conservation practices by different farm types are discussed, followed by an empirical assessment of their importance in the Guanacaste research area. Finally, the results of the empirical analysis are discussed to identify feasible incentives to enhance adoption behavior. The chapter concludes with some comments on the effectiveness of agrarian policy instruments for controlling soil erosion in the Costa Rican hillsides.

Soil erosion problems and soil conservation practices

Soil erosion can be defined as a process of depletion and transport of soil nutrients mainly through the influence of water or wind. Soil erosion represents an important type of soil degradation, characterized as a process of the deterioration of favorable physical and chemical soil characteristics (McConnell, 1983). Soil erosion can result in a range of negative effects on farming systems and the agro-ecological environment as a whole. Pagiola (1994) states that the main categories of costs caused by soil degradation in developing countries are on-farm costs, for example productivity effects. In contrast, off-site effects (for example, costs resulting from soil depositions in rivers and ground water, causing clogging) while hard to quantify, seem to be of relatively minor importance.

Soil erosion often can lead to declining yields or higher input costs to maintain the same yield level. However, the direct relation between soil erosion and productivity losses is hard to establish, mainly because many other factors also influence this relationship, including soil characteristics, crop characteristics and farmers' land use practices. Moreover, the complex process of interaction between these variables makes generalizations about the causes and effects of soil erosion quite impossible. Therefore, the impact of soil degradation on the farm and its wider environment can only be quantified locally.

Soil erosion is not always perceived as a problem by farmers. When talking about declining productivity, farmers frequently mention that they have observed gradually declining yields over the last decades. However, they mostly ascribe this effect to the more frequent occurrence of plagues and pests and refer to the loss of soil fertility (*'la tierra está cansada'*). However, the connection with soil erosion is often not made, although most farmers refer to the heavy impacts of rainfall as a major problem in addition to the losses due to plagues and diseases. This difficulty in observing the direct consequences of soil erosion makes the promotion and adoption of soil conservation practices already a difficult task.

Soil conservation activities can be classified in various manners. A most common distinction is made between physical measures and cultivation practices. The former focus on conservation measures that require a lump-sum investment in terms of labor, capital or land. The latter practices refer to changes in the land use and cropping technologies. Typical examples of physical measures are ridges, ditches or terraces, while cultivation practices refer to activities like contour-plowing, minimum tillage or mulching.

Within the framework of the Guanacaste MAG–FAO project, three types of physical measures for soil conservation are promoted: construction of windshields, building barriers and digging ditches. Windshields (*rompevientos*) protect plots against the soil-degrading effects of wind erosion. Barriers (*barreras*) are built in the field using vegetative or dead material to slow down water runoff and at the same time facilitate penetration of water into the soil. Ditches (*zanjas*) are mostly constructed to facilitate the drainage of water during heavy rainfall without causing extensive soil losses. Although these practices are promoted without discrimination throughout the region, specific types of farmers seem to be more motivated to adopt one measure or another.

Many soil conservation programs face – to an even greater extent than other rural development projects – the dilemma of objectives that are not fully endorsed by the intended clients (De Graaff, 1993). This may be explained by the fact that off-farm effects are not taken fully into account, and farmers' perceptions about on-site soil erosion cannot always be directly related to declining productivity. Moreover, farmers' evaluation of the benefits and costs of various soil conservation measures is seriously hampered by the short time-horizon that especially poor households maintain (Lutz *et al.*, 1994). Thus even a positive cost–benefit relationship cannot be considered as a sufficient reason to expect adoption. Cost–benefit analysis is limited to evaluating an investment on its productiveness from the viewpoint of profit-maximizing behavior of farmers, thereby neglecting the fact that farm households may have multiple objectives. Risk aversion and leisure preference are objectives that equally influence farm household behavior (Ellis, 1988). Efficiency – that is, measuring the productivity of different production factors – can be analyzed by estimating production functions that capture the contribution of relevant inputs that determine the outcome of production (Ruben *et al.*, 1997), but these procedures do not throw light on farmers' motives for either adoption or non-adoption of different soil conservation measures.

Other approaches for the assessment of potential clients for the promotion of improved soil conservation practices pay more attention to different reasons for adoption (Feder *et al.*, 1985). Differences in adoption behavior between farmers can be related to individual farm household characteristics that point to potential willingness to adopt. Commonly mentioned factors include land ownership, farm size, age, gender, education, access to credit, market information and labor availability (Pomp, 1994). Empirical research on these factors and their relationship to the adoption potential of technological innovations by different types of farmers may be very helpful in improving the effectiveness of information systems on the selection of techniques by farmers and incentives for rural extension (Röling, 1988).

Adoption of soil conservation practices

Current research on agricultural technology is strongly focused on the identification of priorities for the generation of potentially effective measures and their subsequent transfer to or diffusion within the farmers' community (Anderson, 1994). Limited adoption is attributed mostly to risk considerations or implicit biases of the technological design in favor of certain types of farmers. More recently, strategies for agricultural research and development recognize that agro-ecological and socio-economic heterogeneity require methodologies for adaptive research, based on targeted intervention and subsequent spillover effects (Bouma *et al.*, 1995; Pomp, 1994). Within this framework, conditions for the successful implementation of soil conservation measures can be reviewed, and farm household characteristics that permit adoption of these practices can be identified.

Neoclassical economic theory devotes major attention to the influence of relative prices on technology choice. Within the framework of the *induced innovation* approach (Hayami and Ruttan, 1985), capital-intensive technologies can be adopted when the wage rental ratio is high. In the case of investment goods, the rate of relative risk-aversion is used for the discounting of future benefits. These pricing mechanisms do not yield acceptable results, however, when market failures occur on factor or commodity markets. Therefore, the frequently heard prescription of 'getting prices right' is not usually sufficient as a policy device to enhance diffusion of soil conservation practices.

Technological choice can be approached from the viewpoint of the technical or economic feasibility of innovations, as well as from the perspective of the prospects for the adoption of technologies. The former question can be addressed using cost–benefit analysis as a methodology for the assessment of potentially profitable technological options (Barbier, 1990). The issue of adoption requires, however, an analytical framework that takes into account also non-price factors, and recognizes the presence of various – sometimes contradictory – farm household objectives.

A distinction should be made between the adoption of certain cultivation practices and the on-farm construction of physical infrastructure. While the former innovation can be adjusted during each cropping cycle, fixed investments are meant to yield benefits during a number of years. Short-term investments can be evaluated within the framework of relative costs, but for the appraisal of long-term investment risk, behavior will also be important. Moreover, the effectiveness of physical measures tends to increase once they are accompanied by simultaneous modifications in cultivation practices, making both technologies highly complementary. Besides the initial investment, maintenance costs also have to be taken into account. Therefore, soil conservation activities are to be considered essentially as a process of *embodied* technological change that involves a simultaneous shift in factor requirements and the organization of production.

A survey of relevant factors that influence the adoption of innovation is supplied by Feder *et al.* (1985). Attention is focused on relevant farm household characteristics that influence decisions on technology choice. The most important factors usually mentioned to explain differences in willingness to adopt include: farm size, tenancy relations, information and knowledge, access to credit, and risks. We will briefly review each of these factors in relationship with the farm-level implementation of soil conservation practices.

Relations between the prospects for implementation of soil conservation measures and the farm size cannot be unambiguously identified. On one hand, there is a clear bias against smaller farms, because these face more difficulties in sacrificing part of the land for the establishment of windshields or barriers, and their time horizon is usually more constrained. Moreover, opportunity costs of labor may be higher for smaller farms that derive a substantial part of their household income from off-farm activities. Finally, technical assistance and credit facilities have a higher coverage among the bigger farms, as land is considered as collateral for lending. On the other hand, smaller farms usually achieve a far higher intensity of land use and are more specialized in intensive cropping activities, where yields are more susceptible to soil erosion. These factors point towards a higher willingness to adopt, as well as better prospects for the maintenance of soil conservation measures.

Property rights have a clear impact on the possibilities for the adoption of soil conservation practices. Land ownership or long-term tenancy contracts favor the implementation of long-term investments to maintain land quality (Hayami and Otsuka, 1993). This is especially the case when returns to revenue streams are sufficiently guaranteed, or rewards to investment can be captured through higher land prices. Most soil conservation measures are, however, effective only when implementation takes place at the watershed level. Therefore, some scale economies are clearly present, and revenues are distributed in the form of externalities.

Factors like access to information, knowledge and educational level are commonly considered to influence decisions regarding factor allocation and adoption of innovations (Moock, 1981). The relationship is twofold: better-educated farmers face higher opportunity costs of labor and are therefore inclined to adopt more capital-intensive innovations, while they also have more abilities ('learning ability') to introduce adjustments within their farming system (Pomp, 1994). These tendencies are usually reinforced by the extension network, as technical assistance services tend to focus on the better-endowed farmers. It should be noted, however, that awareness of and knowledge on soil erosion is part of a wider system of social communication, especially related to the existing information exchange mechanisms and the linkages with factor and commodity markets. Therefore, less-endowed farm households may also decide to adopt certain soil conservation measures if these become part of the commonly accepted 'discourse' in the area.

Differences in risk attitudes among farm households and imperfect access to credit facilities are mutually related. Risk-aversive behavior implies that farmers are less inclined to assume long-term investment for soil conservation, as they cannot carry the fixed costs involved. Most externally financed soil conservation projects try to overcome this constraint through the supply of subsidized credit facilities. The effectiveness of this instrument remains, largely doubtful, however, especially if periodic maintenance activities are required. Pomp (1994) argues that both factors mainly explain differences in the timing of adoption, and not so much in adoption as such.

Finally, the structure of the current production system can be included as a variable influencing the adoption of soil conservation practices. Differences between cropping and livestock systems broadly coincide with farm size. Most physical soil conservation measures are expected on farms with cropping activities, while pasture areas are far less susceptible to erosion. Therefore, soil conservation on small farms with arable cropping activities is essentially meant as a *yield-increasing strategy*. However, differences may occur with respect to the adoption of those measures that are considered as an *investment strategy*. In that case, bigger livestock farmers may capture institutional rents supplied by ongoing projects of international cooperation. Adoption of soil conservation practices then becomes part of a competitive institutional framework that tends to replicate the prevailing tenancy structure.

Farmers' adoption behavior

Fieldwork for this research was carried within the framework of the MAG–FAO project, *'Fomento y Aplicación de Prácticas de Conservación y Manejo de Tierras en Costa Rica'*, which is currently working in eight pilot zones all over the country. This program aims to upscale activities to areas around the pilot areas and other erosion-sensitive areas, while ultimately transferring responsibilities to the Ministry of Agriculture and Livestock (MAG). The pilot area of Monseñor Morera, with its surrounding region, was selected as the site for field research.

The region is situated in the canton of Tilarán in the eastern part of the province of Guanacaste. Its landscape can be characterized as hilly, with altitudes varying between 500 and 1500 meters above sea level. The mean annual temperature is about 24°C and annual rainfall is approximately 2000 mm, the main part falling in the wet season (April until December). Major agricultural activities in the region are livestock, basic grains production (maize, beans), coffee and some horticulture crops (tomato, peppers). Three production systems can be identified in the area: commercial dairy farms, mixed farming combining livestock with coffee, basic grains and horticultural crops, and farms with only arable cropping activities that either are strongly subsistence-oriented (basic grains) or maintain a stronger market-orientation (mostly tomato farmers).

A random sample group of 62 farmers was selected, from both those who participated in the soil conservation program and those who did not. Farm size varied considerably within the sample: about 55 per cent were small farmers with less than 10 ha (40 per cent with even less than 5 ha) and 20 per cent owned more than 25 ha. Minimum farm size within the sample was 0.2 ha and maximum size was 210 ha. Owners comprised 55 per cent and tenants 10 per cent, while the remaining part both owned and rented plots. Half of the farmers were engaged mainly in cropping activities (coffee production and horticulture crops), one-third derived income especially from livestock production, while for 13 per cent off-farm activities were the main income source; 75 per cent had had access to formal or informal credit during the last three years, but only 60 per cent reported a current outstanding loan.

Data collected were classified into three categories of variables: (1) numerical data – for example, farm size, number of animals, years of education, etc.; (2) binary qualitative variables – with labels like 'yes' and 'no' access to credit, participation in the project, etc.; and (3) categorical variables – with labels like 'low', 'medium' and 'high'. For the last category, questions were asked regarding access to markets, frequency of technical assistance and knowledge of soil conservation practices. The numerical variables are measured on an interval or ratio scale and t-tests were used to examine the association between the adoption of certain soil conservation practices and the relevant farm household characteristics. The categorical variables are measured on an ordinal or nominal scale, making use of Pearson association tests for nominal variables and Mantel–Hänszel association tests for ordinal variables to identify a relationship with soil conservation practices.

The upper part of Table 6.1 shows the results of the t-tests of significant differences in mean values between adopters and non-adopters of certain conservation practices. Very few significant differences in average values between users and non-users are observed. Only education and the opportunity costs of labor are significantly related to the adoption of barriers. Apparently, these farm household characteristics cannot offer a sufficient explanation for the adoption of soil conservation measures. Although some significant associations occur (for example, less adoption of barriers with lower levels of education or higher opportunity costs of labor), farming-system-related variables appear to be more important.

The lower part of Table 6.1 shows the results of the association tests between the binominal and categorical variables related to farm management and organization with the occurrence of certain soil conservation variables. The variables 'knowledge of conservation' and 'application of cultural practices' are strongly related to soil conservation. The former represents farmers' knowledge and viewpoints on the conservation of natural resources, and the latter represents whether and to what extent farmers adopt cultural practices within the farming system when soil conservation measures are introduced. As expected, it is confirmed that these two factors are significantly correlated with the application of all three physical soil conservation measures.

The level of assets, an index for the wealth of a farmer, is only significantly associated with the occurrence of windshields. Apparently, wealth or income are less important for the adoption of barriers and ditches. Engagement in off-farm activities and market-orientedness (measured by external input purchase and market selling of the

Table 6.1 Soil conservation adoption intensity in Costa Rica (averages for users and non-users, and tests of association)

	Windshields		Barriers		Ditches	
	Users	Non-users	Users	Non-users	Users	Non-users
1a. Mean differences (T-Test) * significant difference users/non-users (0.05 level)	37	25	17	45	14	48
Age (years)	45	49	46	47	43	48
Number of animals	23	20	6	28	5	26
Cropping index (%)	38	28	43	30	45	30
Education (years)	7.5	8.3	9.3*	7.3*	9.0	7.5
Farm size (ha)	22	28	8	30	5	30
Number of years working in the farm	15	19	12	18	11	18
Opportunity costs of labor (Costa Rican colon)	1820	1830	1220*	2050*	1480	1930

1b. Association tests (Pearson and Mantel–Hänszel)
* = significant at the 0.05 level. ** = significant at the 0.01 level

	Windshields	Barriers	Ditches
Membership of organizations	**	**	*
Market orientation	—	—	—
Knowledge of conservation practices	**	**	**
Distance from the market	**	*	**
Cultural practices	*	**	**
Access to technical assistance	**	**	**
Available assets	*	—	—
Main activity	—	**	**
Off-farm activities	—	—	—
Tenancy status	—	—	—
Participation in project	*	**	**
Access to credit	**	**	**

Source: own fieldwork.

produce) do not significantly differ between users and non-users of certain soil conservation practices. Both variables are related to the availability of purchasing power, which apparently does not seem important for adoption. Otherwise, the access and use of credit is strongly associated with the occurrence of all three conservation practices. This seems to point towards cash constraints that cannot be solved adequately with labor or cropping income.

The membership of organizations or groups and the distance to the town of Tilarán, the center of the region, are in all three cases significantly associated with the adoption of a conservation practice. An explanation could be the importance of access to communication and information through contacts with other farmers and agricultural service organizations, which stimulates adoption. This is also related to the supply of technical assistance, which in all three cases is strongly correlated with the adoption of conservation practices. The significant relationship between participation in the MAG–FAO project and adoption behavior is self-explanatory.

The main activity of a farmer significantly influences the adoption of barriers and ditches. This variable represents the orientation of the production systems towards intensive arable cropping, extensive livestock keeping or semi-intensive mixed farming. Farm investments are realized to reinforce current farming systems of interest to the farmer. Therefore, different farming systems also imply a specific interest for certain soil conservation measures: barriers may be more important for livestock-oriented systems, while ditches are more relevant when arable cropping is the principal activity.

The association tests proved to be less suitable for examining the impact of the tenancy status on adoption behavior. However, since the importance of land ownership rights is mentioned frequently in the literature, it will be included in subsequent logistic regression procedures along with other variables mentioned earlier as being significantly associated with the adoption of a certain soil conservation practice.

Incentives for enhancing adoption

For the appraisal of the possibilities of adoption by certain types of farmers, we relied on the statistical procedure of logistic regression. This procedure can be used for the processing of databases with quantitative and qualitative data and does not require too many assumptions regarding normal distribution (Hosmer and Lemeshow, 1989). It is therefore considered an appropriate tool for practical use in developing countries. The procedure permits the interpretation of data collected in diagnostic surveys for the purpose of identifying relevant variables that influence unequal adoption among different farm types.

The purpose of logistic regression analysis is similar to that of normal multiple regression analysis, which is often used in production function analysis – namely, to determine which independent factors have a significant influence (and to what extent) on a certain dependent variable. In the case of logistic regression, the dependent variable is a binary variable with the two labels 'yes' and 'no,' and it can thus be used to determine the factors that influence the adoption of technical innovations. Similar evaluation parameters can be used as for multiple regression analysis.

From the results of the association tests and the previous literature review, hypotheses were formulated to identify the relevant variables that could be important for the adoption of soil conservation practices by hillside farmers living in the Eastern Guanacaste region of Tilarán. The variables that appeared to be significant in the association tests were subjected to further analysis with logistic regression techniques. The results are presented in Table 6.2.

The variables selected in the model represent the best possible combination of factors that explain the adoption of soil conservation practices by a certain farm household. The combination of these factors provides a significant explanation of the adoption of a particular soil conservation measure, and the estimation procedure permits determination of the factors that contribute to the probability of adoption of specific conservation measures. Therefore, conclusions can be drawn about the order and magnitude of the existing correlations and predictions made about the likelihood of future adoption by certain types of farmers. The logistic regression model selects the most significant combination of variables, thereby indicating implicitly also some priority areas for project intervention and incentives for agrarian policies.

Table 6.2 gives the results of the statistical relations between each of the three soil conservation methods and the relevant variables that explain the likelihood of its adoption by any particular type of farmer. The significant variables are selected through a procedure using the log likelihood criterion and Wald statistics. This leads to the most significant combination of variables explaining the adoption of each of the soil conservation practices. The adoption of windshields is explained largely by three factors: land ownership, availability of assets, and access to technical assistance. The occurrence of barriers is explained largely by the level of education of the farmer, farming

Table 6.2 Factors influencing adoption behavior of soil conservation practices in Costa Rica (logistic regression functions)

Variables		Coefficient	Standard error	Wald statistic	Significance level
Windshields: model chi-square: 45.731 (.000); % correctly predicted: 87.1%					
Assets	High	1		6 575	0.04
	Low	3.03	1.34	5 113	0.02
	Medium	0.46	1.11	0 174	0.68
Technical assistance	High	1		12 852	0.00
	Low	-5.83	1.63	12 800	0.00
	Medium	-3.49	1.27	7 560	0.01
Tenancy status	Rent	1		8 939	0.03
	Settler IDA	10.12	34.64	0 085	0.77
	Ownership	3.63	1.95	3 464	0.06
	Mixed	6.40	2.33	7 535	0.01
Constant		-1.75	2.13	0 674	0.41
Barriers: model chi-square: 69.017 (.000); % correctly predicted: 98.3%					
Education	Years	9.05	130.84	0.005	0.95
Main activity	Other	1		0.005	0.99
	Agriculture	54.34	1 615.61	0.001	0.97
	Livestock	-43.94	1 778.61	0.001	0.98
Technical assistance	High	1		0.005	0.99
	Low	-99.51	1 537.80	0.004	0.95
	Medium	-85.72	1 178.44	0.005	0.94
Constant		-86.91	1 667.14	0.001	0.97
Ditches: model chi-square: 24.043 (0000); % correctly predicted: 87.1%					
Knowledge of soil conservation	High	1		7 655	0.02
	Low	-2.51	0.92	7 418	0.01
	Medium	-1.99	1.12	3 204	0.07
Access to credit	Yes/No	2.43	1.14	4 509	0.04
Constant		-1.18	1.26	0.874	0.35

Source: own fieldwork.

systems oriented towards arable cropping activities, and farms with access to technical assistance. Ditches are adopted by farmers with more knowledge of soil conservation practices and with access to credit.

In all three models, the overall goodness of fit represented by the model's chi-square is satisfactory. Table 6.2 shows that 87.1 per cent of the data are correctly predicted by the model for windshields, while 98.3 per cent of the adoption or not of barriers is explained and 87.1 per cent of the adoption or not of ditches is correctly predicted. These overall results are quite satisfactory, especially for windshields and ditches. However, looking at the individual coefficients and their subsequent Wald statistics, the model for barriers shows that none of the selected variables is significantly different from zero. Also, other significance levels are somewhat low. Apart from the fact that some coefficients are not significantly different from zero, the magnitude of these coefficients makes the Wald statistic unreliable. Therefore, the model cannot be used directly for further predictions on the probability of adopting barriers. However, from the association tests we already know that for the three selected variables – the level of education, the principal activity and technical assistance – significant associations exist with adoption of barriers. Thus, assuming that the signs of the coefficients are correct, we can still make some useful remarks about the adoption of barriers. In the models for windshields and ditches almost all coefficients are significantly different from zero. These are quite reliable for further predictions with farm data.

The results of this analysis confirm some general assumptions regarding the adoption of soil conservation technologies (De Graaff, 1993; Feder *et al.*, 1985). Implementation of barriers is found mostly among farmers for whom arable cropping is their major activity, while farmers dedicated to livestock or with more off-farm activities are less likely to adopt this practice. Moreover, supply of technical assistance tends to increase the probability of adoption of barriers. More highly educated farmers are more prone to adopt this conservation practice, which indicates education as being an important area of attention to stimulate this practice.

Windshields are mostly adopted by farmers who are landowners; farmers who rent land are more reluctant to install windshields than farmers with secure land titles, as this represents a substantial investment with medium- and long-term benefits that improves the value of the land (Kishor and Constantino, 1994). However, rich farmers with more assets are less likely to implement windshields than poor farmers.

This may be explained because richer farmers are more oriented towards livestock production. Moreover, richer farmers with larger farms have the option to choose the best areas in their farm for cropping activities. One of the criteria for selecting such areas is to offer natural protection against wind, which makes the establishment of windshields less necessary. Finally, better access to and higher frequency of technical assistance services tend to increase the probability of implementing windshields. This refers especially to the provision of seedlings and advice in planting and maintenance of the trees.

The probability of the adoption of ditches increases with farmers who possess more knowledge and better information on alternative soil conservation practices, and had had access to credit during the last three years. Apparently, a high awareness of causes and consequences of soil erosion is required to motivate farmers to construct ditches. This practice is more frequently implemented by commercially oriented farmers, who use more external inputs and are more sensitive to declining yields. This seems to contradict the fact that the level of market orientedness is not significant. However, this variable also includes commercially oriented livestock production, which disturbs the relationship. Only farmers with a strong emphasis on cropping activities, and who are commercially oriented, are more inclined to adopt barriers. The application of ditches is the only conservation measure to be implemented by farmers that requires credit assistance.

Apparently, in all three cases, access to information is an important factor for the adoption of soil conservation practices. With windshields and barriers the information constraint is best addressed by practical technical assistance for their implementation. For the implementation of ditches, topical courses on soil conservation to raise consciousness and improve the understanding on soil erosion processes seem to be sufficient. Farmers with a higher level of education are also more inclined to adopt barriers. These variables again strongly confirm the assumption that access to information – in the form of either knowledge or skills or as a process of consciousness-raising on conservation issues – is an important factor for the adoption of soil conservation practices.

Policy implications

Agrarian policies to reduce soil erosion or to enhance the adoption of soil conservation measures usually rely on an incentive framework that tries to reduce the initial costs of establishment. Most soil conservation projects therefore offer facilities for subsidized credit for input purchase (seedlings, planting material, stones, implements), food for work schemes to reduce labor costs and direct finance of external costs such as transport of materials. Their principal effort seems to be directed towards the reduction of input costs and the compensation of labor efforts (Enters, 1998).

While the former policies give priority to supply aspects, far less attention is given to the demand for soil conservation activities by different types of farm households. Looking at the variables influencing adoption behavior reveals that these facilities are of only minor importance. Instead, institutional rules such as tenancy status and factors related to technical assistance, training and education proved to be far more important for actual adoption. Moreover, the current structure of the farming system already implies a specific demand for certain types of soil conservation measures. The availability of credit seems to be an important factor only for ditches.

The statistical procedures used for the interpretation of the differences in adoption rates across farmers offer a fairly good framework to explain the *selective adoption* of various soil conservation measures. The selected variables can be considered as the most important or constraining factors for adoption, given the available data. It should be noted, however, that information on soil productivity or cropping yields under the conservation practices and the analysis of risk behavior are not taken into account, as neither are agro-ecological parameters concerning the suitability of certain soil conservation practices on a specific farm or the erosion sensitivity of certain farm lands.

The analysis permits us to draw some important conclusions. For each of the soil conservation practices, a different mix of variables proved to be significant. Institutional variables like tenancy status (property rights) and access to credit are most important in the cases of windshields and ditches, respectively. More material variables related to the wealth of the farmer, like the level of assets or the principal activity, are significant in the cases of barriers and windshields, respectively. The group of variables related to knowledge and information proved to be relevant for all three practices, with variables like technical assistance, knowledge of soil conservation or education being significant in different cases. Extension services and farmer-to-farmer exchange programs thus offer most incentives for adoption.

These outcomes are all fully in line with the hypotheses derived from the literature review, and all of the variables separately are significantly associated with the occurrence of a soil conservation practice. Three important final conclusions can be drawn: (1) variables like information and knowledge explain a major part of a farmer's behavior; (2) credit is only relevant for the construction of ditches; and (3) adoption of barriers is strongly related to the cropping orientation of the farming system. The latter point could be explained by the fact that smaller farmers with cropping activities as their principal activity pursue soil conservation practices as a yield-increasing or yield-sustaining strategy, while the larger farmers with livestock as their principal activity pursue an investment or rent-seeking strategy. Since small farmers devoted to cropping activities are significant adopters of barriers in contrast to larger livestock ranchers, this could mean that yield-sustaining behavior is encouraged while rent-seeking behavior is discouraged implicitly in the reviewed MAG–FAO project intervention.

7

The Impact of Financial Reform on Rural Credit in Central America

Arie Sanders and Cor J. Wattel

Introduction

Financial reform is omnipresent in Central America. Surprisingly, the financial reform policies are very similar throughout the region, although the macroeconomic and structural conditions of the Central American countries are quite diverse. The reforms all include two basic components: less direct intervention of the state in financial intermediation, and a stronger supervision of the banking system by more autonomous central banks. The basic argument put forward by the servants of the reform is that the liberalization of the financial sector, if adequately supervised, will lead to more savings, hence a broader availability of resources for credit, and generally a more efficient allocation of resources for investment, which in turn will lead to higher economic growth.

In this chapter we will question the above argument, specifically for the case of the rural areas in Costa Rica, Honduras and El Salvador. Our reasons are twofold. First, the macroeconomic basis for financial reform is very fragile, which may lead to counterproductive effects on production and growth, not only in rural areas. Second, the fragmented structure of rural financial markets is a structural development problem, which will not be solved by liberalizing an urban-biased banking market. Third, the policy prescript of financial liberalization leaves little room for the development of semiformal financial institutions that may offer innovative solutions to the fragmentation of the rural credit market.[1]

We will develop our argument in the following four sections. The next section after this one concentrates on macroeconomic issues and summarizes the evidence on the conditions for success of financial reform as shown by experiences of other countries. The succeeding section has a more microeconomic character and analyses the causes and consequences of fragmented rural financial markets. Following this, in the next section empirical evidence is discussed, both on the macroeconomic level (financial deepening) and the microeconomic level (fragmentation of the rural financial market); for the latter, grateful use is made of recent rural credit surveys by the Ohio State University in the three countries mentioned.

The final section offers conclusions and draws some policy implications. The basic point of policy relevance is that in the Central American context it would be naive to trust either the 'free' market forces or the supposedly wise and neutral intervention of the government. It is advocated that policy should promote the emergence of decentralized, semiformal financial intermediaries, which are able to combine sound economic management with the supply of innovative financial services to specific segments of the rural financial markets.

Financial reform and economic development

The empirical evidence on the effects of financial liberalization on savings, investment and growth is far from conclusive. Gibson and Tsakalotos (1994) indicate that much of the evidence in favor of the financial liberalization argument suffers from biased model specifications.[2] The available evidence for Latin American countries seems to indicate at most a very weak, if any positive, effect of financial liberalization on the real economy.

Several authors have tried with empirical tests to verify the chain of arguments of the financial liberalization thesis. We will shortly summarize the findings, and then proceed to the risks of a mistaken financial reform.

Assessments of the effects of financial liberalization on the performance of savings have tended to suffer from a lack of clarity. The neoclassical argument is that interest rate liberalization, and more generally a better performance of banks, will induce the households and firms to deposit more savings into the financial system. On the other hand, post-Keynesians have reasoned that interest rate liberalization might indeed mobilize more financial savings, but does not necessarily lead to higher total savings in the national economy. Both parties have produced empirical evidence for their thesis, but no robust findings have been achieved. Fry (1988) did his empirical work on a set of Asian countries, although others could not confirm the empirical results. The available evidence on Latin American countries would at least cast doubt on the hypothesis that savings are boosted by financial liberalization.[3]

Another point of discussion is whether higher savings will induce more investment, and whether these investments will be selected on profitability criteria rather than political objectives, as argued by the neoclassical economists. The post-Keynesians, however, reply that investment may be positively influenced by a greater credit availability, but that this effect might be offset by two counter-productive effects of financial liberalization: a general rise in real interest rates, and a contraction of economic activity with a resulting decline in the 'animal spirits'. Additionally, our data for Central America suggest that the effect of the higher savings on credit availability may be relatively weak, and seems to be highly influenced by the external sector rather than the financial reform. Again, the empirical evidence is being used to defend both theses, often with partial models, but it has not been possible to accomplish robustness.

Apart from doubts about the theoretical underpinning of the financial liberalization thesis, the literature presents a series of risks of financial reform. These risks may not only affect the financial development outcomes of such reforms, but can also have unexpected effects on economic efficiency and income distribution.

In first position is the risk of financial crash: in his analysis of the Chilean financial reforms of the late 1970s Díaz (1985) demonstrated that the growth of banks and private non-bank financial intermediaries (known as the *financieras*) that followed the 1974–82 financial reform did indeed raise the volume of financial intermediation significantly. The total savings, investment and growth variables, however, did not show any improvement, probably because of too high interest rates and an overvalued exchange rate. On the contrary, the expansion of financial intermediaries proved to be a largely speculative bubble, which was deficiently supervised by the monetary authorities. The ensuing bankruptcies of several *financieras* and a bank in 1976–7, and the crisis of various highly indebted industrial conglomerates (1981–2), forced the government to intervene and spend large amounts of public money to save the financial system from a crash.

In Central America, the crisis of the *financieras* during the aftermath of the second oil crisis generated a broad awareness of the importance of an adequate monetary supervision. In the present financial reforms, the supervision of private banking is therefore one of the cornerstones of the new legislation. Nonetheless, the interconnection of domestic banks with offshore banking makes supervision a very difficult task.[4]

The experience of Chile in the 1970s illustrated another risk of financial liberalization. The rise in banking activity was intimately related to existing business groups that established their own banks to finance their business. These banks mobilized savings from the public, and invested these resources preferentially into the companies of their shareholders. This led to a dangerous concentration of portfolio risks, which in fact resulted in the crash of several banks when the companies of their owners suffered bankruptcy. Although the central bank had declared repeatedly that it would not guarantee the deposits in the private banks, it was forced to intervene and pay the bills, before the financial crisis spread further. Obviously, these events suggest that large budget transfers were used to the benefit of a small group of adventurous new bankers who abused the newly created liberty of financial legislation and exploited the lack of supervision by the monetary authorities (see Díaz, 1985).

A similar phenomenon might occur in Central American countries. In fact, private banks are generally owned by small groups of businessmen, who find an interest in creating a bank to finance their business at lower transaction costs.[5] It is common knowledge that larger corporations sometimes deliberately let some of their companies go bankrupt, and have thus on several occasions been able to transfer unpleasant losses to the state banks.[6] Counting on the responsibility of the central banks to avoid financial crisis, they might repeat the trick in case of debt to (their own) private banks.

It has been demonstrated that the success of financial reform depends strongly upon a favorable macroeconomic environment, and compatible economic policies for the real sector (for instance trade policies). Several authors have investigated the relationship between financial liberalization and economic stabilization, motivated by the extremely contractive effects of the combination liberalization–stabilization in a lot of countries. For the case of open economies, Kapur (1983) advocates a simultaneous growth of the money supply and a coordination of exchange rate policies with the rise of interest rates, in order to avoid too large capital inflows from abroad. Mathieson (1980), on the other hand, advocates an over-depreciation of the exchange rate in order to attract a moderate flow of foreign capital, which could finance an increase in the credit supply without affecting the domestic monetary austerity.

The case of Mexico in 1994 (the tequila effect) proved that a deficient coordination of financial liberalization with macroeconomic policies is a very risky policy, one reason (among others) being the large and uncontrollable capital inflows. These risks had been foreseen by the international financial institutions, and there was awareness that they were very difficult to control by the monetary authorities (Faruqi, 1994).

In the Central American context, similar risks exist. The governments seem to be unable to reduce the current account deficits, and therefore are obliged to turn to foreign capital flows in order to finance the balance of payments. The 'dollarization' of certain sectors of the economy is only a symptom of the increasing importance of the external sector. Although in an open economy the degrees of freedom for monetary policy will anyhow be limited, the financial liberalization process poses new challenges and threats to the monetary authorities.

In the same way, the sequencing of the liberalization process is a crucial risk factor in financial reform. Although conclusive recommendations do not yet exist, it is agreed that the liberalization of the capital account, or external financial liberalization, should be a last step in the liberalization process, and that domestic financial liberalization should be preceded by domestic trade liberalization. In Central America that is often not the case: domestic markets, for example in the case of Honduras, are highly fragmented and oligopolistic in structure, with the result that financial liberalization will not necessarily lead to a more efficient allocation of private investments (see Gibson and Tsakalotos, 1994: 592).

Gibson and Tsakalotos conclude that the concept of financial repression usually applied is too broad, as it censures any state intervention in the financial markets. It does not distinguish between 'bad' interventions that create market failures and 'good' interventions that rather eliminate them.

In our opinion, however, it would be hazardous to draw the conclusion that government intervention in the financial sector in Central America should be automatically promoted. The arguments of the structuralist and post-Keynesian schools in favor of government intervention in the financial markets may be based upon successful East Asian governments (Japan, NIC tigers), but should be mistrusted in the Central American case. In this context, it would be as naive to rely exaggeratedly on the private sector (concentration of economic interests) as it would to believe in a class- and market-neutral state intervention.

Segmentation of rural financial markets

The literature on the access to credit has been dominated during the last decades by the theories of the 'new institutional economics'.

Different analyses and concepts have been developed to explain why some transactions are not organized by the market, but rather by internal contracts within organizations of firms and households, broadly called institutions. Uncertainty in the markets leads in some cases to the impossibility of formulating contingent contracts; therefore transactions that would otherwise be realized through the market are replaced by institutional arrangements, as a more suitable allocation mechanism in situations of imperfect markets. Examples of such institutional arrangements in the agrarian context are sharecropping and the existence of cooperatives.

The existence of different kinds of institutions in the credit markets has been explained from various perspectives. Thus Stiglitz and Weiss (1981) developed the *imperfect information paradigm*, to explain phenomena like equilibrium rationing of credit and the consequent fragmentation of the rural credit market,[7] while others, like Kotwal and Eswaran (1989) and Binswanger *et al.* (1993), are concerned with the agrarian structure to explain the differential access of rural households to credit.

Stiglitz based his studies on imperfect information. The origins of institutions are seen as a solution to various types of information problems, such as incomplete markets, asymmetric information, problems with moral hazard, and others. In the case of rural financial markets, the transaction costs for the principal are caused mainly by asymmetrical information.[8] The problem of the lender is a lack of information about the intentions and behavior of the borrower. The lender must make relatively high investments (screening costs) to distinguish 'good' borrowers from 'bad' ones, by estimating the clients' risk behavior and the probability of default. The risks for the lender are referred to as *moral hazard* problems, *incentive* problems and *enforcement* problems (Hoff and Stiglitz, 1990: 237). As the unit costs of getting enough information increase with lower credit amounts (scale effect), banks tend to classify small-scale clients according to simple standardized criteria (for example crop), instead of seriously investigating the heterogeneity within the potential client group.

To reduce the information costs, the selection of clients is mostly based on information that is easy and cheap to get. In most cases financial institutes use a direct mechanism to select their clients: the requirement of collateral. This requirement leads to the rationing of credits for those groups that cannot comply with the collateral requirements, although they would be prepared to pay the price of the credit or interest and repay the capital. Collateral requirements therefore create a segmentation of markets on the criterion of availability or non-availability of collateral, affecting mostly the asset-poor households with few (formal) property rights. Therefore, the market segment of loans for poorer households is costly to organize and operate (high information costs). The potential gains to a bank from credit operations may not be large enough to justify their presence in this segment. As a result, a whole group of potential borrowers without marketable collateral is pushed into the segment of semi-formal credit markets (NGOs) or informal ones (relatives or moneylenders).[9]

The asymmetric information paradigm pays relatively little attention to the question of which type of household will be rationed. Other authors have emphasized this latter aspect, taking the agrarian structure as a starting point. Rural households have different degrees of market participation, affected and constrained by the institutional setting. This results in the market imperfections being household-specific, rather than commodity-specific.[10]

The characteristics of the households are important for two reasons. First, they influence the household's demand for credit. Second, potential lenders are likely to base their assessment of borrowers' creditworthiness on such characteristics. The latter will be explained: the wealth of borrowers influences the supply of credit, if the costs of collecting debt are high in terms of time, effort, and money. This implies low penalties to the borrowers for defaulting, which in turn provides scope for moral hazard. Lenders react to this situation by insisting on collateral. Because richer agents can offer assets of greater value in the formal economy, they will have access not only to larger loans than poorer households but also to loans with lower interest rates, since these loans are perceived as being less risky (Moll *et al.*, 1996: 5). Therefore authors like Yotopoulos and Floro (1992) draw the conclusion that the availability of credit is directly linked to the agrarian class structure. 'The distinction between the contracting agents, i.e. lenders and borrowers, is also an economic distinction reflecting unequal distribution of ownership/control over the means of production' (Yotopoulos and Floro, 1992: 305).

As Stiglitz and Weiss (1981: 393) indicated, the credit market does not behave like a perfect market, not least because of the intertemporal character of the credit transactions, which implies additional risk and uncertainty compared with other markets. Rural credit markets behave the way they do because of the problems of information asymmetry, moral hazard and the agrarian structure. These market failures do not stem from state intervention, but rather from the inherent features of the credit market and rural households.

It follows that different and more sophisticated infrastructural market institutions are required, in order to promote an efficient functioning of the credit market. The policy implications also differ from the financial liberalization recipes, as credit will be rationed notwithstanding a policy of free interest rates in a competitive banking environment:

> Both the welfare effects of the systematic structural distortions inherent in credit markets, and their distributional implications, call for appropriate state interventions – as opposed to liberalization which is the traditional prescription for distortions. (Yotopoulos and Floro, 1992)

The application of financial liberalization measures in the context of fragmented rural financial markets may do more harm than good. In the first place, eliminating the control over interest rates just may not be sufficient in reducing the selective credit rationing by banks. In the second place, if liberalization results in higher real deposit rates then it will attract investable funds into banks. This might induce a shift of the available funds from the informal credit market to the formal one, and reduce total supply of loanable funds to borrowers. The latter is due to the fact that banks have reserve requirements and curb lenders do not (Thorbecke, 1995: 160).

In the 'asymmetric information' paradigm, the collateral requirements are a relative problem, which can be resolved by reducing the information asymmetry. Lenders can buy information on their clients, as long as the net return to additional information is positive. Treating information costs in this way, these can simply be subject to the marginalist rule that consumption is optimal when the marginal cost of acquiring information is equal to its expected marginal return. There would be no apparent special rationale for the lenders to minimize the information costs, if the benefits are potentially high. Thus it would be possible to incorporate the information costs in the interest rate up to a certain level, to arrange contracts only with a profitable segment of the market.[11]

The information costs could, for example, be lowered through the establishment of (offices of) credit institutions in the rural areas, nearer to the client as in the case of the informal sector. The sole existence of a bank office, however, does not guarantee that small farmers will have better access to formal credit, as the household-specific constraints will remain.

De Janvry *et al.* (1991: 416) include more structural phenomena in their policy recommendations.[12] They focus on how to reduce the structural household-specific constraints, in order to cut down the width of the price bands.[13] Policy implications to narrow the price band are, for example: providing the households with property rights to land, investments in better infrastructure, technology transfers and better access to alternative credit options (ibid.). We might add also the access to alternative marketing channels that could offer a better negotiation position to small farmers in the credit market.

The Central American evidence: credit supply on the macro and micro levels

Credit market policies

Since the 1980s, the governments in Central America have been instituting significant policy and institutional reforms that are intended to stimulate allocative efficiency and restore economic growth by means of policies of economic stabilization and structural adjustment. As a part of this strategy, financial reforms are implemented, which means liberalizing the financial sector from regulations and the direct participation of the state in financial intermediation. The following paragraphs and figures give a brief review of the monetary/macroeconomic tendencies of three countries of the region in the last fifteen years.

Costa Rica (Figure 7.1)

At the end of the 1970s and in the early 1980s, the financial system of Costa Rica collapsed. The fiscal deficit grew out of control. At the same time Costa Rica lost its access to the international financial market. The budget deficit was financed internally by forcing state banks to buy government bonds and by increases in the reserve requirements. As it was impossible to sustain the exchange rate, Costa Rica lost increasing amounts of its international money reserve. The consequence was incremental inflation and shockwise devaluation of the national currency.

During the 1980s the broad money supply (M2) declined seriously. The real value of M2 in 1982 was only 69 per cent compared with 1978. Most affected by the financial crisis was the amount of domestic credit (DC) for the private sector. The increase of the total domestic credit in 1982 looks significant (DC/GDP); however, the real value of the total domestic credit was only 42 per cent compared with 1980.

Figure 7.1 Costa Rica: monetary indicators, 1981–94

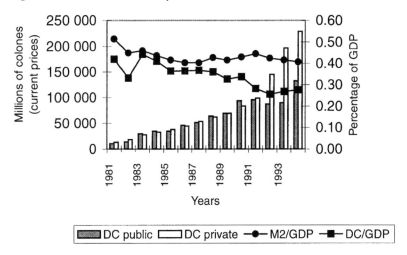

Overall, the financial policy of the Costa Rican government and/or central bank during the 1980s led to a financial contraction. An important change in credit deployment by banks since 1992 is the increase in the share of credit to the private sector in relation to total credit. Credit outstanding to the private sector increased from 47 per cent in 1991 to 63 per cent in 1994. Figure 7.1 shows a decreasing proportion for the public sector after 1983, while the private sector more or less sustained its real value.

El Salvador (Figure 7.2)

In 1980, shortly after the installation of the military junta, the banks in El Salvador were nationalized. The government intervention was based on gaining more control over resource allocation, necessary for financing the civil war and reformist measures. One of the policies was subsidized credit rates to stimulate investment and production. However, as the crisis got worse, the inflation rates and the low interest led to a financial contraction. Almost all credit was used for the public sector, favored by the nationalized banks. Inefficiency and bad management led to an uncontrollable credit portfolio; more than 37 per cent was not recoverable (Cuevas *et al.*, 1991).

At the end of the 1980s and the beginning of the 1990s, the Salvadoran financial system changed drastically. The new government oriented its policy towards an improvement of the financial system, on

Figure 7.2   El Salvador: monetary indicators, 1981–94

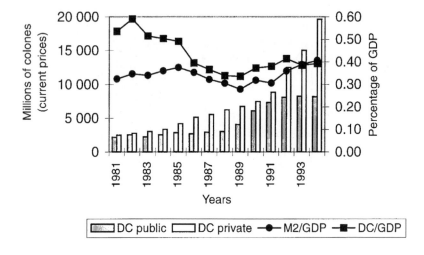

the assumption that the reform of the financial system would lead to economic growth. In the first place the nationalized banks were reprivatized, several banks were closed, the credit portfolio was restructured by transforming loans in severe default into government bonds and other measures were taken. One of the results of the liberalization process of the financial system was the positive real interest rate. The confidence in the bank system increased, resulting in an augmentation of deposit rates and a growing national capital reserve in the last years.

The broad money supply, especially quasi-money, has increased in the last four years. The most important reason for this increment are the millions of remittances from the USA, which stimulate the growth of the net foreign reserves. However, in 1994 there was a small decrease of 0.6 per cent. The rise in NFR means a contraction of the domestic share of the financial system, so that there is less narrow money (M1) available. In fact, El Salvador is faced with a monetary overhang. The central bank cannot control the supply amount of M1, for the reason that a substantial amount of quasi-money can easily be involved in circulation.[14]

In El Salvador, financial policy focused on the private sector. The domestic credit for this sector increased, while the inflation rates became more or less constant. The increment in M2 led to a contraction of the domestic credit compared with the 1980s. In recent years, however, M2 has increased. The composition of the domestic credit supply has changed; in real terms, less money is reserved for the public sector.

Honduras (Figure 7.3)

Until the mid-1980s the financial system of Honduras was in a situation of strong financial repression, characterized by high inflation rates and negative real interest rates on deposits. The central banks imposed high reserve requirements on the banking sector, in order to finance the growing internal debt of the government. The government used part of its budget to subsidize important business groups, for example through debt transfers by the agricultural development bank. The consequence was a contraction of financial intermediation and a concentration of credit in a few hands. The monetary contraction mostly affected the agricultural sector: in 1983 the real value of credits to this sector compared with 1977 was only 62 per cent.

At the beginning of the 1990s the government of Honduras changed its policy to stimulate the efficiency of the financial resource allocation. One of the consequences was a relative decrease in the amount of domestic credit for the public sector. The decrease between 1990 and 1991, in nominal terms, was 9.9 per cent, while in the same period the total domestic credit increased in nominal terms by 15 per cent. The

Figure 7.3   Honduras: monetary indicators, 1981–94

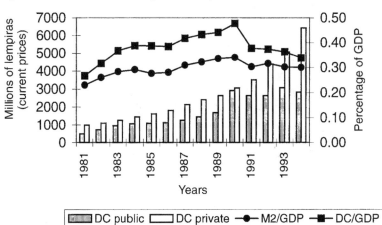

inflation rate in 1991 was about 23.4 per cent, so in real terms the domestic credit supply decreased significantly for both sectors.

In nominal terms the broad money supply increased, being related directly to the increase in the net foreign reserve. It was mostly the quasi-money that increased significantly, especially the term deposits and those in US dollars. The relation between M2 and the GDP has stabilized in the last years, while during the 1980s there was an almost continuous constant increase.

Credit supply and the agricultural sector

The overall tendency in the three countries is a reduction of domestic credit to the public sector. It is the private sector that has gained a more important role in these economies. This does not mean that all economic activities of the private sector are better off than before, in terms of access to credit. Figure 7.4 gives an overview of the agricultural credit assignations as a percentage of the total credit supply in the three countries concerned.

The agricultural sector receives a relatively smaller proportion than before. In the case of Costa Rica, in the early 1980s the agricultural sector absorbed 50 per cent of the total domestic credit, while in the 1990s it was reduced to almost 15 per cent.[15] The decreases affect nearly all categories of agricultural activities, especially basic cereals. Only credits for non-traditional export crops increased. In El Salvador the share of agriculture in credit allocation also decreased, but more

Figure 7.4   Central America: credit absorption of the agricultural sector as percentage of total credit supply (1981–94)

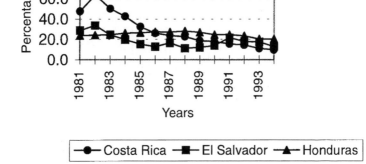

gradually. Historically, the traditional export crops coffee and sugar cane used more than 75 per cent of the total agricultural credit supplied.[16] It is the coffee sector that maintains the percentage of agricultural credit more or less at a stable level. Only in 1992 was there a significant increase of credit supply to the agricultural sector, caused by the high coffee price in the previous year. The credits for basic cereals decreased to less than 1 per cent of all credit supplied to the agricultural sector, while the extension of cultivated area of those crops increased (particularly the area of maize).[17]

In Honduras the credit supply to the agricultural sector remained constant between 1985 and 1992. In the last three years the share of agricultural credit has decreased to an average of 21 per cent, while in the early 1980s the average was 26 per cent of the total credit supply. An important reason was the financial problems of the National Agrarian Development Bank (BANADESA). During the 1970s and 1980s, BANADESA was one of the largest credit suppliers for the agrarian sector.

Rural credit supply at micro level

Access to credit in the rural sector is partly correlated with the development of financial infrastructure like legal rights and the number of banks. The poorer the infrastructure, the less competitive the marketing systems, the less information is available, and the riskier the transactions (see the study of Binswanger and Khandker, 1993). Another important aspect of access to credit, as mentioned above in the discussion of the segmentation of rural financial markets, is the resource endowment of the borrower (mainly land). Table 7.1 shows some variables for a brief description of the conditions of the financial markets in three countries.

Conditions in Costa Rica seem to be the most favorable. According to the reasoning of De Janvry *et al.* (1991), we expect transaction costs to be less in Costa Rica than in the other two countries. In this country, more households have access to credit. Taking into account the incidence of *minifundismo* in the three countries, we can draw the same conclusion.

Costa Rica has a long tradition of facilitating the access to credit for the small scale sector. González Vega *et al.* (1989) noticed that more than 88 per cent of the farmers in their investigation had access to credit at least once in their lifetime, while 74 per cent had access to formal credit. Table 7.2 shows the distribution of credit sources among rural households in Costa Rica.

Table 7.1 Context variables of financial markets in Central America

Variable	Costa Rica	El Salvador	Honduras
Institutional and legal environment	Extensive legislation High transaction costs of enforcement	Moderate legislation Weak enforcement structure	Deficient legislation Weak enforcement structure
Property rights: Distribution of land	Gini 0.79 (1984)[a]	Gini 0.78 (1987)[b]	Gini 0.80 (1993)[c]
Rural households with less than 1 hectare	16 724	178 369 (with less than 2 hectare)	80 088
Physical infrastructure	Well-developed	Well-developed network of telecommunications, buses and highways	Moderate; rural area difficult to reach
Human capital[d]	Literacy rate 92%	Literacy rate 77%	Literacy rate 77%
Financial infrastructure	Well developed: sufficient financial institutes active in the rural sector. Long history of rural financial systems (*cajas rurales*). Total offices banking sector 162 (including savings and credit cooperatives)[e]	Concentration of banks in urban sector: total offices bank sector 255 (including savings and credit cooperatives)[f]	Existence of banks in rural area well developed, high concentration in the three main cities. Total offices bank sector 560 (including savings and credit cooperatives)[g]

Sources: [a] Costa Rica: Censo Agropecuario (1984); [b] Ruben (1991); [c] SECPLAN/SRN (1994); [d] CEPAL (1996); [e] Van Andel and Sminia (1995); [f] Wenner and Umaña (1993); [g] Gonzaléz Vega and Torrico (1995).

Table 7.2 Costa Rica: distribution of credit supply among surveyed households in 1987 (includes only borrowers with access in 1987)

Credit source	Distribution of contracts over households with debts in 1987[a] (%)	Distribution of loans as percentage of total amount (%)	Distribution of total loans in cash (%)
Formal	24.5	67.6	80.3
Semiformal	38.3	23.8	14.8
Informal	58.8	8.6	4.9
		100.0	100.0

Source: González Vega *et al.* (1989).
Note: [a] The distribution of contracts does not add up to 100 per cent, as some households used more than one credit source.

Of all rural households, 57 per cent had access to one of the credit sources. The nationalized banks served only 17 per cent of all households. These results were somewhat surprising for the researchers, because they had expected the state-owned banks to play a more important role. Only a fifth of all households had new loans from the formal sector in 1987, and a quarter had loans from the semiformal and informal sector.

The loss of access to formal credit started in 1984, at the end of the economic crisis in Costa Rica that started at the beginning of the 1980s. The restructuring of the national banks led to a reduction of client numbers and loan volume in real terms. Especially the small-scale producers lost their access to formal sources, as resources for the preferential Rural Credit department of the National Bank were severely restricted.[18]

During the 1960s and 1970s, access to credit in Costa Rica concentrated increasingly into fewer hands. The distribution of credit amounts was more unequal than the distribution of land or incomes (González Vega and Mesalles, 1993: 31). There is no evidence as to whether this concentration of credit has been reduced during the financial liberalization measures since the mid-eighties.

In the study of Cuevas *et al.* (1991) on the financial market in *El Salvador*, only 10 per cent of the rural households surveyed (including all kinds of farmers) had access to formal credit, whereas only 6 per cent had access to the banking sector. Access to the Agricultural Development Bank (Banco de Fomento Agropecuario, BFA) for small producers is restricted for two reasons. In the first place there is the weak financial position of the BFA (high administration costs and difficulties in recovering outstanding loans), resulting in credit rationing that mostly affects small scale producers. In the second place there is the debt overhang of the borrowers. Benito (1993: vii) states that the credit delinquency of private medium-sized farmers with the formal sector banks is a factor that explains the low use of formal credit. However, the overhang is only one of the factors. The low use of credit of medium-sized farmers results from a combination of factors affecting credit supply and demand. The low demand for formal credit results, among other factors, from the low expected profitability in agriculture, the competition from the informal sector, and the attitudes engendered by the subsidized credit of the past (Benito, 1993: 28–32). However, the explanation is doubtful in the case of the small-scale or peasant sector. Peasants cannot choose between the different financial sectors, had only partial access to subsidized credit in the past and have to cultivate (profitably or not) to survive. For the small-scale sector, access to the formal sector is simply denied because of the non-availability of a collateral. These farmers cannot prove their solvency to the Agricultural Development Bank (Mol and Sanders, 1995: 34).

About 45 per cent of the interviewed population had access to semi-formal and informal credit in El Salvador. However, it is the informal sector that plays the most important role in the rural sector, not only in terms of number of contracts but also in the amount of the loans. Table 7.3 shows the distribution of contracts of the households with access to credit. The number of contracts is counted and divided by the total sample.[19]

On the other hand, the data showed that about 30 per cent of the rural households have some kind of financial assets. Collateral requirements of the formal sector are mortgages. An interesting point is that 22 per cent lend money to others, mostly friends or relatives. Only 8 per cent have deposits in formal banks. Cuevas *et al.* (1991) mentioned that an important reason for the low participation of rural households in savings accounts is the absence of banks in the rural area. The totals of liabilities of these households exceed 16 per cent of the total assets. Hence, rural households are net debtors of the formal financial system.

Not only the rural household has difficulties obtaining access to formal credit; so too do urban and rural microenterprises and urban households. Medium and larger enterprises play an important role in the financial markets. Those enterprises interlink the formal and informal sector with each other. Lending from the formal sector is partly used to finance activities of their clients. The study shows that more than 76 per cent of the medium enterprises and 84 per cent of the larger ones lend money to their clients.

Table 7.3 El Salvador: number of households with access to credit: distribution of contracts and loans (percent)

Source	Contracts	Loans
Formal	6.1%	17%
Semiformal	4.5%	17%
Informal	47.4%	66%
		100%

Source: Cuevas *et al.* (1991).

In the rural area, there are twice as many contracts with the informal sector as with the formal. The two most important credit sources are the private lenders and the enterprises. The volume of credits is 19 and 40 per cent respectively of the total credit supply. Mortgages and stocks are used as collateral in the semiformal sector, while in the informal sector hardly any collateral is required. However, the informal financial market seems to be relatively small in comparison with other countries in Latin America like Chile, the Dominican Republic and Costa Rica (Cuevas *et al.*, 1991: 81).

As in both other cases, access to credit for small-scale producers in the *Honduran* financial market is restricted. Access to credit is directly related to the ownership of land. The agrarian census of 1993 found that only 6.7 per cent of all rural households included in the census had access to credit in 1993. Of rural households with less than five hectares of land (71.8 per cent of all households), only 4.6 per cent had access to formal credit in 1993.

Only agricultural producers with less than 50 hectares were included in the study of González Vega and Torrico (1995). The total sample included 361 rural households. Table 7.4 shows the distribution of credit sources among households with access in 1994 and before that in the period 1990–4.

In the last five years, 70 per cent obtained loans from different institutions, mostly in the informal sector. Most of the rural households had a credit loan with more than one institution. The 251 borrowers in this period used 439 financial sources. The amounts of loans were

Table 7.4   Access to credit in Honduras*

	1990–4	*1994*
No borrower	110 (30.5%)	128 (35.5%)
Borrower	251 (69.5)	233 (64.5%)
Formal	18.5%	11.6%
Semiformal	18.6%	12.8%
Informal	84.2%	65.6%

Source: González Vega and Torrico (1995).

* The total percentage does not add up to 100 per cent, as some households used more than one credit source. The results given are the total amounts of contracts divided by total population.

small, with more than 50 per cent being less than US$ 150. While the guarantee requirement is high, and mostly backed with a guaranty (55 per cent), one-third of all guaranteed loans were backed with mortgages. Stock collateral hardly exists, which reflects its weak legal status.[20]

With the financial crisis of the National Development Bank (BANADESA), the access to formal credit for small-scale producers is diminishing. This had resulted in a shift from the formal credit sector to the informal one (see Table 7.4).

Segmentation of rural credit markets

Table 7.5 shows some macroeconomic credit indicators for the three countries. If we compare the period 1991–4 with two previous ones (1981–5 and 1986–90, respectively), the relationship between domestic credit and the broad money supply (M2) decreased in all countries, especially El Salvador (from 1.52 to 1.09). The decrease in this factor means that less domestic credit is available in relation to the broad money supply, as a larger part of the M2 is being invested in foreign assets.

The next proportion, credit to the public sector in relation to the total domestic credit (DC_{pub}/DC_{tot}), shows that at the same time there was a shift within the domestic credit portfolio in favor of the private sector, with less domestic credit transferred to the public sector. Again, the strongest shift was in El Salvador, while the proportion of Honduras remained more or less the same. The decrease in credit and

Table 7.5 Macroeconomic indicators (ratios) of Central America

Indicator (ratio)		Costa Rica	El Salvador	Honduras
$DC_{tot}/M2^a$	1981–85	0.87	1.52	1.28
	1986–90	0.85	1.15	1.36
	1991–94	0.64	1.09	1.19
DC_{publ}/DC_{tot}^b	1981–85	47.8	44.2	39.8
	1986–90	50.7	36.8	40.2
	1991–94	38.7	14.7	40.6
DC_{agro}/DC_{tot}^b	1981–85	47.2	24.2	24.7
	1986–90	22.0	13.3	27.0
	1991–94	13.6	17.4	22.8

Sources:
[a] *Consejo Monetario Centroamericano* (various years).
[b] CEPAL (1996).

the portfolio shift mostly affected the agricultural sector (DC_{agro}/DC_{tot}). Strangely enough, the fall of this sector was sharpest in Costa Rica and least in Honduras, where the macrofinancial proportions remained more or less stable, although there is no clear reason for this.[21]

The overall tendency in the rural credit markets in Costa Rica, El Salvador and Honduras is one towards less government intervention. The agrarian development banks (BANADESA in Honduras, BFA in El Salvador, and the rural credit department of the National Bank of Costa Rica) changed their policies and are searching for clients that are more attractive than small-scale producers (larger amounts with lower administration costs) and are using collateral as the most important screening mechanism.

The semiformal and informal institutions are substitutes for the formal sources. This is especially the case in Costa Rica. In general, however, the data show that the role of the semiformal institutions in the three countries is more or less the same as that of the formal institutions (Tables 7.2 to 7.4). They serve more clients, but the amount of the loans is much smaller.

The informal sector is the most important source in all cases. Without doubt, this aspect is only relative. The data are compared with the access to formal and semiformal credit suppliers, and, as mentioned before, these sources are restricted. In comparison with countries in South Asia, where the informal financial sector varies between 30 and 70 per cent of all credit supplies (Ghate, 1992), the informal sector in Central America is small, and is no substitute for the formal and semiformal institutions (Table 7.6).

In general, we can conclude that the rural financial markets in Central America seem to be segmented. However, a 'financial dualism' between formal and informal systems is difficult to detect. There is some overlap and interaction between the different systems. First, most households

Table 7.6   Microeconomic indicators of rural household access to credit in Central America

Household	Costa Rica (1987)[a]	El Salvador (1990)[b]	Honduras (1994)[c]
With access to formal (bank) credit	24.5%	6.0%	18.5%
Without any credit	44.2%	45.0%	35.5%

Sources: [a] Costa Rica – González Vega *et al.* (1989); [b] El Salvador – Cuevas *et al.* (1991); [c] Honduras – González Vega and Torrico (1995).

use more than one credit source, of which combinations of credit loans of formal and informal are not uncommon. Second, formal credits are 'channeled through' to informal sectors (for example, input suppliers), as in the case of El Salvador. This does not mean that the mobility between the sectors is unrestricted. The different credit suppliers tend to display certain biases, particularly in the case of the formal sector. The group of rural clients is selected by this sector on the basis of the collateral requirements, so the non-availability of collateral pushed a large group of households into the semi-formal and informal sectors. There are a lot of semi-formal financial institutions, but they can only serve a part of all households. So, many households can use only the informal sector, but for some households the transaction costs are too high. For these cases, a credit market does not exist at all.

Conclusions and policy implications

In this chapter we have reviewed the theoretical and empirical basis for financial liberalization, and its relevance for the supply of rural credit in Central America. We have seen that financial reforms do not lead necessarily to more savings, more investment and more growth. The international debate between neoclassical and post-Keynesian economists about this line of reasoning still continues, and each party presents partial empirical evidence for its thesis.

The Latin American experiences with financial reform have shown that there are several risks involved in liberalization strategies. The danger of financial crisis exists when the monetary authorities do not exercise effective control over the banking sector – which actually happened in Central America with the *financieras* in the first half of the 1980s. The risk of moral hazard and regressive income distribution effects within the financial system is most often mentioned where governments intervene, but is equally likely within the private banking sector. Also, for the liberalization strategy to be successful, certain macroeconomic preconditions must be met that are very difficult to control in the open economies of Central America. All these arguments, however, do not mean that financial liberalization is useless or harmful, but rather that a very prudent strategy is required from the government in order to control the process.

The financial reforms in Costa Rica and El Salvador have led only partially to financial deepening. The broad money supply has increased, but mainly because of the growth of secondary liquidity (including dollar deposits) creating a monetary overhang that represents a risk for medium-term financial policy. The increased financial intermediation is not reflected in a higher availability of domestic credit, but rather is used to improve the position of the countries in the international financial markets (paying external debts or accumulating foreign exchange reserves).

The financial reforms have indeed induced drastic changes in the composition of the credit portfolios. Credit to the public sector has significantly reduced, and the share of credit to the private sector has increased. The agricultural sector has suffered a severe drop in its share of the total allocation of credit.

The spreads in the banking system continue to be quite high (above 10 per cent). In Costa Rica, the partial measures of financial reform did not reduce the intermediation margins, but rather opened the way for the private banks to exploit the rents of an oligopolistic financial market dominated by two or three state banks.

Strangely enough, it seems that Honduras was somehow not affected by these phenomena. This might indicate that in Honduras the economic stabilization measures have not been applied effectively, although there is little evidence to support such a thesis.

The surveys done by Ohio State University in the three countries provide at least suggestive evidence for the segmentation of the rural financial markets. Despite the relatively developed nature of the Costa Rican economy, the access of small farmers to formal credit is not significantly higher than in Honduras. Also, the use of informal credit is more or less the same in Costa Rica as in Honduras.

The segmentation of credit is determined by two types of factors: structural determinants (household characteristics) and non-structural determinants (like the macroeconomic environment and the soundness of the financial sector). The financial reforms affect only the latter, while for rural financial markets and small farmers the former seems to be the real bottleneck. Therefore it is improbable that financial liberalization would lead to any significant improvement in the access of small rural entrepreneurs to finance.

On the other hand, the same argument can be used to state that financial reform does not lead to a significant deterioration of small farmers' access to rural finance. The reduction of agricultural bank credit will fall mostly on the shoulders of rent-seeking groups like big cattle farmers, military entrepreneurs, and some of the land reform groups. The rise in bank interest rates might, however, induce a shift of resources from informal intermediaries to the banks, which may affect the availability of informal credit for small-scale rural entrepreneurs.

Rather than by financial reform, the rural credit problem should be tackled by attacking the structural causes of the lack of access to credit, which are reflected in the segmentation of the rural financial markets. Therefore, more attention should be given to existing market failures and institutional barriers in the financial markets with respect to access to credit for small firms and farms. In a world of imperfect markets, financial liberalization does not always promote better access to credit, especially not for the poor.

Notes

1. Usually regarded as semiformal institutions are non-governmental organizations (NGOs) and organizations such as cooperatives and credit unions. Although regulated in certain aspects, they retain the essential informality of the informal sector.
2. For instance, the model specifications used by Fry (1988) often do not endogenize the main relationships between the relevant variables, and in some cases apparently misspecified equations lead to incomplete interpretations (see Gibson and Tsakalotos 1994: 596, for more details).
3. Gupta (1987) found that the interest rate effect is weaker in Latin American countries than in Asia. Warman and Thirlwall (1994), in a study on Mexico, confirmed a positive interest rate effect on financial savings, but could not find a significant effect on total or private savings.
4. In Costa Rica, for instance, where the banking system was nationalized in 1948, the private banks emerged after the 1981–2 world economic crisis, mainly on the basis of supplying dollar deposit facilities to the private sector and to the public. Because of legal restrictions, these dollar activities were channeled through their own offshore banks, outside the reach of the Costa Rican monetary authorities. The Costa Rican Central Bank recognizes that this phenomenon may severely hamper the effectiveness of the supervision by the superintendance. This is further aggravated by the presence of narco-dollars, which are obviously not being effectively supervised by the monetary authorities (at best, some of this money appears under 'errors and omissions' in the balance of payments), but whose scale seems to be large enough to unbalance the financial system. Whether and on what scale there exist relationships between private banks and these irregular dollar flows is still unknown.
5. There seem to be indications of a process of concentration of banking activity in fewer hands, under pressure from the opening of the banking sector to new entrants from abroad. For example, the largest private bank in Honduras recently bought all the shares of the Banco de Occidente, which is the fourth largest bank in the country and the most active in rural areas. Similar phenomena took place during the reprivatization of the Salvadoran banks (1992–6).
6. There are enough examples of this behaviour: the FODEA Law in Costa Rica (1983), the 'banana crisis' of the 1990s in the same country, the debt condonations in favor of the large cattle holders and military by BANADESA in Honduras – to mention only a few.

7. 'Equilibrium rationing of credit' refers to the situation where free market forces establish an interest rate, but nonetheless rationing of credit persists (see Cosci, 1993).

8. In the new institutional economics, the transactions are explained in terms of two contractual parties: the principal and the agent. The principal provides resources to the agent and must assure himself that the resources are efficiently utilized and that the agent will grant him his right share of the benefits.

9. We are aware of the fact that to explain market segmentation only as a result of non-availability of collateral is too simplistic. Credit rationing also includes a lot of subjective social and political factors. For instance, female-headed households or etnnic minorities in general encounter more difficulties in obtaining credit than do (white) male-headed households.

10. Stiglitz and Weiss (1981), for instance, indicate that the intertemporal character of the credit market is responsible for the rationing phenomenon, which would make credit rationing a commodity-specific market failure.

11. Hoff and Stiglitz (1990) explain in their article that the interest rate on loans has a certain ceiling, that can be lower than the market clearing level. Higher interest rates would attract borrowers with riskier investment behavior (adverse selection and incentive effects). Therefore there is a limit to the incorporation of information costs in the interest rate.

12. However, while De Janvry *et al.* (1991) include structural constraints in their approach, they cannot explain why, when the interest rate is lower than the shadow price of capital for a household and the household would thus become a net buyer of capital, the access of certain households to credit is still restricted. This cannot be explained through borrower transaction costs only. Neither do they indicate what kind of policy prescriptions are necessary to relax the credit constraint for certain households.

13. In the case of the rural credit market, the price band is the difference between the net remuneration of monetary savings and the implicit costs of informal loans.

14. The monetary overhang can destabilize the exchange rate, resulting in an overvalued Salvadoran colón, which has negative results for the (agricultural) export sector, while imports increase, affecting for example the domestic market for basic cereals.

15. The data only report direct credit to the agricultural sector. No accounts are available of credits to agribusiness and agro-trade that could be used to finance production indirectly. These indirect credit flows may have offset part of the reduction in agricultural credit.

16. For a century, the coffee elite was the most powerful group in El Salvador. 'The domestic banking industry was entirely based on coffee wealth, and the leading banks were controlled by coffee families until they were nationalized in 1980' (Paige, 1993: 10). However, while the economic importance of the coffee elite has decreased, they still have a lot of influence in the political arena.

17. The credit supply as a percentage of total added value differs greatly between coffee and maize. In 1993 the added value of cereals was more than the added value of the traditional export crops – 2454 and 1792 millions of Salvadoran

colónes respectively. Meanwhile the credit absorption of the coffee sector was more than 85 times that of the basic cereal sector.

18. The National Bank of Costa Rica (BNCR) has a rural credit department that is specialized in credit lines for small farmers, and during the first half of the twentieth century it was the most important formal source for this sector. The quantity of loans declined drastically during the last decades, from more than 52 000 in 1976 to less than 11 400 in 1993. The average real loan amount increased from 7500 to 9820 colones (Colones of 1978) (*La Nación*, 22 September 1994).

19. Cuevas *et al.* (1991) analyzed only the number of contracts and the market relations, and ignored the structural aspects that exist behind the markets. It is not possible with the data available to analyze which type of household has access to credit and how the credit is distributed among households.

20. At the moment the Honduran government is working on a new law for stock collateral. This will improve the legal enforcement of stock collateral.

21. It might indicate that Honduras is the only country where the standard effect of structural adjustment, an improvement of the terms of trade for the agricultural sector, is actually being realized. An alternative explanation, however, might be that the adjustment or stabilization measures just have not been fully implemented. The stable proportion of public credit gives an indication of this.

8

Rural Off-Farm Employment and Food Security Policies in Honduras

Ruerd Ruben and Harry Clemens

Introduction

Agricultural development policies in Honduras focused for a long time on issues of rural production and commercialization. Since the beginning of the land reform process in 1972, most attention has been dedicated to the redistribution of national land and the allocation of ample credit resources in order to stabilize the rural population in the countryside while controlling rural political unrest (Ruhl, 1984; Brockett, 1988). These policies culminated in the 1980s in a massive program of land titling – trying to establish stable property rights for small and medium farm households.

While the redistributive impact of these policies was highly limited, it proved to be surprisingly effective in the creation of a new dynamism on the rural labor market. Instead of establishing viable family farms where rural families are able to fulfill their reproduction requirements, a high proportion of marginal sub-family farm households became increasingly engaged in off-farm employment and seasonal intra-rural migration, especially towards coffee-producing regions (Baumeister, 1996: 45). Consequently, prospects for food security depend less on farm production and far more on the available purchasing power generated from rural employment and wage levels.

This rather particular migration pattern tends to be typical for semi-arid areas with high risks and weather variability, where access to rural financial markets is severely restricted (Reardon *et al.*, 1992; 1994). Rural off-farm employment may then serve as a substitute for lending, while restricting permanent out-migration towards urban centers. The recent restructuring of the financial system, imposing restrictions on access to (formerly subsidized) credit, has obliged farmers to accept wage labor in order to maintain household expenditures and to stabilize their subsistence production.

The increasing importance of rural off-farm employment implies that farm households are looking for options to overcome capital market constraints. Remaining farm production will first become more extensive, while expenditure effects of off-farm income may lead later on to farm investments that permit a transition towards more stable and sustainable production systems. Moreover, the procedures to guarantee food security have also been adjusted, as less emphasis is required to support production with inputs or technical assistance, and better results are expected from rural employment programs.

The main objectives of this chapter are: (1) to analyze the income composition of small farm households and the contributions of off-farm income to food security, (2) to discuss the role of off-farm labor allocation in farm household decisions on consumption, saving and investment, in order to cope with food insecurity and (3) to acknowledge the policy implications of the increasing role of off-farm income for rural food security. These issues are discussed against the background of the current food security situation and policies in Honduras.

Food security situation and policies in Honduras

The issue of food security in Honduras can be analyzed from the viewpoint of general availability of food, as well as from the perspective of access to food. Until the beginning of the 1980s, most attention was devoted to measures to increase food production, while the latter perspective of food consumption and purchasing power gained importance during the structural adjustment process (World Bank, 1994). This shift in emphasis is directly related to the increased market involvement of peasant producers during the agrarian reform process, and the recent liberalization of rural commodity and financial markets.

Land reform policies in Honduras devoted major attention to the conversion of formerly underutilized national land into cropping land, through the assignment of land titles and the establishment of cooperative enterprises. Although redistributive effects remained rather limited, the impact on rural commercialization was very substantial. After thirty years of land reform, the level of monetarization of production in Honduras increased from 13 per cent in 1960 to 36 per cent in 1990, reaching second position in Central America, just behind Costa Rica (Wattel *et al.*, 1994: 22). Simultaneously, the general credit disbursement increased from less than 12 per cent in 1960 to more than 30 per cent of the national product in 1990, indicating a strong engagement with more technology intensive and commercially oriented production (ibid.: 23).[1] This emphasis on market production was especially promoted by the government, offering subsidized credit and state marketing services to capture an important share of basic grains production in order to guarantee national food security (Brockett, 1988).

This dynamic experienced an important modification after the introduction of structural adjustment policies and the implementation of the so-called Agrarian Modernization Program. Formal credit supply for basic grains production was reduced to only 3.2 per cent of all credit disbursements and interest rates were severely increased (Arce, 1995: 13). Internal trade was completely liberalized, while regional trade within the Central American Common Market was encouraged. Within this framework, less emphasis was given to production-enhancing measures, as food security could be equally reached through market exchange. In fact, purchasing power appeared as the major limiting factor to maintain food security prospects, and involvement of the rural population in the labor market became a critical component in the strategies to combat poverty and malnutrition.

Empirical assessments of the development of supply aspects of food security measured by per capita apparent consumption between 1975–9 and 1990–4 indicate a continuous decrease in the availability of maize, while the availability of rice, milk and eggs virtually stagnated and wheat, sugar and meat production clearly increased (see Figure 8.1). These aggregate figures reflect a tendency towards more urban-oriented consumption patterns based on high energy and fat intake and reduced levels of protein consumption.

Recent figures on national basic grains production confirm the steady low levels of yield compared with neighboring countries, but also indicate a recovery of cropped area of almost 7 per cent a year after market liberalization in 1990 (World Bank, 1994: 43). During the last six years, however, food imports have remained important, with maize, rice and wheat under the PL480 US aid program arrangement in the most prominent position, accounting on average for 23 per cent of national consumption. The Western and Southern regions in particular face continuous food deficits owing to their poor agro-ecological conditions, the limited diversification of cropping patterns and illegal exports to El Salvador (Pino and Perdomo, 1990). Malnutrition is significantly higher in the Western region than in any other region of the country (Rogers *et al.*, 1996: 37–52).

Figure 8.1 Honduras: apparent consumption of basic food products (1975–94)

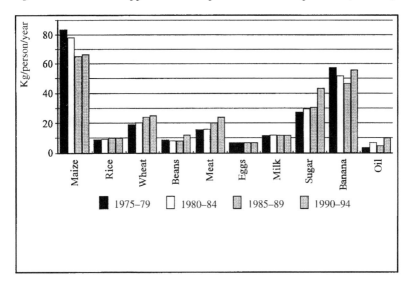

Source: USAID, 1994, based on DGEC data various years.

With respect to incomes and purchasing power to guarantee access to food products, in 1992 about 42 per cent of rural households were living below the poverty level (World Bank, 1994: 67), indicating some improvement compared with figures of the 1980s (Menjívar and Trejos, 1990). As rural producer prices increased at a faster rate than rural wages, farm households in a net supply position benefited most, while urban and rural net consuming households will have suffered losses. Real wages are also being eroded by the increasing inflation and the still overvalued exchange rate.

In recent years, the food security policies of the Honduran Government have focused mainly on production of basic grains, although the importance of access to food is increasingly recognized. When the Reina administration took power in 1994, an Action Plan for Food and Nutritional Security was formulated and an inter-institutional technical team was formed (Gobierno de Honduras, 1996: 5). A first step in the process towards operationalization of this Action Plan was the design of an Immediate Action Plan for 1994–95, which concentrated on basic grains production. Next, a more comprehensive strategy was elaborated, which culminated in a document presented to the World Food Summit in November 1995 (ibid.).

This document details policies within three main programs, aimed at increased and more stable availability of food, better access to food and improved nutritional intake. Most attention is devoted to policies aimed at improving and stabilizing food availability within the framework of the agrarian modernization program. An important role is foreseen for a modernized national research and extension system with high participation of private agents and NGOs and extension services by internationally financed rural development projects. Improved tenancy security, private investment in basic grains and other food production stimulated by free markets, as well as other specific measures, should promote basic grains production. The latter include interest rate subsidies and a guarantee fund created by the Central Bank, as well as low import tariffs for agricultural equipment. Free trade within the Central American regional market is promoted, with relative protection from external imports through a system of floating tariffs within a price band. Specific policies are proposed to reduce market imperfections of product markets at a national level (market information, creation of a maize-exchange market, and provision of decentralized food storage). In addition, the establishment of a strategic stock of maize and beans is proposed.

Policies to improve access to food include the promotion of rural development projects and programs, as well as social compensation programs. The latter include a large-scale program of food distribution through schools and health centers (the Family Assignment Program, PRAF), and employment creation by the Honduran Social Investment Fund (FHIS). Moreover, programs to improve nutrition intake are being developed with local institutions, both governmental and non-governmental. Better health conditions are seen as a basic requirement to improve biological utilization of food.

It can be concluded that the food security policies are of a rather general nature. The main focus is on increasing production and marketing of food commodities. In addition, social programs are being developed to improve nutrition of marginalized groups and to compensate for negative effects of adjustment policies. Policies to increase access to food are only implemented solely in the context of aid and social compensation, and only marginally address prospects to improve the purchasing-power capacities for sustainable food access by the rural poor. A thorough assessment of rural poverty and food security prospects at the household level, based on the analysis of income composition and simultaneous engagement of households in various factor and commodity markets, is generally lacking. As we will show, off-farm employment is an important part of household strategies to cope with food insecurity, in the face of the high risks associated with traditional agricultural production and of the failures of markets for finance and land.

The role of off-farm employment for food security

Most macroeconomic studies on agricultural development provide a perspective on food security and agricultural transformation by focusing on phenomena like the transfer of labor from agriculture to other sectors of the economy, the change of technology for agricultural modernization, and the role of public investment (Hayami and Ruttan, 1985; Timmer, 1988). These approaches mainly consider growth potentials outside the agricultural sector, and tend to neglect available options for the transformation of farm household economies based on intra-rural linkages.

Microeconomic studies tend to deal with the rural transformation process from various perspectives. Early research on the role and consequences of off-farm employment for farm households focused on the low opportunity costs of labor permitting easy mobilization of surplus labor without causing major distortions in prevailing agricultural production systems (Sen, 1966; Todaro, 1969). Traditional neoclassical theory is based on the marginal cost principle to explain current labor allocation and land use (Schultz, 1964; Rosenzweig, 1980). In this 'poor but efficient' approach, most attention is devoted to policy measures to enhance technical efficiency, while internal mechanisms for resource allocation decisions by the farm household are not clearly acknowledged, and options for off-farm employment are neglected. Similarly, political economy for a long time considered engagement in the labor market to be a manifestation of disintegration of the peasant economy.

Within the framework of institutional economics, the rationality of off-farm employment and its potential positive role for the survival of the farm household economy receives new attention. Based on contributions from agricultural decisions analysis, uncertainty and risk behavior are recognized as guiding principles for factor allocation (Moscardi and De Janvry, 1977). Moreover, within the framework of agricultural household modeling, expenditure effects of labor use receive thorough attention (Singh *et al.*, 1986). Supply response, however, proved to be strongly dependent on the possibilities for the adjustment of factor allocation and the flexibility in production techniques (Fafchamps, 1993). Therefore, off-farm employment could be evaluated like an investment decision within the framework of factor substitution, risk preferences and seasonality (Rosenzweig and Binswanger, 1993).

Income diversification is considered an important device to enhance food security, since specialization in traditional agricultural production is associated with high risks (Moscardi and De Janvry, 1977). Engagement in off-farm employment can also be used to respond to specific failures on the local markets for finance and/or land. Increasing labor demands from the rapidly expanding coffee sector facilitate intra-rural migration, enabling the payment of wages sufficient to compensate for opportunity and transaction costs (Skoufias, 1994). Otherwise, some households are able to develop local alternatives for non-agricultural self-employment, but these activities are open mainly to a small segment of medium-size households that can get access to finance for the initial capital investment.

Market interactions proved to be an important element in explaining decisions on farm household labor allocation. Under conditions of market fragmentation or missing markets, internal adjustment of factor intensity tends to replace market response (De Janvry *et al.*, 1991). Price bands at factor markets affect tradability and reduce prospects for factor substitution. In the case of selective failure on the financial market, seasonal engagement in off-farm employment could serve as a substitute to maintain consumptive and capital expenditures. This implies a temporal adjustment of crop and technology choice at farm level.

Linkages between seasonal labor allocation decisions and farm-household savings and investment behavior provide a new perspective on issues of food security and sustainable land use. With absent or ill-functioning finance and insurance markets, off-farm employment is an important device for portfolio diversification and risk management (Saha, 1994; Rosenzweig and Binswanger, 1993). Off-farm employment can also become a substitute for collateral, thus contributing to improved access to financial markets (Collier and Lal, 1986). Expenditure analyses indicate that a substantial share of the income derived from off-farm employment is used for initial investment in perennial crops (Burger, 1994) or for the purchase of productive inputs, equipment or livestock that permit a subsequent improvement of the farm-level resource base (Reardon *et al.*, 1994). Marginal savings depend on the kind of activities and the source of earnings. Expenditure effects from farm and off-farm income will result in different propensities to save out of each income category (Kelly and Williamson, 1968).

Recent studies reveal that off-farm activities provide an increasing share of household income in developing countries (Anderson and

Leierson, 1980; Weber *et al.*, 1988; White and Wiradi, 1989; Haggblade *et al.*, 1989; Reardon *et al.*, 1992, Burger, 1994). Some of these studies concentrate on endogenous factors that induce farm households to undertake activities outside agriculture, such as motives of consumption smoothing, risk avoidance, or ensuring food security under adverse weather conditions (Reardon *et al.*, 1988; Deaton, 1990). Other studies focus more on relative prices. The farm household model of Low (1986) addressed off-farm employment of food deficit households as determined by the ratio of labor opportunity costs and the retail price of purchased food. Within the same line of reasoning, Goetz (1992) developed a selectivity model of market participation and tradability of production factors and commodities. These studies devote most attention to the income-generating effects of off-farm employment and the resulting increased expenditure opportunities.

This question is especially relevant for agro-ecological marginal regions (semi-arid tropics, hillsides, etc.) where erratic rainfall conditions, degraded soils and highly variable yields make lending operations highly risky, and financial institutions are reluctant to supply rural credit, owing to high risks and transactions costs for serving small peasant farm households. Resource-poor farm households can become more easily engaged in the labor market, since labor is an abundant and highly divisible resource, and off-farm employment can be used as a substitute for lending, as well as for risk diversification. Precautionary savings are required to guarantee subsistence consumption in case of adverse weather conditions or unexpected family expenditures, explaining the diversity in off-farm labor engagement among households according to their life cycle. Demand for labor is on the increase, both from the cities and from commercial agricultural enterprises, for example coffee. When commodity markets are more developed and investment opportunities at farm level are available, the willingness to work and to invest can be evaluated from the viewpoint of differential earning opportunities in spatially distinct labor markets. Taking into account transaction costs, seasonal intra-rural migration may be preferred over rural–urban migration.

Labor allocation decisions that induce farm households to spend part of their labor resources outside their own farm depend on productive and consumptive preferences, as well as specific household characteristics. Farm size, market distance, age, education and gender are considered major factors that influence transaction costs and substitution elasticity between capital and labor. Large households and younger, more educated household members normally face lower transaction costs in finding off-farm employment, while small families and female-headed households with a high dependency rate tend to be less mobile (Bradshaw, 1995). Moreover, the quality of land resources and distance to markets and market information may cause differences among farm households with respect to their engagement in off-farm employment.

The consequences of off-farm employment for factor substitution at farm level are twofold. First, off-farm labor use will lead to less intensive production systems. Returns from off-farm income can be used subsequently for intensification of production and ultimately may result in a higher labor productivity at farm level, thus reducing incentives for further migration. The expenditure effects of off-farm income thus compensate for financial market failure. This flow of remittances will contribute ultimately to the stabilization of family farms if these are used for investment purposes. These farm-level investments increase fixed costs and will thus encourage farm continuation. Off-farm employment can be considered as a risk-reducing device, as non-cropping income is less covariant with local agricultural production, and thus contributes to stabilization of rural purchasing power (Reardon *et al.*, 1988).

The understanding of the interlinkages between off-farm labor allocation and farm household decisions on consumption, saving and investment, as well as their consequences for land use and technology choice within farm households, may lead to important policy consequences. Current rural or agricultural development programs aim predominantly at intensification of resource use and/or improvement of input efficiency, and are often implemented through a mixture of technical assistance and financial incentives such as input price subsidies. Labor opportunity costs are mostly neglected, and off-farm employment is erroneously considered as a 'drain' and thus only mobilized for temporary food-for-work activities. Misspecification or neglect of the potential saving and investment function of off-farm employment may easily lead to inadequate policy recommendations. Attention to the linkages between off-farm employment and savings and investment decisions provides a more comprehensive perspective and may result in policies enabling lending for the creation of rural non-farm employment opportunities, as well as incentives for the investment of off-farm income to improve agricultural production systems.

Farm household incomes and off-farm employment in Honduras

Rural households depend on different sources of income, and therefore food security can be guaranteed in different ways. Simultaneous engagement in various factor and commodity markets may contribute to food consumption, whether the items eaten are produced at the farm, purchased through market exchange or both. For most small farm households, home production of basic grains represents only a minor part of total family income (up to 30 per cent in farms of up to 3.5 hectares). Additionally, wage income from local employment and/or from seasonal migration towards other rural regions is of fundamental importance to generate additional cash flow, which is used both for consumption purposes as well as for the purchase of necessary farm inputs. In Honduras, the overwhelming majority of rural households are found within the farm size category of less than 3.5 hectares; in 1993, 39 per cent of the rural households were registered as landless laborers (202 000 families), and 37 per cent of the households possessed less than 3.5 hectares (192 000 families), while only 24 per cent had access to more than 3.5 hectares of farm land (EC, 1994; SECPLAN/SRN, 1994).

According to the National Socio-Economic Household Survey of 1993–4 (USAID, 1994), average rural income is lowest for the stratum of farm households with less than 3.5 hectares. While on-farm labor allocation generates only 31 per cent of total income, off-farm activities generate as much as 69 per cent of total income, compared with 23 per cent for the larger farm household categories (see Table 8.1). This implies that – on average – small farm households spend 58 eight-hour working days on farm activities generating on average 17 lempiras (L) per day, while off-farm activities are undertaken during 186 days and generate a daily income of 11.7 L (USAID, 1994: 18–23). Although the income share from off-farm activities is far more important, the

Table 8.1 Income composition of rural households in Honduras.
(The average exchange rate of the Honduran lempira during the period was between 7 and 8 per US dollar.)

	On-farm income		Off-farm income		Total income
	L*	%	L*	%	L*
Rural non-agricultural households	0	0	4 368	100	4 368
Farm households < 3.5 ha	986	31	2 176	69	3 162
Farm households > 3.5 ha	4 836	77	1 416	23	6 252

Source: USAID (1994: 18–23).

* Honduran lempiras.

remuneration level for seasonal wage labor is still below the farm-level opportunity costs of labor. Compared with the average wage level for permanent wage labor supplied by rural non-agricultural households (17.9 L per day), off-farm labor from small farm households is clearly less remunerative.

A POSCAE–UNAH Survey during the 1991–2 cycle registered a particularly high dependence on off-farm income for the Southern department of Valle (76 per cent of household income) and for the Western departments of Ocotepeque (72 per cent), Intibuca (71 per cent), Santa Barbara (63 per cent) and Lempira (60 per cent), while these figures are only slightly less for departments in the Northern Atlantic Coast: Cortes (62 per cent), Atlantida (54 per cent) and Colon (52 per cent) (POSCAE–UNAH, 1992: 43). It can be argued that dependency on off-farm income is highest in those departments where the average rural per capita income is lowest, mainly in Western Honduras (USAID, 1994: 14–17; SECPLAN/OIT/FNUAP, 1992).

Off-farm employment is provided in both agricultural and non-agricultural activities. Engagement in rural non-agricultural employment of a more permanent nature is most important for rural wage laborers or tenants without fixed access to land, while small farm households rely more on seasonal labor in agricultural activities. The Continuous Labor Force Survey in Rural Areas of 1986–7 compiled detailed information on seasonal fluctuations of rural employment. Non-agricultural rural activities (small industries, trade and services) offer employment to about 28 per cent of the rural economic active population. Fairly small seasonal fluctuations were found, with a peak in February–March (31 per cent), when employment in maize and sorghum is at its lowest point (13 per cent, including both on-farm and off-farm employment). Its lowest level is reached in May–June (26 per cent), when labor demand by the latter crops is high (39 per cent) (Howard-Borjas, 1989: 49, 59).

Small landholders earn income mainly from arable cropping and small livestock activities, while off-farm agricultural labor is a complementary income source. A survey executed by the food security program of CADESCA in 1987–8 analyzed gross income composition of distinct categories of basic grain producers. The lower stratum, with less than 2.5 ha, derived 38 per cent of gross income from crops, 23 per cent from livestock and 39 per cent off-farm (see Table 8.2). Off-farm income was provided mainly by agricultural employment (22 per cent) and other non-agricultural employment (12 per cent), and far less by small industries, trade and transport services (5 per cent).

Table 8.2   Honduras: composition of gross income of small basic-grains producers[a] 1987–8 (per cent)

Agricultural production		
Basic grains	34	
Other crops	4	38
Livestock		
Pigs	2	
Chicken meat/eggs	14	
Cattle raising/milk	7	23
Off-farm income		
Small industry	1	
Trade	4	
Other agricultural	22	
Other non-agricultural	12	39
Total		100

Source: CADESCA (1989: 67–80).
Note: [a] Producers with less than 2.5 hectares of land.

In the case of Honduras an important source of off-farm income is provided by wage labor during the coffee harvest, and its importance has been growing over the last two decades. Labor demands for coffee production are highly seasonal, creating employment for 14 per cent of the rural labor force in the month of December, compared with 3 per cent in June (Howard-Borjas, 1989: 49, 59, based on the 1986–7 Rural Labor Force Survey). In the beginning of the 1990s, the contribution of the coffee sector towards rural employment has steadily increased, as coffee production was 70 per cent higher in 1994–5 compared with 1986–7 (UPSA–SRN, 1995: 23). Labor demand for coffee harvesting in December can be estimated at 198 500 persons by 1995, compared with 317 000 farm households. Part of this demand is covered by off-farm employment, while another part is supplied by on-farm sources, as 29 per cent of all farm households already incorporated coffee in their production system (Baumeister, 1996: 270–1).

Most coffee harvesting is done by members of small farm households, and provides them with a major income source. It has been estimated that total income generated by coffee harvesting (excluding other harvesting activities) must have been equal to 78 per cent of total added value of basic grains production (maize, beans, sorghum and rice) in 1992, a year of low coffee prices and low wages in coffee picking. This weight increased to 97 per cent in 1995 when coffee prices rose and subsequently higher wages were paid.

No precise information is available on incomes earned by small farm households from non-agricultural activities. However, most of these activities in rural areas tend to be low-paid, as indicated by the average earning in off-farm employment (11.8 L per day for off-farm activities, compared with 17 L per day for on-farm labor). Earnings in coffee harvesting are generally higher, but in the remaining months rural labor demand is low and earning opportunities decline considerably. Apart from agricultural wages, income from non-agricultural wage labor and from a wide range of own account activities is important for total household income. According to the 1993–4 Household Survey, contribution by remittances from family members to household income is fairly limited in Honduras, contributing less than 6 per cent of total income in rural areas (Rogers *et al.*, 1996: 78).[2] Migration to urban centers is dependent on the availability of savings, as transport and settlement are capital-intensive activities. It is doubtful whether the poorest rural strata can 'afford' migration towards the cities or abroad.

Limited research has been done on the use of off-farm income by Honduran small farm households. It can be expected to differ according to the type of income source, the time of the year and, related to this, the level of payments. Daily family income from coffee picking tends to be higher than income from off-farm activities in the low season. Part of the income derived from coffee picking will be used for consumption expenditures, but another part may be applied for buying inputs (weed control, fertilizers) to grow maize and other basic food items in subsequent months. Off-farm income in the low season, when employment opportunities are scarce, wage levels low and food stocks decreasing, can be expected to contribute to food security when a high proportion will be spent on consumption priorities in order to survive. Otherwise, remittances from family members living in urban areas or abroad might, however, also contribute to investment in agrarian production (purchase of inputs, equipment, cattle, or, even, land).

In conclusion, rural households, and particularly small farm households, are inclined to diversify their income composition. Basic grains production is only a minor component of income, and food security depends on a wide spectrum of income-generating activities. Income diversification is necessary because of high risks associated with traditional agricultural production, while off-farm employment is also used to respond to specific failures on the local markets for finance and/or land. In the case of Honduras, increasing labor demands from the rapidly expanding coffee sector have facilitated intra-rural migration, enabling the payment of wages sufficient to compensate for opportunity and transaction costs. Some other households are able to develop local alternatives for non-agricultural self-employment, but these activities are mainly open only to a small segment of medium-size households with sufficient access to finance for the initial capital investment.

Policy implications

In an environment of increasing market integration and liberalization of national and regional food markets, food security of households depends critically on purchasing power to buy food. Income diversification strategies of rural households mean that policies to encourage food security should go far beyond promotion of basic grains production. In essence, food security policies become very similar to poverty alleviation policies.

There is a growing consensus that the design of rural poverty alleviation policies will benefit from distinguishing different types of poor rural households and their specific sources of income (Valdés and Wiens, 1996: 23). A distinction can be made between three types of poor rural households: (1) small farms with real prospects for increasing their agricultural productivity, (2) rural households whose real destiny lies in the off-farm labor market or non-farm self-employment, and (3) rural households that have no prospects for escaping abject poverty.

Enhancing agricultural productivity of small farm households can include both basic grains production and diversification of crops. In large parts of Honduras, diversification through partial substitution of basic grains production by coffee growing has proven to be a suitable way to increase income and improve food security of small farmers (Baumeister, 1996). Access to land suitable for growing coffee or other commercial crops is an essential condition for this strategy. Policy instruments to overcome constraints and imperfections on the land and capital markets are important to facilitate agricultural intensification and the conversion of sub-family farms with insufficient production to feed the peasant family, into viable production units.

With respect to basic grains production and self provision by small farmers of the first type, which may maintain an important role in a diversified production system, risk-reducing strategies, including crop association, improved selection of seeds, and so on, can be encouraged through research and extension programs. Because many rural households buy food in pre-harvest time, price policies should focus particularly on improving inter-seasonal stability of prices at the local level by reducing market imperfections (Fafchamps *et al.*, 1995). Information dissemination on market prices, implementation of import price bands at the Central American level (which requires the cooperation of the Government of El Salvador), promotion of local storage facilities, improved access to pre- and post-harvest credit for producers, and public investment in rural access roads may contribute to these objectives.[3]

Owing to existing capital market imperfections, off-farm income may well play a pivotal role in the conversion of sub-family farms into viable production units. The size and nature of the linkages between rural off-farm employment and the farm household economy can be divided into demand effects and productivity effects (Haggblade *et al.*, 1989). At the household level, the latter are of particular importance. They include the use of generated savings to reinforce the farm-level resource base or for the improvement of resource use efficiency. Off-farm labor allocation may thus be enhanced without sacrificing production, and will lead eventually to an increasing on-farm level labor productivity. Secondary effects of off-farm employment in obtaining additional skills and experience reinforce this tendency. These may favor earning opportunities in subsequent periods, and could also improve farm management capacities.

In the case of Honduras, coffee harvesting provides an important opportunity for earning seasonal off-farm income that can be invested in the farm. Intra-rural migration facilitates this mechanism for a large group of rural households. Another group of households may use income opportunities in urban areas (family members working in domestic services, industrial processing zones, and so on) to overcome financial market restrictions for farm development.

For the second group of rural households, whose destiny lies in the off-farm labor market or in non-farm self-employment, direct promotion of rural off-farm employment creation tends to be important. Major bottlenecks for productive employment in rural areas are fragmented financial and commodity markets (De Janvry *et al.*, 1991). Since rural financial markets are highly segmented, institutional innovations and new financial technologies are required to improve access to financial services by rural households and entrepreneurs (Zeller *et al.*, 1997). Development of local credit and savings institutions could be promoted, based on the articulation of these schemes within a wider network, enabling an adequate portfolio diversification of risks among sectors and territories. Providing access to credit without conditions for tying it to investment in specific crops or technologies could reduce the high default rates experienced by many former agricultural credit schemes in the region. In fact, recent experiences with community banks and other local credit and savings institutions show that the provision of credit for non-agricultural rural activities meets high demand, while access was highly restricted by former credit programs (Clemens and Wattel, 1997).

Education and training of rural people seems to be another crucial policy area for enhancing the possibilities for success of this group in off-farm activities (Valdés and Wiens, 1996). This holds for both wage labor and for self-employment, even though the kind of skills required may differ. Current educational or training programs in rural areas are highly underdeveloped, and even worsening because of public expenditure cuts. Giving priority to public education expenditure in rural areas is therefore required.

However, the efficiency of promotion of rural off-farm employment creation also depends on the agrarian structure, because of the demand effects of linkages between rural off-farm employment and the agricultural economy. Weller (1997: 85–8) shows that a more homogenous agrarian sector, in terms of average labor productivity by different farms and agricultural enterprises, creates better conditions for more productive and well-paid off-farm income opportunities. Therefore, priority of policies to facilitate small and medium farm development, over policies to promote large agricultural enterprises, is also essential for those rural households whose destiny lies in off-farm employment. Small and medium farm development depends mainly on addressing constraints for the functioning of factor and commodity markets, while these are less relevant for larger agricultural enterprises.

Finally, there remain rural households that cannot escape from abject poverty, at least in the short term. Policies directed toward this group could place less emphasis on productivity increase and more on easing hardship. Improvement of access to basic social services such as primary education, water supply and primary health care seem to be of prime importance. Social investment funds can contribute in the short term to the creation of seasonal employment opportunities and temporarily improve income of rural families and thus their food security. The Honduran Social Investment Fund (FHIS) has proved to be an effective and efficient institution for this purpose. Moreover, the Fund contributes to the reinforcement of rural social and physical infrastructure, which is essential for improving productivity of rural production.

Targeted interventions to improve food security of vulnerable house-hold categories (for example female-headed households) could focus on the diversification of diet through extension programs directed at home garden production, taking into account local knowledge of fruits, vegetables and other plants – including those with medicinal values – as well as of minor animal species. Such programs have to be subsidized in their initial phase, but can provide an efficient way to improve long-term food security prospects for low-income families (Bradshaw, 1995).

Only a combination of policies, directed at improving income-generating opportunities in the short and long term, can enhance food security prospects in a sustainable way. Therefore, constraints for the functioning of factor (in particular capital and land) and commodity markets are to be addressed, in order to increase on-farm and off-farm income. Off-farm income may contribute to financing the required investments directed at intensification of farm production and the con-version of sub-family farms into viable production units. The develop-ment of these farms is also essential to create demand for productive off-farm labor.

Conclusion

Engagement in rural off-farm employment tends to be a major element of farm household food security strategies in Honduras. Instead of con-sidering this as a disintegrating tendency, emphasis is given to the rationale of off-farm labor to overcome financial market constraints and to contribute to the diversification of risks. Off-farm employment leads to an adjustment in factor proportions in agricultural activities, as decisions on labor use determine to a high extent the efficiency with which quasi-fixed land resources are utilized. The initial effects depend on the elasticity of substitution between capital and labor and on a possible substitution of labor for leisure as a result of a higher total family income (Fafchamps, 1993). When labor becomes a more scarce factor, crop and technology choice will most likely be oriented towards activities with a higher labor productivity.

In order to enable the subsequent mobilization of savings from off-farm income for the intensification of agricultural production, expen-diture effects have to be analyzed. Within the framework of the life-cycle permanent income hypothesis, off-farm income can be considered as a transitory income component (Modigliani and Ando, 1963; Bhalla, 1987). A substantial part of this income is normally maintained as precautionary savings that respond to consumption-smoothing objectives (Deaton, 1990). Otherwise, investment linkages may also occur when part of the transitory income is used for intensification of cropping systems or improvement of the farm-level resource stocks. In the latter case, positive effects may also be expected for the sustainable management of the natural resource base (Repetto, 1987).

As food security of rural households increasingly depends on purchasing power to buy food, policies to encourage food security should go far beyond promotion of basic grains production. In essence, food security policies become very similar to poverty alleviation policies. Design of these policies can benefit from distinguishing different types of poor rural households and their specific sources of income. This includes small farmers with real prospects for increasing their agricultural productivity, rural households whose real destiny lies in the off-farm labor market or non-farm self-employment, and rural households that have no prospects for escaping abject poverty (Valdés and Wiens, 1996: 23).

With respect to the first group, policies to improve agricultural markets and institutions are essential. In addition, due to existing capital market imperfections, policies to increase off-farm income (earnings from coffee harvesting, family income from wage labor in industrial processing zones etc.) may well play a pivotal role in the conversion of sub-family farms into viable production units.

For the second group of rural households, employment creation, and enhancing skills of rural people by education and training tend to be most important. Improving access to financial services by rural households and entrepreneurs, far beyond traditional agricultural credit policies, appears to be important for employment creation in rural areas. However, the efficiency of promotion of rural off farm employment creation also depends on the agrarian structure, because of the demand effects of linkages between rural off-farm employment and the agricultural economy (Weller, 1997: 85–8).

Finally, policies directed at rural households that cannot, at least in the short term, escape from abject poverty should place emphasis on easing hardship. Improvement of access to basic social services seems to be of prime importance. Temporal employment opportunities created by social investment funds (the FHIS), and well-targeted food distribution, plus other interventions like extension programs directed at home garden production, may well contribute to the desired easing of hardship.

Acknowledgements

This chapter is based on research carried out within the framework of the preparation for the programming mission on food security in Honduras for the European Union. Most theoretical issues are derived from the ongoing research program on off-farm employment within the Department of Development Economics at Wageningen Agricultural University. The USAID mission in Honduras is acknowledged for providing access to the results of the Encuesta Nacional de Indicadores Socioeconómicos 1993–4.

Notes

1. Besides the impact of financial deepening as a result of the increasing market integration associated with the land reform process, there is also a more independent effect caused by the expansion of coffee production and the rise in coffee prices during the same period.
2. Remittances from family members living in the USA contribute to about 40 per cent of the rural family income in El Salvador. The importance of remittances is thus much lower in Honduras.
3. Public investment in rural roads is important to lower transaction costs, enhancing competition on commodity markets and improving the purchasing power of rural families.

Bibliography

Acevedo C., D. Barry, H. Rosa: El Salvador's Agricultural Sector: Macroeconomic Policy, Agrarian Change and the Environment, *World Development*, 23: 12 (1995) 2153–72.

Acuña E., I. Rodriguez, W.G. Wielemaker: *Reconocimiento de los Sistemas Alternativas de Uso, Manejo y Conservación de Suelos en Nueva Guinea*. CDR-ULA, San José, 1990.

Aguilar Olmedo C., M.A. Espinoza: *Mercado de Insumos en Nicaragua. El Caso de la Cadena de Comercio a Jalapa, El Jicaro y Quilialí*. Monografía, ESECA, UNAN, Managua, 1994.

Alfsen K.H., M.A. DeFranco, S. Glomsrod, T. Johnsen: The Cost of Soil Erosion in Nicaragua, *Ecological Economics*, no. 16 (1996) 129–45.

Ambrogi R.: *Caracterización de los Sistemas de Producción en Trópico Húmedo. Colonistas en el municipio de Nueva Guinea*. ESECA, Managua, 1995.

Amsden A.H.: Taiwan's Economic History, in Bates R. (ed.), 1988.

Anderson D., M.W. Leierson: Rural Non-farm Employment in Developing Countries, in *Economic Development and Cultural Change*, 28: 2 (1980) 227–448.

Anderson J.R. (ed.): *Agricultural Technology: Policy Issues for the International Community*. CAB International for the World Bank, Washington, 1994.

Antle J.M.: Infrastructure and Agricultural Productivity: Theory, Evidence, and Implications for Growth and Equity in Agricultural Development, in *Growth and Equity in Agricultural Development: Proceedings of the Eighteenth International Conference of Agricultural Economists*. Gower, Aldershot, 1983.

Arce C.: *Honduras: Panorama Financiero y el Sector Agropecuario*. CDR-ULA, San José, 1995.

Bade J., H. Hengsdijk, G. Kruseman, R. Ruben, P.C. Roebeling: *Farm Household Modelling in a Regional Setting: The Case of Cercle Koutiala, Mali*. DLV-report no. 6, AB-DLO/WAU, Wageningen, 1997.

Bakker M.L.: *Colonization and Land Use in the Humid Tropics of Latin America*. BOS, Wageningen, 1993.

BANADES (Banco Nacional de Desarrollo): *Costos de Producción Agrícolas, Ciclo 93/94–95/96*. Gerencia General de Crédito, Managua, 1993–6.

Barbier B.: *Economics for Sustainable Production*, in Prinsley R. Tamara (ed.), 1990.

Bardhan P. (ed.): *The Economic Theory of Agrarian Institutions*, Clarendon Press, Oxford, 1989.

Barquero J.: *Costos de Producción Agrícola; Rubros: Granos Básicos, Oleaginosas, Productos Exportación, Dirección de Análisis económico*. Ministerio de Agricultura (MAG), Managua 1995.

Bates R. (ed.): *Toward a Political Economy of Development*. University of California Press, Los Angeles 1988, 133–75.

Baumeister E.: *Tendencias de la Agricultura Centroamericana en los Años Ochenta*. FLACSO Cuaderno de Ciencias Sociales no. 7, FLACSO, San José, 1987.

Baumeister E.: Rasgos Básicos y Tendencias Estructurales de la Actividad Cafetalera en Honduras, in Baumeister E. (ed.), 1996.

Baumeister E. (ed.): *El Agro Hondureño y su Futuro*. Editorial Guaymuras, Tegucigalpa, 1996.

BCN (Banco Central de Nicaragua): *Informe sobre la Evolución de los Precios Macroeconómicos*, desde no. 1–93 (enero 1993) hasta 11–94 (noviembre 1994). Managua, Noviembre 1994a.

BCN (Banco Central de Nicaragua): *Gerencia de Estudios Económicos Indicadores de Actividad Económica, varios años*. Managua, 1994b.

Behrman J., T.N. Srinivasan (eds): *Handbook of Development Economics*, vol. 3B. Elsevier, Amsterdam, 1995.

Bell C.: Credit Markets and Interlinked Transactions, in Chenery H., T.N. Srinivasan (eds), 1988.

Benito C.: *Debt Overhang and other Barriers to the Growth of Agriculture in El Salvador*. Agricultural Policy Analysis Project II, USAID, San Salvador, 1993.

Bhalla S.S.: The Role of Sources of Income and Investment Opportunities in Rural Savings, *Journal of Development Economics*, 45 (1997) 259–81.

Binswanger H.P., K. Deininger, G. Feder: Power, Distortions, Revolt and Reform in Agricultural Land Relations, in Behrman J., T.N. Srinivasan (eds), 1995.

Binswanger H.P., S.R. Khandker: How Infrastructure and Financial Institutions Affect Agricultural Output in India, in *Journal of Development Economics*, 41 (1993) 337–66.

Bouma J., A. Kuyvenhoven, B.A.M. Bouman, J.C. Luyten, H.G. Zandstra: *Eco-Regional Approaches for Sustainable Land Use and Food Production*. Kluwer, Dordrecht–Boston, 1995.

Bouman A.M., Nieuwenhuysen, H. Hengsdijk: PASTORA Technical Coefficient Generator for Pasture and Livestock Systems in the Humid Tropics, Version 2.0, in *Quantitative Approaches in Systems Analysis*. AB-DLO/C.T. de Wit Graduate School in Production Ecology, Wageningen, 1998.

Bradshaw S.: Women's Access to Employment and the Formation of Female-headed Households in Rural and Urban Honduras, in *Bulletin of Latin American Research*, 14: 2 (1995) 143–58..

Brockett C.D.: *Land, Power and Poverty: Agrarian Transformation and Political Conflict in Central America*. Unwin Hyman, Boston, 1988.

Bulmer-Thomas V.: *The Political Economy of Central America since 1920*. Cambridge University Press, 1987.

Bunch R., G. López: *Soil Recuperation in Central America: Sustaining Innovation after Intervention*. IIED, London, 1995.

Burger K.: *Farm Households, Cash Income and Food Production: The Case of Kenyan Smallholders*. Free University Press, Amsterdam, 1994.

Byres T.: *The Agrarian Question and Differing Forms of Capitalist Agrarian Transition*. Paper, Institute of Social Studies, The Hague 1989.

CADESCA: *Caracterización de los Productores de Granos Básicos, eje II: Sistema de Producción*. CADESCA/CEE, Programa de Seguridad Alimentaria del Istmo Centroamericano, Tegucigalpa, 1989.

Calkins P., W.S. Chern, F.C. Tuan: *Rural Development in Taiwan and Mainland China*. Westview Press, Boulder, 1992.

Carter M.R., Mesbah: Can Land Market Reform Mitigate the Exclusionary Aspects of Rapid Agro-Export Growth?, *World Development*, 21: 7, (1993) 1095–100 .

Cartín S., Piszk I.: La Producción de granos básicos en Costa Rica, Instituciones Estatales y Fuerzas Sociales. Período de Diversificación Económica, in *Revista de Ciencias Sociales*, no. 19–20, Universidad de Costa Rica, 1980.

Castro C., G. Barrantes, F. Saenz: *Información Socioeconómica sobre la Zona Atlántica de Costa Rica*. CINPE Universidad Nacional Autónoma, Heredia, 1996.

Censo Agropecuario 1984. Ministerio de Economía, Industria y Comercio y Dirección General de Estadística y Censos, San José, 1984 .

CEPAL, United Nations: *Información Básica del Sector Agropecuario, Subregión Norte de América Latina y el Caribe 1980–1994*. Mexico City, 1996.

Chen C.: *Land Reform in Taiwan*. China Publishing Company, Taipeh, 1961.

Chenery H.B.: *Redistribution with Growth*. Oxford University Press, London, 1974.

Chenery H., T.N. Srinivasan (eds): *Handbook of Development Economics*, vol. 1. Elsevier, Amsterdam, 1988.

Clemens H. (ed.): *Por la Búsqueda de una Estrategia de Desarrollo para Nicaragua, Foro Agropecuario Nacional, la Estrategia de Desarrollo Agropecuario*. ESECA-UNAN, Managua, 1993.

Clemens H.: *Competitividad de Nicaragua en la producción Agrícola, Consultoria para COSUDE*. Serie CIES/ESECA 94.1., CIES/ESECA/UNAN, Managua 1994.

Clemens, H., D. Green M. Spoor (eds): *Mercados y Granos Básicos en Nicaragua – hacia una Nueva Visión sobre Producción y Comercialización*. ESECA-UNAN, Managua, 1994.

Clemens H., J. Simán: *Caracterización del Manejo del Cultivo del Café en la IV Región, Ciclo 1990/91*. Serie CIES/ESECA, 93.2, CIES/ESECA/UNAN, Managua 1993.

Clemens H., C.J. Wattel: Rural Lending by Projects: Another Cycle of Unsustainable Interventions in Rural Credit Markets? An Analysis of Case Studies in Central America, in De Groot J.P., R. Ruben (eds), 1997.

Clercx L.: *Régimen de Tenencia de la Tierra en la Zona de Nueva Guinea*. CDR-ULA, Costa Rica, 1990.

Collier P., D. Lal: *Labour and Poverty in Kenya:* 1900–1980, Clarendon Press, Oxford, 1986.

Collins J.L.: Farm Size and Non-traditional Exports: Determinants of Participation in World Markets, in *World Development*, 23: 7 (1995) 1103–14.

CONCAFE (Comisión Nacional del Café): *El Café en Cifras, Boletín* no. 1–3. Managua, 1994.

Consejo Monetario Centroamericano: *Boletin Estadistico*, various years, cmc, San José (1990–7).

Corbo V., A. Bruno: *An Economic Assessment of Nicaragua*. Swedish International Development Agency, Stockholm 1993.

Cosci S.: *Credit Rationing and Asymmetric Information*. Dartmouth, Aldershot, 1993.

Cuevas C.E., D.H. Graham, J.A. Paxton: *El Sector Financiero Informal en El Salvador*. FUSADES, Ohio State University, Columbus, 1991.

Deaton A.S.: Savings in Developing Countries: Theory and Review, *World Bank Economic Review*, 4 (1990) 61–96.

De Bruin, S.: *Estudio Detallado de los Suelos del Asentamiento Neguev*. Serie técnica, Informe técnico no. 191, Atlantic Zone programme, Phase 2, Report no. 25, Centro Agronómico Tropical de Investigación y Enseñanza, Turrialba, Costa Rica, 1992.

De Graaff J.: *Soil Conservation and Sustainable Land Use: An Economic Approach.* Royal Tropical Institute, Amsterdam, 1993.

De Groot J.P.: Policies in Soil Conservation, in Castro E. and G. Kruseman (eds): *Policies in Sustainable Land Use in Costa Rica,* Editorial Guayacan, Tegucigalpa, 1996.

De Groot J.P., R. Pasos (eds): *Propuestas Campesinas para el Desarrollo Sostenible, un Recuento sobre Experiencias Piloto en Centroamérica.* CDR-ULA and FUN-DESCA, Panama, 1994.

De Groot J.P., R. Ruben (eds): *Sustainable Agriculture in Central America,* Macmillan – St Martin's Press, London – New York, 1997.

De Janvry A., M. Fafchamps, E. Sadoulet: Peasant Household Behaviour with Missing Markets: Some Paradoxes Explained, in *The Economic Journal,* 101: November (1991): 1400–17.

De Janvry A., E. Sadoulet: A Study in Resistance to Institutional Change – the Lost Game of Latin American Land Reform, in *World Development,* 20: 10 (1992): 1397–407.

De Janvry A., E. Sadoulet, E. Thorbecke: Introduction, in *World Development,* 21: 4 (1993): 565–75.

De Janvry A., E. Sadoulet, E. Thorbecke (eds): *State, Market and Civil Organisations: New Theories, New Practices and their Implications for Rural Development.* Macmillan, London, 1995.

Delforce, J.: Seperability in Farm-Household Economics: An Experiment with Linear Programming in *Agriculture Economics,* 10 (1994) 165–77.

Demery L., M. Ferroni, C. Grootaert, Jorge Wong-Valle (eds): *Understanding the Social Effects of Policy Reform. A World Bank Study.* World Bank, Washington, 1993.

Devé F.: *Caracterización de los Productores de Granos Básicos del Istmo Centroaméricano.* Collección Temas de Seguridad Alimentaria no. 4, CADESCA, Panama:1990.

DGEC (Dirección General de Estadística y Censos, San José, Costa Rica):
Agricultural Census 1963, 1966.
Agricultural Census 1973, 1976.
Censo Agropecuario 1984, 1987.
Metodología. Encuesta Nacional de Ingresos y Gastos de los Hogares, Informe no. 2, 1988.
Avance de Resultados. Encuesta Nacional de Ingresos y Gastos de los Hogares, Informe no. 1, 1990.
Costa Rica – Cálculo de Población, 1992.

Díaz Alejandro C.: Goodbye Financial Repression – Hello Financial Crash, *Journal of Development Economics,* 19:1–2, (1985), 1–24.

Diskin M.: El Salvador, Reform Prevents Change, in Thiesenhusen W. (ed), 1989.

Dorner P.: *Latin American Land Reforms: Theory and Practice.* University of Wisconsin Press, Madison, 1992.

Eberlin R.: The Development Potential of the Nicaraguan Agricultural Sector under the Conditions of a Structural Adjustment Program, The Policy Analysis Matrix as a Methodological Instrument and a Empirical Application to the Case of Nicaragua (Central America). *Doctoral thesis,* Zürich 1998.

EC: *Encuesta Permanente de Hogares de Propósitos Multiples 1993.* Dirección General de Estadística y Censos, Tegucigalpa, 1994.

Edwards S.: *Real Exchange Rates, Competitiveness and Macroeconomic Adjustment in Nicaragua*. University of California Press, Los Angeles, 1992.

El-Ghonemy R.: *The Political Economy of Rural Poverty: The Case for Land Reform*. Routledge, London, 1990.

Ellis F.: *Peasant Economies*. Cambridge University Press, 1988.

Ellis F.: *Agricultural Policies in Developing Countries*, Cambridge University Press, 1992.

Enters T.: *Methods for the Economic Assessment of the On- and Off-Site Effects of Soil Erosion*. IBSRAM, Bangkok, 1998.

Evans P.: Government Action, Social Capital and Development: Reviewing the Evidence on Synergy, *World Development*, 24: 6 (1996) 1119–32.

Fafchamps M.: Sequential Labor Decisions under Uncertainty: An Estimable Household Model of West-African Farmers, *Econometrica* 61: 5 (1993) 1173–97.

Fafchamps M., A. de Janvry, E. Sadoulet: Transaction Costs, Market Failures, Competitiveness and the State, in Peters G.H., D.D. Hedley (eds), 1995.

Faruqi S.: Financial Sector Reforms, Economic Growth and Stability: Experiences in selected Asian and Latin American Countries. EDI Seminar Series, World Bank, Washington, DC, 1994.

Feder, G., R.E. Just, D. Zilberman: Adoption of Agricultural Innovations in Developing Countries: A Survey, in *Economic Development and Cultural Change*, 33 1985: 254–97.

FIDEG:
El Observador Económico, Various issues, 1993.
El Observador Económico, no. 2:10, Managua, 1997.

FMLN – Coordinación Nacional del Sector Campesino: Propuesta Nacional Abierto al Sector Agropecuario, San Salvador, 1995.

Fry M.J., *Money, Interest and Banking in Economic Development*. Johns Hopkins University Press, Baltimore, MD, 1988 .

Ghate P.B.: Interaction between the Formal and Informal Financial Sectors: The Asian Experience, *World Development*, 20: 6 1992: 859–72.

Gibson H.D., E. Tsakalotos: The Scope and Limits of Financial Liberalisation in Developing Countries: A Critical Survey, in *Journal of Development Studies*, 30: 3 April (1994) 578–628.

Gobierno de Honduras: Lineas de acción del Plan de Seguridad Alimentaria Nutricional. Documento preparado para la Cumbre Mundial sobre la Alimentación, Roma, 13–17 noviembre 1996. Tegucigalpa, 1996.

Goetz S.J.: A Selectivity Model of Household Food-Marketing Behavior in Sub-Saharan Africa, *Journal of Agricultural Economics* 74 (1992) 444–52.

Gómez O.L.: *La Política Agrícola en el Nuevo Estilo de Desarrollo Latinoamericano*. FAO, Oficina Regional para América Latina y El Caribe, Santiago de Chile 1994.

Gonzáles M.H.: Desarrollo Agropecuario y Políticas Macroeconómicas en la Década del 80 en Costa Rica, in Mora Alfaro J. *et al.*, 1994.

González Vega C., R. Jiménez, L. Mesalles: Costa Rica: *Fuentes de Crédito para los Agricultores*. Agricultural Finance Program, Department of Agricultural Economics and Rural Sociology, Ohio State University, Columbus, 1989.

González Vega C., L. Mesalles Jorba: *La Economía Política de la Nacionalización Bancaria en Costa Rica: 1948–1990*, in González Vega C., T. Vargas (eds), 1993.

González Vega C., J.I. Torrico: *Honduras: Mercados Financieros Rurales no Formales.* Proyecto para el Desarrollo de Políticas Agrícolas de Honduras (PRODEPAH), Tegucigalpa, 1995.

González Vega C., T. Vargas (eds): *Reforma Financiera en Costa Rica: Perspectivas y Propuestas.* Academia de Centroamerica, Ohio State University, San José, 1993.

Grabowski R.: Economic Development and the Rise of Market Systems, *Studies in Comparative International Development,* 30: 3, Fall (1995), 49–69.

Grindle M.S.: *State and Countryside.* Johns Hopkins University Press, Baltimore, MD, 1986.

Guardia J., A. A. Di Mare, T. Vargas, V.H. Céspedes, J. Corrales, M. Baldares M.: *La Política de Precios en Costa Rica.* COUNCEL-CIAPA, AID, Trejos, San José, 1987.

Gupta, K.L.: Aggregate Savings, Financial Intermediation and Interest Rates, in *Review of Economics and Statistics,* 69: 2, (1987): 303–11.

Haggblade S., P. Hazell, J. Brown: Farm–Non-farm Linkages in Rural Sub-Saharan Africa, *World Development,* 17: 8 (1989) 1173–201.

Hart G., A. Turton, B. White (eds): *Agrarian Transformations: Local Processes and the State in Southeast Asia.* University of California Press, Berkeley, 1989.

Hayami Y.: Land Reform, in Meier G. (ed.), 1991.

Hayami Y., K. Otsuka: *The Economics of Contract Choice: An Agrarian Perspective,* Clarendon Press, Oxford, 1993.

Hayami Y., V.W. Ruttan: *Agricultural Deveopment: An International Perpspective.* Johns Hopkins University Press, Baltimore, 1985.

Hengsdijk H., G. Kruseman: *Operationalizing the DLV Program: An Integrated Agro-Economic and Agro-Ecological Approach to a Methodology for Analysis of Sustainable Land Use and Regional Agricultural Policy.* Report no. 1, AB-DLO/WAU DLV, Wageningen, 1992.

Hengsdijk H., A. Nieuwenhuysen, B.A.M. Bouman: LUCTOR: Land Use Crop Technical Coefficient Generator; Version 2.0. A Model to Quantify Cropping Systems in the Northern Atlantic Zone of Costa Rica, in *Quantitative Approaches in Systems Analysis.* Wageningen University Press, Wageningen, 1998.

Ho, Y.: *Agricultural Development of Taiwan 1902–1960.* Vanderbilt University Press, Nashville, 1966.

Hoff K., J. Stiglitz: Introduction: Imperfect Information and Rural Credit Markets – Puzzles and Policy Perspectives, *World Bank Economic Review,* 4: 3 (1990) 235–50.

Holmann F.: *Costos de Producción de Leche y Carne, Inversión de Capital, y Competitividad en Fincas de Doble Propósito en Cinco Regiones de Nicaragua.* Comisión Nacional de Ganadería, Managua, 1993.

Hosmer D.W., S. Lemeshow: *Applied Logistic Regression.* Wiley, New York, 1989.

Howard-Borjas P.: *Empleo y Pobreza Rural en Honduras, con Enfoque Especial en la Mujer.* SECPLAN/FNUAP/OIT HON/87/P02, Tegucigalpa, 1989.

Howard-Borjas P.: *Cattle and Crisis: The Genesis of Unsustainable Development in Central America. Case Studies of Honduras and Nicaragua.* FAO, Rome, 1992.

Hsieh P.C.R.: *Land Reform and its Impacts on Taiwan's Development in the Republic of China.* LRTI paper, Guatemala City, 1989.

Huang S.: Structural Change in Taiwan's Agricultural Economy, *Economic Development and Cultural Change,* 41 (1993) : 43–65.

Ibrahim M.A.: Compatibility, Persistence and Productivity of Grass-Legume Mixtures for Sustainable Animal Production in the Atlantic Zone of Costa Rica. *Doctoral thesis,* Wageningen University, 1994.

Irwin G.: New Perspectives for Modernization in Central America, *Development and Change,* 22 (1991) 93–115.

Jansen H.G.P., A. van Tilburg, J. Belt, S. Hoekstra: *Agricultural Marketing in the Atlantic Zone of Costa Rica. A Production, Consumption, and Trade Study of Agricultural Commodities Produced by Small and Medium-Scale Farmers.* CATIE, Turrialba, 1996.

Jones Jeffrey R.: Colonization and Environment. *Land Settlement Projects in Central America.* United Nations University Press, Tokyo, 1990.

Kannappan S.: The Economics of Development: The Procrustean Bed of Mainstream Economics, *Economic Development and Cultural Change,* 43 (1995).

Kapur B.K.: Optimal Financial and Foreign Exchange Liberalisation of Less Developed Economies, in *Quarterly Journal of Economics,* 98: 1, (1983) 41–62.

Karshenas M.: *Industrialization and Agricultural Surplus.* ISS Research Seminar, The Hague, 1992.

Kelly A.C., J.G. Williamson: Household Savings Behavior in the Developing Economies: The Indonesian Case, *Economic Development and Cultural Change,* 16: 3 (1968) 385–403..

Killick T.: *Markets and Governments in Agricultural and Industrial Adjustment.* Working Paper 34, Overseas Development Institute, London, March 1990.

Kishor N., L. Constantino: (1994) Sustainable Forestry: Can it Compete?, *Finance and Development,* 31 (1994) 4.

Kotwal A., Eswaran M.: Credit and Agrarian Class Structure, in Bardhan P. (ed.), 1989.

Kruseman G., R. Ruben, H. Hengsdijk: *Agrarian Structure and Land Use in the Atlantic Zone of Costa Rica.* DLV Report no. 3, AB-DLO/WAU, Wageningen, 1994.

Kruseman G., R. Ruben, H. Hengsdijk, J. Bade, H. Djouara: *Policy Instruments to Address Market and Institutional Constraints for Sustainable Land Use at Farm Household Level.* Paper presented to the International Symposium Institutions and Technologies for Rural Development in West Africa, University of Hohenheim, 1996.

La Gaceta: Decreto No.Y26639, Ministerio de Agricultura y Ganadería, CXX: 23, 1–4 (1998) .

Leftwich A: Bringing Politics Back in: Towards a Model of the Developmental State, *Journal of Development Studies,* 31: 3, 500–27 (February 1995).

Leonard H.J.: *Natural Resources and Economic Development in Central America: a Regional Environmental Profile.* International Institute for Environment and Development, Transaction Books, New Brunswick, 1987.

Lipton M.: Land Reform as Commenced Business: The Evidence against Stopping, *World Development,* 21: 4, 641–57 (1993).

Low A.: *Agricultural Development in Southern Africa: Farm Household Theory and the Food Crisis.* James Curry, London, 1986.

Lutz E., S. Pagiola, C. Reiche (eds): *Economic and Institutional Analysis of Soil Conservation Projects in* Central America and the Caribbean. World Bank Environment Paper no. 8, Washington, DC, 1994.

MAG (Ministerio de Agricultura de Nicaragua, Managua):
   Dirección General de Información y Apoyo al Productor, Anuario de Información de Precios y Mercados 1993, 1994. 1993.
   Análisis Situacional de los Productos e Insumos Agropecuarios (monthly bulletins, Noviembre 1994).
Maldidier C.: *Tendencias Actuales de la Frontera Agrícola en Nicaragua*. NITLAPAN-UCA, Managua, 1993.
Mathieson D.J.: Financial Reform and Stabilization Policy in a Developing Economy, *Journal of Development Economics*, 27: 3 (1980) 359–95.
Mattos M.M., C. Uhl: Economic and Ecological Perspectives on Ranching in the Eastern Amazon, *World Development*, 22: 2, 145–50 (1994).
McConnell K.E.: An Economic Model of Soil Conservation, *American Journal of Agricultural Economics* , 65 (1983) 83–9.
Meier G. (ed.): *Politics and Policy Making in Developing Countries*. International Center for Economic Growth, San Francisco, 1991.
Mendoza O.: *Ajuste Estructural, Términos de Intercambio Internos y la Pequeña Producción de Granos Básicos: el Caso de Nicaragua*. PRIAG, CORECA–CEE/IICA ALA 88–23. 1992, Universidad Libre de Amsterdam, Oficina Regional Centroamericana, San José, 1992a.
Mendoza O.: *Distribución del Ingreso y Seguridad Alimentaria en un Ambiente de Ajustes Cambiarios, los Precios Relativos en Nicaragua (1986–1992)*. Serie CIES/ESECA 92.2, CIES/ESECA/UNAN, Managua, 1992b.
Menjívar R., J.D. Trejos: *La Pobreza en América Central*. FLACSO, San José, 1990.
MIDEPLAN: *Plan de Desarrollo Region Huetar Atlántica*. San José, 1991: 79.
Miller D. *Handbook of Research Design and Social Measurement*, Sage, London (1991).
Mitchell R., Bernauer Th.: Empirical Research on International Environmental Policy: Designing Qualitative Case Studies, *Journal of Environment and Development*, 7: 1, 4–31 (March 1998).
Modigliani F., A. Ando: The Life-Cycle Hypothesis of Saving, *American Economic Review*, 63 (1963) 55–84.
Mol E., A.A. Sanders: Who Meets the Needs: A Case Study to the Financial Landscape in El Salvador. MSc thesis, Wageningen Agricultural University, 1995.
Moll H.A.J., R. Ruben, E.W.G. Mol, A.A. Sanders: *Segmentation of Rural Financial Markets: An Exploration of the Borderline in El Salvador*. Wageningen Agricultural University, 1996.
Monke E., S. Pearson: *The Policy Analysis Matrix for Agricultural Development*. Cornell University Press, Ithaca and London 1989.
Monke E., S. Pearson: Evaluating Policy Choices in Developing Countries, the Policy Analysis Matrix, in *Proceedings of the XXI International Conference of Agricultural Economists*, 22–29 July 1991, Tokyo, Japan. Dartmouth, London, 1991: 166–80.
Montoya A.: *El Agro Salvadoreño Antes y después de la Reforma Agraria*, Cuadernos de Investigación, San Salvador, 1991.
Moock P.R.: Education and Technical Efficiency in Small-Farm Production, *Economic Development and Cultural Change* , 29 (1981) 723–39.
Mora Alfaro J., O. Oviedo Sánchez, L.F. Fernández Alvarado: *El Impacto de las Políticas Macroeconómicas en el Agro Costarricense*. UNA, Facultad de Ciencias Sociales, Editorial Universidad Nacional, San José, 1994.

Morisset J.: *Unfair Trade? Empirical Evidence in World Commodity Markets over the Past 25 Years*. Policy Research Working Paper 1815, Foreign Investment Advisory Service, World Bank, Washington D.C., August 1997.

Moscardi E., A. de Janvry: Attitudes Towards Risk among Peasants: An Econometric Approach, *American Journal of Agricultural Economics*, 59 (1977) 710–16.

Mundlak Y., D. Larson, R. Butzer: *The Determinants of Agricultural Production*. Policy Research Working Paper 1827, Development Research Group, Washington D.C., September 1997.

Norton Roger D.: *Integración de la Política Agrícola y Alimentaria en el Ambito Macroeconómico en América Latina (Integration of Food and Agricultural Policy with Macroeconomic Policy: Methodological Consideration in Latin American Perspective)*. Estudio FAO: Desarrollo Económico y Social, no. 111, FAO, Roma 1993.

NRC (National Research Council USA): *Sustainable Agriculture and the Environment in the Humid Tropics*. Committee on Sustainable Agriculture and the Environment in the Humid Tropics, National Academy Press, Washington, DC, 1993.

NZZ: Absage an die marktfreundliche Entwicklung. Weltbank sieht komplementäre Rolle von Markt und Staat, *Neue Züricher Zeitung*, no. 145, 26-6-1997.

Ozorio de Almeida A.L., J.S. Campari: *Sustainable Settlement in the Brazilian Amazon*. World Bank–Oxford University Press, Washington, DC, 1995.

Pagiola S.: Cost–benefit Analysis of Soil Conservation, in Lutz E. *et al.* (eds), 1994 .

Paige J.M.: Coffee and Power in El Salvador, *Latin American Research Review*, 1993.

Paniaga Nuñez C., M. Fernández Ampie, F. Torrez Castillo: *Impacto del Ajuste Económico en el Periodo 1988–91 en los Sistemas de Producción de los Pequeños Y Medianos Productores de Granos Básicos: Caso Nandaime*. Monografía, ESECA, Managua, 1992.

Pasos R.: *Desarrollo Sostenible y Producción Campesina en Centroamérica: Enfoques y Propuestas*. SIMAS, Managua, 1994.

Pelupessy W. (ed): *Perspectives on the Agro-Export Economy in Central America*. Macmillan, London, 1991.

Pelupessy W.: *The Limits of Economic Reform in El Salvador*, Macmillan–St Martin's Press, London–New York, 1997.

Pelupessy W., J. Weeks: *Economic Maladjustment in Central America*, Macmillan–St Martin's Press, London–New York, 1993.

Peters G., D. Hedley (eds): *Agricultural Competitiveness: Market Forces and Public Choice, Proceedings XXII Conference IAAE*, Dartmouth, Aldershot, 1995.

Pino N., R. Perdomo: *Política Macroeconómica y sus Efectos en la Agricultura y la Seguridad Alimentaria en Honduras*. CADESCA, Panama, 1990.

Platteau J.P.: *Land Reform and Structural Adjustment in Sub-Saharan Africa*. FAO, Rome, 1992.

Platteau J.P.: Behind the Market Stage where Real Societies Exist, Parts I and II, *Journal of Development Studies*, 30: 3 (April 1994) 533–77 .

Pomp M.: Smallholders and Innovation Adoption: Cocoa in Sulawesi, Indonesia. *PhD thesis*, Free University Amsterdam, 1994.

POSCAE–UNAH: *Los Campesinos Centroamericanos ante los Retos de los Años 90. El Caso de Honduras*; Postgrado Centroamericano en Economía y Planificación del Desarrollo. Oxfam, Tegucigalpa, 1992.

PRODES:
   Programa de Desarrollo Rural en la Zona de Nueva Guinea: Diagnóstico Socio-
   Económico, Nueva Guinea, Managua, 1992.
   Ministerio de Cooperación Externa Nicaragua and DGIS: Proyecto PRODES,
   Resultados Y Perspectivas, Nicaragua Mission Report. DGIS, The Hague, 1996.
Prosterman R.L., J. Riedinger: *Land Reform and Democratic Development.* Johns
   Hopkins University Press, Baltimore, 1989.
Prosterman R.L., M.N. Temple, T.M. Hanstad (eds): *Agrarian Reform and*
   Grassroots Development. Lynne Rienner, Boulder–London, 1990.
Quiros, R., F. Barrantes, H. Clemens, M. Ugalde: *Estudio de Oferta y Demanda de*
   Crédito Rural en Costa Rica, a partir de estudios de casos en tres regiones del
   país. Mesa Nacional Campesina, Centro de Estudios para el Desarrollo Rural,
   Universidad Libre de Amsterdam, Instituto para el Desarrollo y la Acción
   Social, San José, 1997.
Ranis G. (ed.): *Taiwan, from Developing to Mature Economy.* Westview Press,
   Boulder, 1992: 15–70.
Ranis G., F. Stewart: Rural Linkages in the Philippines and Taiwan, in Stewart F.
   (ed.), 1987.
Reardon T., E. Crawford, V. Kelly: Links between Non-farm Income and Farm
   Investment in African Households: Adding the Capital Market Perspective,
   American Journal of Agricultural Economics, 76 (1994) 1172–76.
Reardon T., C. Delgado, P. Matlon: Determinants and Effects of Income
   Diversification Amongst Farm Households in Burkina Faso, *Journal of*
   Development Studies, 28: 2 (1992) 264–96.
Reardon T., C. Delgado, P. Matlon: Coping with Household-level Food
   Insecurity in Drought Affected Areas of Burkina Faso, in *World Development ,*
   16: 9 (1988) 1065–74.
Reinhardt N., Contrast and Congruence in the Agrarian Reforms of El Salvador
   and Nicaragua, in Thiesenhusen W.C. (ed), 1989.
Repetto R.: Economic Incentives for Sustainable Production, in *Annals of*
   Regional Science, 21 (1987) 44–59.
Rogers B., A. Swindale, P. Ohri Vachaspati: *Determinantes de la Seguridad*
   Alimentaria Familiar en Honduras, informe sobre la Encuesta Nacional de
   Consumo, Ingreso, Gasto y Nutrición, 1993–94. USAID, Tegucigalpa, 1996.
Röling N.: *Extension Science: Information Systems in Agricultural Development.*
   Cambridge University Press, Cambridge, 1988.
Rosenzweig M.R.: Neoclassical Theory and the Optimizing Peasant: an
   Econometric Analysis of Market Family Labor Supply in a Developing
   Country, *Quarterly Journal of Economics,* 94 (1980) 31–55.
Rosenzweig M.R., H.P. Binswanger: Wealth, Weather Risk and the Composition
   and Profitability of Agricultural Investments, *Economic Journal,* 103 (1993)
   56–78.
Ruben R.: *El Problema Agrario en El Salvador: Notas sobre una Economía Agraria*
   Polarizada. CENITEC, El Salvador, 1991.
Ruben, R., P. v.d. Berg, M.S. van Wijk, N. Heerink: Aspectos Económicos
   de Sistemas de Producción de Alto y Bajo Uso de Insumos Externos en la
   Agricultura de Laderas, in S. Scherr *et al.,* (eds) 1997.
Ruben R., G. Kruseman, H. Hengsdijk: *Farm Household Modelling for Estimat-*
   ing the Effectiveness of Price Instruments on Sustainable Land Use in the

Atlantic Zone of Costa Rica. AB-DLO/WAU, DLV Report no. 4, Wageningen, 1994, 44.

Ruhl J.M.: Agrarian Structure and Political Stability in Honduras, *Journal of Interamerican Studies and World Affairs*, 26: 1 (1984) 33–68.

Ruthenberg H.: *Farming Systems in the Tropics*, 2nd edition. Oxford University Press, Oxford, 1976.

Saborio L., H. Clemens: *Ajuste Estructural y Producción de Granos Básicos, Sistemas de Producción en la Zona de Nandaime, Región II, Nicaragua (1987–1990)*. Departamento de Economía Agrícola UNAN, 1991, DEA-UNAN, Managua, 1992.

Sadoulet E., A. De Janvry: *Quantitative Development Policy Analysis*. Johns Hopkins University Press, Baltimore, 1995.

Saha A.: A Two-Season Agricultural Household Model of Output and Price Uncertainty, *Journal of Development Economics*, 42 (1994) 245–69.

Sanclemente Oscar H., R. Ligia Maria Salas, B. Molijn: *Resultados de los Ensayos de la Producción de Maíz en Rotación con Frijol Abono (Ciclos 1992/93 y 1993/94)* (PRODES, Nueva Guinea), Ministerio Cooperación Externa, Managua, 1994.

Scherr S., B. Miranda, O. Neidecker-Gonzales (eds): *Investigación sobre Políticas para el Desarrollo Sostenible en las Laderas Mesoamericanas*. IICA–OFPRI, San Salvador–Washington, 1997: 157–82.

Schiff M., C.E. Montenegro: Aggregate Agricultural Supply Response in Developing Countries: A Survey of Selected Issues, *Economic Development and Cultural Change*, 45: 2 (January 1997), 393–410.

Schiff M., Valdés A: *The Plundering of Agriculture in Developing Countries*, World Bank, Washington D.C., September 1992.

Schneider R.: *Government and the Economy on the Amazon Frontier*, World Bank, Washington, DC, 1995.

Schultz T.W.: *Transforming Traditional Agriculture*. Yale University Press, New Haven, CT, 1964.

SECPLAN/OIT/FNUAP: *Honduras: Libro Q: Pobreza, Potencialidad y Focalización Municipal*. HON/90/P03, Tegucigalpa, 1992.

SECPLAN/SRN: *IV Censo Nacional Agropecuario 1993*. Secretaría de Planficación, Coordinación y Presupuesto, y Secretaría de Recursos Naturales, Tegucigalpa, 1994.

Sen A.K.: Peasants and Dualism with or without Labour Surplus, *Journal of Political Economy*, 74 (1966) 425–50.

SEPSA (Secretaria Ejecutiva de Planificación Sectorial Agropecuaria de Nicaragua, Managua).
Sostenibilidad, Estratégia de Desarrollo del Sector Agropecuario. 1995.
Políticas del Sector Agropecuario (Revisión y Ajuste). 1997.

Simons L.R., J.C. Stephens Jr: *El Salvador Land Reform 1980–1981, Impact Audit*. OxFAM, Boston, MA, 1981.

Singh I.J., L. Squire, J. Strauss (eds): *Agricultural Household Models: Extensions, Applications and Policy*. John Hopkins University Press, Baltimore, MD, 1986.

Singh R.H.: The Impact of Structural Adjustment Policies on the Performance of Agriculture: The Case of Jamaica, in Weeks J. (ed.), 1995.

Siu O., H. Rose: *La Protección Nominal de los Granos Básicos en Nicaragua: 1991–1993*. Programa Agrícola, CONAGRO/BID/PNUD, MAG, Managua, 1994.

Skoufias E.: Using Shadow Wages to Estimate Labor Supply of Agricultural Households, *American Journal of Agricultural Economics* , 76 (1994) 215–27.

Sobhan R.: *Agrarian Reform and Social Transformation.* Zed Books, London–New York, NJ, 1993.

Stewart F. (ed.): *Macro-policies for Appropriate Technology in Developing Countries.* Westview Press, 1987, Boulder, 140–91.

Stiglitz J.E., A. Weiss: Credit Rationing in Markets with Imperfect Information, *American Economic Review,* 71: 3 (1981) 235–50.

Stoorvogel J.J., G.P. Eppink: *Atlas de la Zona Atlántica Norte de Costa Rica.* Programa Zona Atlántica, CATIE-AUW-MAG, Guapiles, Costa Rica, 1995.

Takase K., J. Watanabe: *Agriculture in Latin America and Global Structural Reform.* International Development Center of Japan (IDCI), Tokyo, 1997.

Tangermann K.D., I.R. Valdés: *Alternativas Campesinas: Modernización en el Agro y Movimiento Campesino en Centroamérica.* CRIES/Latino Editores, Managua, 1994.

Thiesenhusen W. (ed.): *Searching for Agrarian Reform in Latin America.* Unwin Hyman, Boston, 1989.

Thiesenhusen W.: Land Reform Lives! *European Journal of Development Research,* vol. 7 (1995a) 193–209.

Thiesenhusen W.C.: *Broken Promises. Agrarian Reform and the Latin American Campesino,* Westview Press, Boulder, co, 1995b.

Thorbecke E.: The Process of Agricultural Development in Taiwan, in Ranis G. (ed.), 1992.

Thorbecke E.: Impact of State and Civil Institutions on the Operation of Rural Market and Non-Rural Market Configurations, in De Janvry A. *et al.* (eds), 1995.

Thorpe A.: Adjusting to Reality: The Impact of Structural Adjustment on Honduran Agriculture, in Weeks J. (ed.), 1995.

Tijerino A.C.: *La Formación de Precios de Maíz y Frijol desde el Productor de Jalapa y el Jicaro hasta el Comerciante Mayorista en Managua, Ciclo 1992–93.* Monografía, ESECA, Managua 1993.

Timmer C.P.: The Agricultural Transformation, in Chenery H., T.N. Srinivasan (eds), 1988.

Timmer C.P. (ed.): *Agriculture and the State.* Cornell University Press, Ithaca, NY, 1991.

Timmer C.P., W. Falcon, S. Pearson (tr. Carmelo Saavedra Arce): *Análisis de Políticas Alimentarias (Food Policy Analysis; 1983).* Banco Mundial, Washington, DC, 1985.

Todaro M.: A Model of Labor Migration and Urban Unemployment in Less Developed Countries, *American Economic Review,* 59 (1969) 138–48.

Toniolo, A., C. Uhl: Economic and Ecological Perspectives on Agriculture in the Eastern Amazon, *World Development,* 23 (1995) 959–73.

Trinidad de Almeida O., C. Uhl: Developing a Quantitative Framework for Sustainable Resource-Use Planning in the Brazilian Amazon, *World Development,* 23, 12 (1995) 1745–64.

Tsakok I.: Agricultural Price Policy. *A Practitioner's Guide to Partial-Equilibrium Analysis.* Cornell University Press, Ithaca, NY–London, 1990 .

Uphoff N.: Grassroots Organizations and NGOs in Rural Development: Opportunities with Diminishing States and Expanding Markets, *World Development,* 21: 4 (1993) 607–22.

UPSA-SRN: *Compendio Estadístico Agropecuario 1995.* Unidad de Planificación Sectorial Agrícola. Secretaría de Recursos Naturales, Tegucigalpa, 1995.

USAID:
Framework for an Agribusiness Strategy in Nicaragua, vols I and II. Consultancy Report for USAID by CARANA Corporation and Sparks Companies. Managua, 1991.
Nicaraguan Grain Marketing Systems, vols I (summary report) and II (technical analyses). Consultancy report for USAID by CARANA Corporation and Sparks Companies. Managua, 1992.
La Seguridad Alimentaria en Honduras. Resultados de la Encuesta Nacional de Indicadores Socioeconómicos de 1993–1994. Tegucigalpa, 1994.
Utting P.: *The Social Origin and Impact of Deforestation in Central America.* Discussion Paper 24, UNRISD, Geneva, 1991.
Valdés A., T. Wiens: Rural Poverty in Latin America and the Caribbean, *Annual Bank Conference on Development in Latin America and the Caribbean.* World Bank, Washington, DC, May 30 1996 .
Van Andel M., R. Sminia: *Competitiveness and Efficiency of the Banking System of Costa Rica: A Study of the Consequences of the Implemented Financial Liberalisation Program (1978–1994).* CDR Serie Estudios no. 6, San José, 1995.
Van der Walle D., K. Nead: *Public Spending and the Poor: Theory and Evidence.* Johns Hopkins University Press for the World Bank, Baltimore MD–London, 1995.
Van der Noord P.J.: Globalisation and the European Disease, *The Economist*, 144 (1996) 195–222.
Van der Pol, F.: *Soil Mining. An Unseen Contributor to Farm Income in Southern Mali.* Bulletin no. 325, Royal Tropical Institute, Amsterdam, 1993.
Vargas E.: Análisis de la Competitividad de los Granos Básicos: Maíz, Sorgo, Arroz y Frijol Rojo. MAG (un shed), Managua, 1996.
Wang Rong: *A Comparison of Agrarian Reforms between Taiwan and El Salvador.* Unpublished internal report, NAU/IVO, Tilburg, 1992.
Warman F., A.P. Thirlwall: Interest Rates, Savings, Investment and Growth in Mexico 1960–1990. Tests of the Financial Liberalisation Hypothesis, *Journal of Development Studies*, 30: 3 (April 1994) 629–49.
Wattel C.J., R. Ruben: *El Impacto del Ajuste Estructural sobre los Sistemas de Producción de Granos Básicos en Centroamérica.* IICA-PRIAG, San José, 1992.
Wattel C.J., R. Ruben, E.L. Caballero, E. Krikke: *Financiamiento Rural Alternativo: Experiencias con Crédito No-bancario en Honduras.* Editorial Cuaymuras, Tegucigalpa, 1994.
Weber M.T., J.M. Staatz, J.S. Holtzman, E.W. Crawford, R.H. Bernstein: Informing Food Security Decisions in Africa: Empirical Analysis and Policy Dialogue, *American Journal of Agricultural Economics*, 70: 5, 1988: 1044–52.
Weeks J. (ed.): *Structural Adjustment and the Agricultural Sector in Latin America and the Caribbean.* Macmillan, London, 1995.
Weller J.: *La Generación de Empleo e Ingresos en las Exportaciones No-tradicionales Agrícolas: el Caso de los Pequeños Productores en Centroamérica.* OIT–PREALC, Panama–Geneva, 1993.
Weller J.: El Empleo Rural no Agropecuario en el Istmo Centroamericano, *Revista de la CEPAL*, 62 (1997) 75–90.
Wenner M., R. Umaña: *Evaluación del Mercado de Crédito Agrícola en El Salvador.* Agricultural Policy Analysis Project II, USAID, San Salvador, 1993.
White B., G. Wiradi: Agrarian and Non-agrarian Bases of Inequality in nine Javanese Villages, in Hart G. *et al.* (eds), 1989.

Williams R.G.: *Export Agriculture and the Crisis in Central America*. University of North Carolina Press, Chapel Hill, 1986.

World Bank:

  Making Adjustment Work for the Poor. A World Bank Study. World Bank, Washington, DC, 1991.

  Nicaragua: Stabilisation and Adjustment. Enabling Private Sector Growth. Consultative Group Meeting, Paris, 1993.

  Honduras: Country Economic Memorandum and Poverty Assessment, World Bank Report no. 13317-HO, Washington, DC, 1994.

Yang M.: *Socio-economic Results of Land Reform in Taiwan*. East-West Center Press, Honolulu, 1967.

Yotopoulos P.A., S.L. Floro: Income Distribution, Transaction Costs and Market Fragmentation in Formal Credit Markets, *Cambridge Journal of Economics*, 16 (1992) 303–26.

Zeller M., G. Schrieder, J. von Braun, F. Heidhues: *Rural Finance for Food Security for the Poor. Implications for Research and Policy*. Food Policy Review 4, IFPRI, Washington, DC, 1997.

Zuñiga N.: Estimación de la Tasa de Interés Promedio, *El Financiero*, San José, 1996, 6.

Index